AN
AMERICAN
MOSAIC

AN AMERICAN

MOSAIC

PROSE AND POETRY
BY EVERYDAY FOLK

EDITED BY

Robert Wolf

ILLUSTRATIONS BY
Bonnie Koloc

OXFORD UNIVERSITY PRESS
New York Oxford
1999

OXFORD UNIVERSITY PRESS

Oxford   New York
Athens   Auckland   Bangkok   Bogotá   Bombay
Buenos Aires   Calcutta   Cape Town   Chennai   Dar es Salaam
Delhi   Florence   Hong Kong   Istanbul   Karachi
Kuala Lumpur   Madrid   Melbourne   Mexico City
Mumbai   Nairobi   Paris   São Paulo   Singapore
Taipei   Tokyo   Toronto   Warsaw

and associated companies in

Berlin   Ibadan

Published by Oxford University Press, Inc.,
198 Madison Avenue, New York, New York 10016

Library of Congress Cataloging-in-Publication Data
An american mosaic : prose and poetry by everyday folk / edited by
Robert Wolf.
   p.   cm.
ISBN 0-19-513264-5 (cloth). — ISBN 0-19-512712-9 (pbk.)
1. Working class writings, American. 2. Homeless persons' writings, American.
3. United States—Social life and customs—20th century—Literary collections.
4. American literature—20th century. i. Wolf, Robert, 1944– .
PS508.W73A83   1999
810.8'0920623—dc21   98-55998
CIP

design: David Thorne

9 8 7 6 5 4 3 2 1

Printed in the United States of America
on acid-free paper

To the Memory of
Margaret Marino Wolf

Contents

Contents

Contents

RURAL AMERICA: THE MIDWEST

Contents

THE RIVER AND THE DELTA

Introduction   231

THE RIVER

THE DELTA

Acknowledgments

This book is the outcome of ten years of effort on the part of many people. The first workshop was encouraged by LaRue Moss and later by Mary Goldman, both with the Nashville Board of Education. Others who made the homeless project a reality include Steven Meinbresse, Cherry Smith, and others at the staff of the Tennessee Department of Human Services; Steve Pruitt, Fletch Coke and the board of directors of MATTHEW 25; the staff of the Tennessee Arts Commission; Coke Sams, Dave Webb, Meredith Ludwig (who named Free River Press), Lynn Gunzenhauser, the Lynn R. and Karl E. Prickett Fund, the Junior League of Nashville and Tipper Gore.

Thanks for participation and assistance are due more recently to: Murray Hudson and his family; Larry Rettig and the Amana Clear Creek Community Library board; the Clermont Community Club; Connie Brown and Mark White of Independence, Iowa; Linda Klinger, Raleigh Buckmaster, and the other trustees of the R. J. McElroy Trust; Christine Zinni, Roger Isaacs, and others who have organized or participated in workshops.

Acknowledgments

Thanks to my friend and editor, Elda Rotor, and to Ellen Cho-
dosh, Director of Trade Paperbacks at Oxford University Press, this
volume became a reality.

AN
AMERICAN
MOSAIC

General Introduction

American Mosaic is a record of American life focusing primarily on the second half of the twentieth century. It is a collection of stories and essays written for the most part by men and women without literary ambition, and developed in Free River Press writing workshops. The idea for the book came from my desire to get people from all regions of the country and as many occupations as possible to document their lives and work in an ongoing series of books. *American Mosaic* is a miniature version of what I hope to accomplish over the next twenty-five years.

The press was created in 1990 in Nashville, Tennessee as a non-profit corporation whose purpose was to publish the work of homeless men and women. The corporation in turn was an outgrowth of a writing workshop held at MATTHEW 25, a short-term residence facility for homeless men in downtown Nashville. The workshop began almost accidentally. I had been hired by the Nashville Metro Board of Education to teach G.E.D. subjects to the men at MATTHEW 25. Most of MATTHEW 25's then-current population, as I had been told, had either G.E.D. certificates or high school diplomas. Some had college degrees, one had a masters. There was no point in teaching the G.E.D. curriculum. Instead, I started talking with the men, asking how they became homeless. They were willing to tell their stories, and, with the school board's approval, I soon had them writing their accounts.

Almost from the start the workshop was open to homeless women as well as men. One MATTHEW 25 resident was particularly good at recruiting, and brought two talented female writers. Another G.E.D. teacher for the homeless brought a woman. Four months after the workshop started, we gave a public reading at a popular restaurant and music venue to a standing-room only crowd.

At its best, however, the workshop included men and women with jobs and homes. We—the homeless and the nonhomeless—became a tight-knit group of seven persons who met Thursday afternoons to write, and to socialize at other times as well.

Three months after our first public reading we gave another which was taped for National Public Radio's "All Things Considered." The subsequent fourteen-minute piece on the workshop gave us credibility, and convinced a friend, Steven Meinbresse, and I to found Free River Press. Our point was to give the homeless a voice, to put a face to the statistics, to humanize the problem. I had assembled a group of five poets, each with a strong personality. My intention was to publish a volume by each, for I felt their voices would capture readers' interest and imagination. If they made their way into the right hands, I thought, the books might help to influence a few lawmakers.

The writing workshop ran for nearly two and a half years. Before I left Nashville for Iowa in June 1991, the press had published five slim books by the homeless and was to publish yet another. Before the move I had decided to expand the press's mission and to document as much life as I could in contemporary America. Our books, I hoped, would be the literary equivalent of the WPA photo project.

When I moved to Iowa, I began assembling a workshop for farm families, who needed a public voice as much as the homeless. When the last homeless book appeared, it was accompanied by the press's first farm book, an anthology written by five farm families and a local dentist. We met for over two winters, mostly around one large dining table, and eventually produced three books.

Since then the press has published books from other regions and on other subjects. Stories from many of those books are contained in this volume, along with others developed especially for it.

∽

Most of the pieces in this volume were developed in Free River Press writing workshops. The workshops are orally oriented, which means two things. First, participants tell their stories before they write them; second, they are urged to write them as closely as possible to the way they told them. This takes all the mystery out of writing. It emphasizes story line, and tells people that they don't need special training to write intelligibly.

That solves the biggest obstacle to obtaining stories: namely, the conviction many have that they are ill-prepared to write. This is the result of years of poor English instruction. For years teachers told us to be extremely careful with our spelling, punctuation, and grammar, then handed back our compositions filled with red lines and comments. It convinced most students that they had no aptitude for writing. For those of us who persevered, it planted a nasty editor inside our heads who stopped us every few minutes to worry over whether we had chosen the right word, whether it was spelled correctly, whether a comma went here or there, and so on. Now English teachers are letting students write first drafts in an uninterrupted rush, telling them not to worry about matters that can be handled later.

To get a reluctant person to attend a workshop I tell them that anyone who can tell a story can write one. Once they realize that writing consists of imitating oral tellings, the problem of getting them to write is usually solved. Very few of those who attend a workshop have not followed through with a written piece. The workshop process evokes the common wisdom that we all have regarding storytelling. We may not be able to articulate our knowledge, but we have it. And if we are placed in a workshop where we are not threatened or threatening, we draw it forth. After all, we all know a good story when we hear it, we also know a dud. And we can tell, if pressed, why this or that story is one or the other.

I had been told long ago that the more prewriting exercises the instructor uses, the better the results. Thus the writing portion of the workshop is the culmination of an hour and a half of prewriting exercises, including a reading and discussion of two published stories.

With regard to editing, my primary consideration is to preserve the author's voice. In the case of Jim Mince, who hailed from Texas, I wanted the reader to hear Jim's accent and inflections. Since Jim spelled phonetically, I left his spelling intact. (This is perhaps the single case in which I've done that; the occasional misspellings of other writers did not contribute to their tone and were just annoyances.)

In a few cases the writers had their own fractured syntax, consistent throughout their work. When they had it, as Rebel Yell does, I left it. Where a writer's verb forms are consistently nonstandard, I have left them too. The rural Midwesterners with whom I have worked will say "it don't" for "it doesn't," and seldom use adverbs. They'll say, for example, "We done it easy" instead of "We did it easily." These, too, I have left.

The case is different for writers who approach standard English, or, for the most part, write it. If the nonstandard writer is consistently nonstandard, the reader can make sense of the work. But when standard and nonstandard jostle together, the reader is jerked around on a wild ride; in these cases I go with standard.

With writers who have a mastery of standard and develop their pieces in a workshop, little is usually called for except light editing, such as working with punctuation or making sure that a list of items is in parallel order.

A third to a half of all stories called for some degree of cutting. Because most workshops involve at least three three-hour sessions, and because the writers read their work aloud to others, they have the opportunity to have others tell them when a passage is repetitive or otherwise unnecessary. Many workshops go on for three days, with three sessions per day. In these, participants have the time to type what they have written and can have it read to them. They can hear what needs cutting or rewriting.

Two stories were developed for this book long distance, without the workshop process. In those cases drafts were sent back and forth and I made cuts that I probably would not have had to make if the work had been reviewed by peers.

⌒

From at least age sixteen I have wanted to know the United States— its regions, their people, and work.

As a youth my imagination was fed with the poems of Carl Sandburg and Langston Hughes, the short stories of William Saroyan and the novels of John Dos Passos and Jack Kerouac, the paintings and murals of Grant Wood, Diego Rivera, and Thomas Hart Benton. They fed my desire to see all of the country. Not only were they depicting places I wanted to visit, but most had hoboed or otherwise traveled extensively. Sandburg had ridden freights around the country and followed the harvests; Benton had tramped the South on foot and driven out West on sketching expeditions, gathering raw materials for the American epics that he painted on walls across the country; and Kerouac, of course, was famous for having gone on the road. His best known work was a call to my generation.

I learned of others who had taken off. I read John Muir's accounts of his thousand mile treks across country, of Woody Guthrie's days riding the rails, and Burl Ives's Depression-era search for the truth about America, days spent in hobo jungles and on freight trains.

Charles and Mary Beard's *America in Midpassage* contained wonderful chapters on Depression-era painting and writing. Two of the artists and writers they described stayed in my mind for years. One was an artist who had vowed to paint a mural in every post office of every town he entered as he crossed the United States. The other was a writer who had gone off across country in search of the American soul. I had just finished reading some novels of Dostoevsky and was convinced he had depicted a soul or character distinctly different from our own: one that loved to confess and weep, that was highly agitated, that upon first meeting another would leap in to discuss ultimate questions, such as the soul's immortality or the existence of God.

Was there a distinctly American soul? I was certain there was and at sixteen I ran away from home in search of it. For years I wandered about the country, hitchhiking and riding freights, searching for the underlying unity. I sought this American soul with ranchers, cowboys, farmers, academics, hoboes, bums, drug addicts, businessmen, artists. I worked on a ranch in New Mexico, hitchhiked across country, drank cocktails at New York's Algonquin Hotel, slept with bums at the Salvation Army in Phoenix, golfed on Connecticut and New York courses. At nineteen I was the only Anglo living in a New Mexican village. In later years I taught at a penitentiary, at an inner city high school in Brooklyn, at Chicago colleges and universities. I was a newspaper columnist and a house parent at a residence for retarded men.

And even when I concluded that we were too disparate a country to have a common character or soul, I kept trying to figure out what made this country tick. Over the years I have held at least a score of jobs and lived in ten states. And the jobs I have had and the places I have lived have never been enough. This desire was not merely a matter of wanting to mimic what I had read. One had to know, and knowing would not come through books. The young vag in Dos Passos' *USA* "must catch the last subway, the streetcar, the bus, run up the gangplanks of all the steamboats, register at all the hotels, work in the cities, answer the wantads, learn the trades, take up the jobs, live in all the boardinghouses, sleep in all the beds. One bed is not enough, one job is not enough, one life is not enough."

Dos Passos' vag reminds me of Thomas Wolfe and his persona, Eugene Gant. Wolfe's books are testament to his own ravenous hunger to understand America. His torrent of words is an attempt at exactness, to capture the complexity of what he had experienced.

It is the same with Whitman's catalog of America, of the jobs, the workers, the sights, the sounds. It is epitomized in his poem "A Carol of Occupations."

The catalog is an essential ingredient for any American trying to write of the whole continent. Otherwise, how do we weld this disparate thing into a whole?

〜

Probably the single greatest influence on my own vision of the country was Thomas Hart Benton's mural *America Today*, painted in 1932 for the New School for Social Research. I remember seeing it for the first time, in my teens, and the impact it had on me. It is a work of enormous energy. Benton's forms are sinewy, eternally moving, his conclusion on the American character.

The mural is composed of six panels. Two panels compose City *Activities*. One panel shows trapeze artists flying in midair, moviegoers watching a film, a woman at a soda fountain flirting with the soda jerk, dancers gliding across a nightclub floor, a man reading a tickertape, a physician examining a child in its mother's lap. The other panel depicts men and women kneeling in prayer as a Salvation Army band plays nearby, prize fighters in a boxing ring slugging it out, a couple necking on a park bench, burlesque dancers shaking their cans, passengers sitting and standing in a subway car.

Another panel, *Steel*, depicts work in a foundry and blast furnace. Mining shows power plants and freighters, and bent laborers leaving mines. *ChangingWest* depicts a cowboy on horseback with grazing cattle; a man welding a metal pipe; a surveyor with a transit; a cowboy, a woman, and an Indian in a bar; an oil boomtown. *South* shows cotton being combined and cotton-laden sacks on wagons loaded onto a paddlewheeler. Finally, *Instruments of Power* depicts a speeding train, a plane, a power line, an engine.

As with any attempt at so large a canvas, it was incomplete. Even Whitman with his seemingly endless catalogs was incomplete. *American Mosaic* is a catalog of stories which I have tried to unify with my introductions, commentaries, and afterword—with a structure suggested by *America Today*. Like Benton's mural, *American Mosaic* is composed of sections which I think of as panels. There is one each for the Mississippi River, the Midwest, and the Mississippi Delta. There is another for the homeless. As a vision of American it is fragmentary and incomplete, but it is a start.

The order of sections follows the chronology in which the works were developed. Other panels for a larger mural are in the process of being created, panels for the Southwest, Chicago, and suburban Connecticut. Eventually each panel, including those in *American Mosaic*, will be developed into a full length work.

POETRY
AND PROSE
BY THE
HOMELESS

Introduction

In January 1989, when the homeless writing workshop began, downtown Nashville was no longer the collection of two-story brick buildings that it had been up until the sixties. It was filling with sky-scrapers. The Grand Ole Opry, once located in an austere brick build-ing and former church known as the Ryman Auditorium, had moved out of town in 1974 and relocated near the airport. Music industry people were moving in from Los Angeles and New York. Broadway, a downtown drag once the domain of tourists, was filled with the homeless, who spent their days (and sometimes nights) in its honky-tonks or outside them on the sidewalks. The homeless were coming to Nashville from all over the country, many in the hope of breaking into the music business and becoming the next Willie Nelson or Waylon Jennings.

MATTHEW 25, where I ran a writing workshop for two years, was located on the corner of 8th Street and Broadway, a ramshackle, three-story building that sheltered approximately forty men. In ret-rospect, it was the perfect place for the writing project. It had the right feel and was close to the honky-tonks. The life on the streets came with the men into the shelter. In the first six months there was nothing depressing about it; it was, in fact, exciting. Much of the credit for that probably goes to Steve Pruitt, the shelter's director for that period.

The Nashville Metro Board of Education had hired me to teach G.E.D subjects to the residents, but as my supervisor at the Board of Education said, the current residents had high school diplomas, G.E.D certificates, and college degrees. Go there, she advised, and think of something to do until the time is right to begin teaching. I arrived with some trepidation. I had once worked at the New Mexico State Penitentiary, but it had been years since I had been with a down-and-out population. I sat around the upstairs common room filled with old busted-up, greasy furniture, drinking bitter coffee out of Styrofoam cups and talking to the few men who hung around in the afternoons I was there.

I did try to teach math and formal writing but had few takers. I started talking with the men about how they became homeless and got them writing their stories, but attendance was erratic. So-and-so couldn't be there that day; he had to work. Or else he just didn't want to write again. But a few stuck with it and showed up the two afternoons a week for the class. They were a mixed bunch, not only blacks and whites, alcoholics and drug users, but sober and drug-free men as well. Gary was a shipyard worker from Wilmington whose wife had cheated on him; he was intelligent and did not have an alcohol or drug problem. It was the few men like Gary, who I met at this time, who convinced me that many of the homeless had just had bad breaks. One friend, who ran another homeless agency at that time, referred to those days of the late 1980s as "the romantic period," when many of us did not realize the extent of the drug and alcohol problem among the homeless and believed that some creative efforts at self-actualization could solve the problem for many.

The workshop began in January. By April we held our first public reading. The Nashville press was very receptive to the project and gave us good coverage. As a result, that first reading was jammed with people.

The writers included not just men but women, too, and not all the men were from MATTHEW 25. The MATTHEW 25 writers included Keith McMahon, a Nicholas Cage look alike with forty different versions about his mysterious and fabulous youth, and Tony, his buddy, who had a master's degree in zoology and information on a major government conspiracy that included extraterrestrials. They also included Wayne Leonhard, a little guy from Minnesota, in many ways naive but enthusiastic about life, and Jim Mince, an older man and Willie Nelson look alike with a bandana around his long hair. Jim found Anna Shaw and Liz Gilbert at a McDonald's; they lived with an older couple who had taken them in. Both became regular attendees.

In those early days, Allison Smith, another G.E.D teacher, brought Rebel Yell and Pat Guild to the workshop. Rebel, whose real name is Lori Lee, was tall and gawky. She wore jeans and a plaid shirt and carried a backpack. Like Liz Gilbert, whose pen name was El Gilbert, she was a prolific writer. Rebel lived under an interstate bridge and had trained herself to write in the dark. Pat Guild was a cowboy poet who had built a shack in the woods by the Cumberland River. Pat usually showed up drunk, and later bragged about severely beating a homeless man who had intruded on his property—gloating over his claim that he had kicked one of the man's eyes out and left him crawling around the woods.

Not only did the workshop writers read for that first event, but several of them, including Joe Goller and Jim Mince, sang songs that they had written. Joe was a counselor at MATTHEW 25, a strong personality who had served time in prison, had been on the Nashville streets, later lived at MATTHEW 25, and eventually joined its staff. He had written countless country western songs which he was trying to promote. I asked him to join the workshop, but he only came a few times. To get rid of me, he handed me a manuscript of poems, which Free River Press later published.

The publicity from the reading brought a call from Steven Meinbresse, homeless coordinator for the State of Tennessee's Department of Human Services (DHS), who was enthusiastic about the workshop and wondered if some of the poets would read for a meeting he had organized. The audience included Tipper Gore, wife of then-

Senator Albert Gore, Jr. Anna and Liz both read, and Mrs. Gore, who was very much involved in homeless issues, was impressed with them and their work.

Steven brought another poet to the group, Diana Schooler, a formerly homeless woman then on disability, who lived in Knoxville. When she read her poems, many of which she had written in prison, you heard a blues shouter. Diana had a strong public presence, spoke well to groups, and was involved in youth drug education. About the same time Robert Roberg, a Mennonite street preacher and folk artist, had read about the workshop and wanted to join. He, too, had written poetry; in fact, he had self-published several of his own volumes.

My wife was the one who suggested that I publish their work. In May, following the first public reading, the Board of Education photocopied and bound a slim volume of their prose and poetry that I had edited. In July, when the workshop had its second public reading, a producer and journalist for National Public Radio drove down from Washington to cover it. The subsequent fourteen-minute piece on "All Things Considered" further boosted my feeling that we were doing something important. At that point I decided to found a nonprofit press that would be devoted to giving the homeless a voice.

Over the next year various combinations of the homeless poets—sometimes joined by prose writer Wayne Leonhard—read at various functions across Tennessee. They became an effective means for DHS to humanize the homeless problem. Steven was keen on the poets, and for some reason most of the strongest work written by the homeless was in verse. Poetry seemed a more natural form of expression, possibly because many came from a tradition in which feelings, problems, and loves were expressed in song.

Several times we did programs with Mrs. Gore, who would present a video funded by a committee of Senate wives. When the homeless writers went on a bus trip to Washington for the Housing Now! March, Mrs. Gore and her daughters marched with us. It was an exciting time. We all felt we were a part of something. The formation of Free River Press and the fact that we were being nurtured by DHS and congratulated by the media made us feel that we could, somehow, make a difference.

Steven worked hard to make the press a reality, including getting lawyers who helped with the nonprofit application. Mrs. Gore persuaded the Junior League of Nashville to fund *Five Street Poets*, written by Liz, Robert, Joe, Diana, and Rebel. At the same time, MATTHEW 25 decided to fund a companion volume of writings, *Passing Thru*, by the men from the workshop.

At the end of two years, I seemed to be finding fewer interesting writers. MATTHEW 25 moved to a building that had once housed the elderly. Everything looked and felt institutionalized. We were far from downtown. Members of the original workshop had long since scattered; those who remained in town were not going to make the trip to the new building. Steve Pruitt was long gone too. It was clear that if Free River Press was going to survive, it would have to publish more than the work of the homeless. While Nashvillians continued funding the nonprofits which serviced the homeless, the public at large was losing interest in the subject.

Now, five years after the workshop closed, I remember the writers and our meetings as a time of excitement and experiment, engendered in large part by naiveté. Without the naiveté, however, the project would have been far different, and, I think, not as fruitful.

POETRY

■ *El Gilbert*

Before coming to Nashville, El Gilbert had been assistant to John Hammond, the legendary producer at Columbia Records. In the last three years El has moved from Nashville to New York to Alabama and back to Nashville, where she continues to write poetry.

WELL SEASONED

Friday night, Nashville, Captain D's fish chain
on West End Avenue where the elite meet to
crunch, chomp, guzzle, & slurp,
unaware of the perpetual draft from the
air conditioner or the monotony of
Muzak in the distance.

Counter girls appear at intervals to wipe off
tables, fill napkin holders, keep the ketchup
flowing & the customers content.
That's what they're paid to do, so when they holler,
"Y'all come back!" in their best finishing school
voices, don't take it personally.

You're not a person first of all.
You're a seafood platter & a coke
or black coffee and a banana tart.
Nothing more. Don't forget that.
Hush. Be quiet. Eat your grub as quickly
as possible & get out.
These are the unspoken rules of the restaurant
game in these parts.
No room for poachers or poets,
just as no dogs allowed.

100% TEXAN

I have loved cowboys (urban or otherwise)
   in their stack-heeled boots, close-fitting jeans,
   hats bent to the curve of the head,
   brass belt buckles, and I have said,
   "God help me for this weakness, this
   shooting gallery/pinball alley mentality,
   this final ride into the hills of what used to be,
   can never be again."

I have loved Waylon, Willie & the Boys,
   who-done-me-wrong songs,
   jukeboxes playing in roadside diners,
   deserted horsemen and Texans stuck with themselves,
   whittled from the inside out, stranded and forgotten,
   left to fight half-worlds with unloaded guns.

I have loved good ole boys, rednecks, rebels,
   outlaws, men brave enough to defend their rights,
   even when they weren't right, who dreamed of
   owning themselves and freeing the prisoners.

I have loved taverns and bars, restaurants devoid
   of decorations or beauty, plain places filled
   with plain people, dethroned princes, commoners,
   laborers and fieldhands too exhausted to expound on
   Pound, Poe, or Proust,
   extraordinary examples of courage in a
   less than courageous society.

I have loved truck drivers for being themselves,
   whoever they are, wherever they are,
   their spirit of freedom flashing across the
   freeways in fluorescent colors,
   their independence and individuality

in spite of the countryside cluttered with
copies of copies.

And I have loved you even though you didn't fit
into my VW and couldn't be shrunk to size.

DRUNK

Drunk
in this after 5 escape valve
rearranging peanuts
on the ridged deck of the bar,
I climb to the top
of my martini glass
and fall in.

The vermouth is soothing
enough to keep me quiet
until I bump into you
sitting on my olive:
naked, smiling.

WINTER BOY

Crawl into bed now.
Slide between the
wrinkled sheets.
Hold me
in your arms
& tell me
nothing changes.
Let me hear you say
it only rains over there.
Make me believe
it's true.

I'M SORRY BUT

Meeting you this afternoon
made me think of
other afternoons
alone.

TEMPORARY RELIEF

"I love you," he said,
"even though you are
old enough to be
my mother."

He was wearing week-old
jeans and a Linda Ronstadt
T-shirt. His breath
smelled of White Russians.

"We dance this way in
New Jersey too," he
grinned. The band eased
into "For the Good Times."
He stumbled, rested his
beard against my face.
There was enough dirt
under his fingernails to
plant a marijuana patch.

"I'd like to make love
to you," he said between
hiccups/repressed farts.
That's what they all say
after the fifth drink
when the vision gets
clouded and younger

prospects disappear with
well-heeled honchos.

I let him sleep on the
spare cot. He made two
trips to the bathroom to
throw up, said he was
sorry if he caused me
any trouble, hoped I had
a good time.
The next morning I felt
hungover. Cokes do that
to me now.

He put on his boots, kissed
me goodbye at the door (some
things are expected). I folded
up the cot, lit a cigarette,
watched him cross the street
from the kitchen window.

EXEMPT FROM DEATH

I walk an eternal walk,
Wade through time,
wait as no one has ever waited before
or will wait again,
burnt into majestic oak,
charred from all sides
and smoldering,
passed unnoticed in a wind storm,
moving with distant sands,
farther and farther away,
flattened to a faint whisper
before faceless gods
obediently operative despite

defective machinery.
Bound within, free without,
I walk an eternal walk
dragging behind the carcass of
the form you fail to
recognize as mine.

WOULDN'T YOU KNOW IT

Fools rush in where angels fear to tred
& the fools are packed in here tonight,
each one trying to look hipper than the next,
each one sucked into Music City Melodrama,
pasty phonies from New York, Chicago, L.A.,
the cosmo-playboy whirlwind/tornado,
the "in" scene, the boredom.

I sit at the front table wearing my five-year-old
Steppenwolf t-shirt, which isn't very in by
local standards. But what's the difference?
I've been out so long I'm in.
You noticed. How sweet. I'm trembling with
excitement. The only thing that prevents me from
jumping up to kiss you is the fact that you
look like a gargoyle.
You say you're not a gargoyle . . . A musician?
That's too bad. That's really too bad.
Well . . . Look, I'll see you around.

What? What am I doing with that old man?
That old man is a year younger than I am.
Yeah . . . Ha-ha, it's funny, I know.
No, there's no sex. I accompany him to places
like this so he'll look less like a madman.
He feeds me in exchange.
Otherwise I'd go hungry.

Jobs aren't that easy to get now.
I guess I'm sort of a musician too.
Trouble is, the only instrument I've got
is broken & the concert hall is empty.

■ *Diane Schooler*

*Diana Schooler spent seventeen years in the Tennessee State
Prison for Women, during which time she wrote the poems printed
here. During the early nineties Diana was active in Knoxville social
service programs, talking to youth about the dangers of drug use.*

I. Poems Written in Prison

FRIGHTENED BY THE SOUNDS OF NIGHT

Frightened by the sounds of night,
laying still for days, it seems,
 before I realize
  'twas only a dream
 or a memory
  of the
   many
    days
    and
     nights
spent inside of steel and brick.

I open my eyes
 to the darkness
  of a
  brand
  new
   world . . .

A world where the
only fears I have
are of
 bills and
of bill collectors
 and I smile and say . . .
 "Thank God."

THE NIGHT IS COOL . . .

The night is cool . . .
the air is damp
the sky is dark
 could use a lamp . . .
My heart is heavy
 as are my eyes . . .
Too much thinking
 'bout family ties . . .

Feel like laughing
 but not tonight,
don't need confusion
 can't lose sight . . .
of the misery
 that I feel . . .

Sitting alone
 deep in thought
Misery lives
 deep inside me
never shows . . .
 Nobody knows
 cause I smile.

I'VE DREAMED MANY DREAMS THAT NEVER CAME TRUE

I've dreamed many dreams that never came true,
I've seen them vanish at dawn . . .
But I've realized enough of my dreams, thank God,
To make me want to dream on.
I've prayed many prayers, when no answer came,
Although I waited patient and long,
But answers have come to enough of my prayers,
To make me keep praying on.
I've trusted many a friend who failed
And left me to weep alone,
But I've found enough of my friends true blue,
To keep me trusting on.
I've sown many seeds that fell by the way
For the birds to feed upon,
But I've had enough golden sheaves in my hand
To make me keep sowing on.
I've drained the cup of disappointment in pain
And gone many days without song . . .
But I've sipped enough nectar from the roses of life
To make me want to live on.

SOMETIMES YOU HURT ME TERRIBLY

Sometimes you hurt me terribly,
More than anyone in the world . . .
There are times you make me feel
That you're sorry I'm your girl.
The tears you bring from within me
Are caused from loving you
'Cause if I didn't love you
The tears could not get through.
You call me names and tell me that
I don't listen to a word you say . . .
Why is it then, my darling,

I put up with you each day?
You become so angry
You fail to stop and see . . .
Without the love that comes from you
I would cease to be.
I hate it when you hurt me
When you tear my soul apart . . .
There's nothing that can change
The love that's in my heart.
So I will keep on caring
Taking the pain you give . . .
Because I know, my darling,
Without you I could not live.

YOU'VE AWAKENED IDEAS, THOUGHTS

You've awakened ideas, thoughts.
 I'm beginning to feel alone.
  Maybe I was . . . simply lonely,
   but loneliness is nothing
    unusual . . . for me.

You've put to sleep bad thoughts.
 Gone are the nightmares . . .
  or bricks . . . of steel . . .
   of screaming women.

You've opened up another world,
 one in which I can be
  whoever in the world
   I think I am or
    maybe want to be.

SAD, ASHAMED

Sad, ashamed
 Lonely and afraid
  Seeking peace
   Needing rest.

Sick
 Disgusted
 Ashamed
  Wanting to be free
   From . . . myself.

I've said
 I'm free . . . yet
  You say
   I still owe . . .
    You!
Endless days
 Sleepless nights
  Too many memories
   Some good
    Most nightmares.

II. Poem Written after Prison

YOU ASK JUST WHAT YOU CAN DO FOR ME

You ask just what you can do for me
With all sincerity in your voice.
To me this seems kind of ludicrous,
As if I had a choice.

The things I need are just the same
As those things you need each day . . .
Food, clothing, and utilities,

And, of course, a place to stay.

I need decent employment too,
A job that would pay well . . .
For otherwise I'm no better off.
Cans to make a difference, I must sell.
Please don't think me lazy,
Just living off the land . . .
It's just that I'm having a hard time.
It's almost more than I can stand.
There are times when I speak to civic groups
I try to make them see
That I'm no longer confined to jail
But support must have if I'm to be free.

■ Robert Roberg

*In Nashville Robert Roberg was a street preacher for the Men-
nonites and illustrated his sermons with dayglo paintings. He and his
family now live in Palmetto, Florida, where his paintings first achieved
recognition. He is now a nationally known Outsider artist.*

DRESSED IN DOUBT

I the pilgrim
dressed in doubt
set out one morning to see God
and I didn't see him in any of the
rich new churches where the people
dress like movie stars
 nor in the dusty tomb-cold cathedrals
  (the last place he'd be seen dead in)
nor in the womb-warm roll-in-the-aisle joints

I didn't see him in the trees at Mission Park

I didn't see him in the green sky
or blue grass
nor in the faces of babies
or the laughter of children
I saw God in a night alley
behind a Chinese restaurant
digging thru the trash
with wild hungry flaming eyes
and wonderously crippled hands

THE SHADOW

I saw a lonely shadow on a barroom wall
I thought it might be Mike
his second wife left him just last fall
I turned to say hello, but he was gone.

Later as the juke box played *The Broken Rose*
I saw the shadow flicker thru the candle glow
I thought it might be Jane
After Eric left her she was never quite the same
I turned to say hello, but she was gone.
I was returning from the bathroom when I saw it in the hall
just for a brief moment I thought
it might be Tom
then I remembered his plane went down
over Viet Nam.
After midnight when I left the bar
I saw the shadow sitting in my car
(They say loneliness can play tricks
on your mind. I've got to stop this drinking
while I still have the time.)
For the shadow on the barroom wall was mine
I turned to say hello, but I was gone.

CHURCH HOUSE BLUES

I was hungry
and you pledged millions of dollars to build
yourselves a new building

I was thirsty
and you bought the most luxurious organ you
could find

I was naked and you put in new carpeting
I was homeless and your doors were locked
I was sick and your youth group had a
Mickey Mouse banquet
I was in prison and you visited me thru
your radio show. The voice was warm, but far
away and untouchable
I was lonely and you sent missionaries
overseas

I was broken hearted and I couldn't help
blaming someone
Can you guess who?

THE WAY UP IS DOWN

Who needs more learning than a teacher?
Who needs more preaching than a preacher?
Have you ever felt lonely in a crowd?
Have you ever noticed how silence can be loud?

The world makes more sense, if you
turn it upside down
where those who weep the most
are the laughing clowns

Look at those high on the ladder of success
Can't you see their lives are a mess?
Money's not the name of the game.
Those who go for the gold
are those who go lame.

Yes the world makes more sense
turned upside down
where those who weep the most
are the laughing clowns.

The prouder they come the harder they fall.
Only the humble can truly stand tall.
In my search for the truth this much I've found
The way up's not up, but way up is down.

THRU A POOR MAN'S EYES

A poor man's eyes are stretched wide by hunger
so he sees a different world.
I've been imprisoned in Mexico, the U.S. and Colombia
sold my blood in Greece for a boat ticket to Israel
begged for bread on the streets of India
I've slept under bridges, eaten from soup kitchens
walked all night many nights because I had no money or
    friends

Look into my mind let me be a window to show you how
the poor think:
We think constantly of the rich . . . we hate them
The rich are the cause of all our suffering
we are blind to any good they may do.
We hate all governments which favor the rich.
We hate congressmen who vote themselves raises
We hate rich farmers who are paid not to plant

We hate little shopkeepers who exploit their workers with
low wages
We are blinded by people eating from garbage cans
We hate fences that say "Keep Out, No Trespassing"
We hate well clipped lawns where money that could go
to the poor goes to
lawn mowers and fertilizers
We hate pets who gobble up meat and fish dinners
We hate cars that gulp gallons of gas, paint, oil, and wax
We hate to see people skiing behind boats for the fences
keep us even from dipping our tongues in the lakes
We hate churches with tall steeples and stained glass windows
We know we are not welcome there
We doubt if the sweaty carpenter of Nazareth would be
welcome there
We hate preachers on TV begging for money
We hate people trying to stop Nuclear War

The poor say let it come
Let the bombs rain down
then the rich will reap what they have sown and the poor
will inherit their Lazaran reward.

(I wrote this poem before I became a Christian . . .
I still struggle
with negative thoughts about the rich . . .
I am now trying to love everyone
"but it ain't easy")

■ *Rebel Yell*

*Rebel Yell, whose real name is Lori Lee, works for a Nashville
church in exchange for housing. When she was a member of the
homeless writing workshop, she was well known among the*

Nashville homeless, a tall figure in blue jeans and plaid shirt, who often carried all of her effects in a backpack.

WHAT REALLY HAPPENED TO US

What Really Happened To Us, And Why We Went Different Ways. I Went North Across Three States To Forget About You.

When I Was In East Texas, Where There Was Only Pines And Spruces, Fir Trees Covered The Land, You Didn't Want To See This With Me.

And In Louisiana, You Didn't Want To Share My Lonely Nights And Going To The State Fair With Me. And You Didn't Want To Watch The Thoroughbred Racing Beside Me, And See the Mighty River of The Mississippi.

When I Was In Mississippi State, Looking At Vicksburg, Where Part Of The Civil War Took Place So Long Ago.

And Looking At The Cotton Fields And Hearing The Civil War Of Long Ago And Watching The Traffic Going Past Me.

And When I Was Sleeping In Alabama, Where A Group Got Started Singing Their Song And Looking At The Spanish Moss That Draped On The Tall Cedar Trees, The Heart Of Dixieland.

And Looking At The Old Mansion Of The South And Hearing Ghostly Music Inside The Dunleith Mansion, Where Miss Percy Could Still Be Heard Playing A Harp Only At Dusk.

I Still Miss My Love, When You Are Living In And Working In Dallas, Texas.

HERE I SIT ACROSS THE STREET

Here I Sit Across The Street From Union Planters National Bank. The Lights Are Going On Inside The Bank And Merrill Lynch Pierce, Fenner & Smith Has Men Going In With Business Suits And Looking Nice And Cases In Their Hands.

Merrill Lynch Is A Stock Market, Always Talking About

Stock And Selling. Or Buying Stock.

Pierce, Fenner, Smith Are Working Hard As A Team. They Worked In The Third National Banking In Nashville, Tenn.

When The Points Going Higher, You Are Making Money And When The Points Going Down Below 0.00 They Are Losing Money. When That Happened Men Will Be Jumping Out The Window.

The Building Standing On The Corner Of Church St. And 4th North. The Building Is Well Alarmed With Locks, Only Guards And Bankers Know The Money And Stocks Are very Safe All The Time.

The Pillars Stand In Front Of The Building And With Green Bushes And Few Trees In Front Of Them And The Windows Are Clean And The Ticket Board Always Moving And The Market Closed Down At 5 P.M.

A Business Runs By A Business, The Stock Market Is First, If All The Banks Will Come To A End All the Small Business Will Go Down, Then The People Will Have No Food On The Table, Then No Job Will Be There At All.

TRAVELING FEVER

When Springtime Comes All The Hitch Hikers Are Hiking Around The Nation. There Is One Hitch Hiker Who Can't Travel Again.

Tears Rolling Down My Face Where People Can't See The Tear Rolling Down My Cheeks, I've Got The Moods, Traveling Fever Just

Like The Trucker Who Travels Down The Road And I Am A Hiker Crossing This Land.

Now This Person Had A Debt To Pay To This City And I Am Tired Of Seeing This City.

The Traveling Fever Is Starting Up Again And I'm Trying To
Fight It, It's Hard For Me Tonight.

Traveling Fever Is Hard To Fight, There Will Be Times I
Want To Leave And Can't.

So I Will Keep Fighting It And It Will Take A Long Time
But I Will Be On The Road Again.

LORD, TAKE MY WEAKNESS

Lord, Take My Weakness, Throw It Away From Me. You Are
Slowly Changing Me, Lord.

Lord, Take My Weakness, And Give Me A Spiritual High All
The Time.

I Know You Can Make Me Strong With Your Word And

I Know You Can Make Me Intelligent In Your Sight And In
Your Word, Also.

■ *Joe Goller*

*Joe Goller served ten years in prison, where he wrote a volume
of verse from which this selection is taken. Formerly a counselor at
MATTHEW 25, Joe is now married with two children. Joe's
Diner, a fifties-style, colorful restaurant he created in 1996 was
destroyed by tornado in 1998. He has since rebuilt it.*

I WATCHED A ROSE

I have witnessed Woman's full cycle of life and all her
wonderful variations of beauty and stages of life.
I watched a Rose
ascend from its stem into a bud,
to a young and tender flower,

watching its petals slowly open,
yet not fully,
until in a burst of exhuberance and sensual dancing
discard all shyness and reveal her youthful beauty
to the world,
drawing deeper colors from the sun
and complementing the stars at night
until its journey along life's path
developed her total bloom of womanhood
strong,
radiant,
breath-taking,
luring me closer,
feeling the rich tones,
finding myself surrendering to the pure
aromatic scent of femininity.
Then ever so painfully my eyes witnessed
its petals melting away, one by one,
withering into age, ashes, oblivion . . .
Yet even during her dying gesture,
retaining beauty through its swan song.
I have witnessed Woman. I watched a Rose . . .

WHEN MY LIFE IS GONE

When my life is gone
don't ever bury me
don't want no flowers
or trees growing over me

When my life is gone
keep my name forever silent
lest the winds carry it
and destroy my eternal peace

When my life is gone

shed no tears for me
it would be such a waste
to weep over your enemy

When my life is gone
set my soul aflame
lest it get away from me
and hinder my escape

???

GOLD
     is precious, paid for with countless lives . . . .
DIAMONDS
     are valued, ask the old and ugly wives . . . .
RUBIES
     are worth their weight in shape and size . . . .
EMERALDS
     are favorites, but beyond the poor man's prize.
WATER
     who needs it, except to drink and pollute . . . .
AIR
     well I can use it, but I like it with soot . . . .
EARTH
     has its use, but looks better under cement . . . .
NATURE
     yes I once saw it, on a postcard stamp . . . .
VALUES
     what a wonderful thing to possess . . . .
MORALITY
     means loving thy neighbor's wife best . . . .
CHARACTER
     play the next man's part, instead of self . . . .
FAITH
     a stack of old Bibles on a dusty shelf . . . .

LOVE

LOVE
  is
WAR
  not
FLOWERS
  is
HATE
  not
FRIENDS
  is
VANITY
  not
BEAUTY
  is
COLD
  not
RED
  is
DEAD
  is
NOT
  *
  *
  *
  *
  *
  IS

FEMALE GUARD

She traded her blue jeans
          and her Sunday dress
gave her a new uniform
          off-green at best

she walks the beat now
> grounds forbidden so long
just another cop on the prowl
> trying to meet the test
do you think she can hear the growl
> deep within the prisoner's chest
the uniform is on
> badge in place
smile erased
but we look, and she feels the heat
> right through her bare feet
Thank God she isn't wearing boxers
> too . . . .

PHRASING

Grey walls, steel bars
put them in a jar
& flush it down the toilet

Pretty boys lifting weights
& spending time
broken down at the waist

The morning's without sun
so I stare at the glare
of the 50 watt freak

Lying on my bunk
thinking about the punk
who winked at me!

Bedsprings start to sing
to the only tune
& the face on the wall

Guards changing shifts
but not the rules
doesn't matter, got my own
Received a letter
a week old
& means just as much

Too bad hate's not
shaped like a key
I'd have a Masters

Don't tell me
what time it is
it may be too late

The great promise!
Two cars in every garage
& a T.V. in every cell

Nothing really new
about my style,
just the way it's expressed . . . .

I HATE

I hate
the smallness of your thoughts
I hate
your obssession with man-made store-bought
I hate
your beauty above the ugly inside
I hate
all the things you're trying to hide
I hate
the one you'll never be
I hate

you, because you're blind to me
I hate
the things you think you represent
I hate
you on Sunday as you repent
I hate
everything you leave to fate
I hate
the hate, I hate the hate
I hate

PROSE

■ *Wayne Leonhard*

After leaving MATTHEW 25, Wayne Leonhard went back to work for a road construction company that builds highways in Texas and Louisiana. In 1995, somewhere in his thirties, he had made enough money to return home to northern Minnesota and begin building his own house.

THE RIGHT ROAD

1974 we rolled into Denver from the north, riding in a van packed full of cameras, clothes, sleeping bags, and bodies of hopeful men in their mid-twenties.

Excitement was in the air. All of us had our own dreams. I was going to be a songwriter and performer. Bob, who owned the van, was setting out from his home in Appleton, Wisconsin, to start a new life as a photographer. The other two guys were also going to do things their own way. We all were hoping to find the world we'd heard of in the sixties, the world of free love and independent living styles.

It was sunny the day we pulled into Denver. We'd left Wisconsin with its 40 below zero weather behind and now as we came south from Cheyenne the weather was 50-60 degrees. Shirts and shoes weren't needed. We drove down Colfax Avenue around the capital and back east until Bob thought he must be close to a friend's house. He stopped at a public phone to call.

I jumped out, full of enthusiasm and wished him and the others well and started absorbing the atmosphere. I was going to whip the world. It was probably the pot still curling out the doors of the van that made me feel that way. So now, with my banjo in hand, I was ready to show the world what they were missing. I would learn to play that banjo if I could find some banjo picker to teach me. I just tuned it like the first four strings on a guitar. I didn't know what that short string on top was for.

I just stood there feeling everything. It would be easier to call my brother, who was in the Air Force, and stay with him than sleep in the streets as I dreamed I would. Mark was actually living in a neighborhood only twenty blocks east of where I stood. I called him. He said to stay right there, he'd come and get me. He arrived in a 1970 Maverick, white and nice looking. He pulled up and said, "Hi! What you doing here?" I jumped in, and we went to his apartment. He looked okay, a little tired maybe. His wife, Kathy, and his children, Kelly and Mark Jr., were doing well. They lived on the third floor of an apartment complex.

It turned out I had called at a good time because Mark was home between the Air Force and a night custodial job. I rode along when he went to work. He showed me what he did and where he kept the supplies he needed for his job. There wasn't much to it. We cleaned the toilets, mopped and waxed the floors, emptied the trash, cleaned ashtrays, and followed a list of things that needed to be done once a week, once a month, or every six months. I went with him every night the week I stayed with him, and I found out most of what he did. We cut his time almost in half that week.

Mark took me to visit my Uncle Alan and Aunt Laura Lee in Arvada. I'd been in touch with them through the years, at least what I thought was in touch. They and their kids were all right.

The day I left Mark cooked a big kettle of chili. He thought I'd stay long enough to help eat it. I did have one bowl before I left. Mark, Kathy, Kelly and Mark Jr. took me down the interstate just south of Pueblo where, with much regret, they dropped me off and headed back to Denver, waving goodbye.

I got a ride before sundown from three young people in a 1950's pickup truck. A woman sat between two men. We put my knapsack and banjo in the back. When we made Santa Fe it was dark. It seemed it was all low adobe buildings.

Albuquerque lay in a valley and I could see every light in the whole city. Other cities had impressed me by their size or the height of their buildings, but Albuquerque impressed me by just being there.

The people in the truck weren't going much farther, so they dropped me off on the west side, out in the desert. It was almost daylight when I unrolled my sleeping bag. I lay down in the desert to sleep for the first time. I loved it. It was cool, quiet, and comfortable to lay on. I slept until after daylight. I got up, stashed everything, put my banjo in the bushes, and walked into town.

In Denver I'd found places where a person could play music for twenty minutes on stage for auditions. The Oxford Hotel, Denver Folklore Center, The Global Village and Ebbets Field had open mike nights. I went into Albuquerque looking for the same thing.

I was wearing my old knee-length, blue Air Force coat. My hair and beard were growing. I had my best clothes in my knapsack. My brother, Tim, had given me that knapsack for Christmas. I wouldn't need clothes until I started playing somewhere. I'd clean up in filling station rest rooms, so I wasn't worried about cleaning up. Still, I looked the part of a drifter.

I found a clean little cafe in the old part of town where they let people play. Three musicians were playing, and I listened to them for a few hours. Then I went out to roam the streets. One man I talked to told me he'd met Glen Campbell hitchhiking down the same road five years ago. That must mean I was on the right road! I walked into another place where a classical guitar player was on stage. I watched him play for a few minutes. I plucked a string on my banjo to check its tune. He said to keep that thing quiet. He didn't miss a beat. I kept it quiet and left. I headed back to find my things. They were where I left them. I checked around for snakes and insects and rolled my sleeping bag out for another night on the desert. I can't forget the quiet of the desert or the stark starlit skies. I felt great lying there, I was heading for big things. I just knew I was.

The next morning with everything rolled up and stashed, I started into town. I could see a semi parked on the hill to the west. I wondered if I could catch a ride, so I got my stuff and started up the hill. It was over a mile to the semi. When I got within a quarter of a mile I saw activity around the truck. I started running, hoping they wouldn't take off. I made it there just in time to yell to the passenger as he was closing his door. He stuck his foot out to hold the door and asked me where I was going. Los Angeles was the only town on my mind so I told him that. He opened the side compartment and I threw my things into it.

As we took out along Highway 40 they took time to introduce themselves. Red was in the sleeper and Slim was driving. Slim told me about the fires in California we were heading into. He also talked about the bad hills that we were heading for and hills he'd driven in the past, before the roads were improved. I felt I wasn't traveling in a very safe world. Slim liked to talk and point to places along the road, like the trails that curved out of sight on the location where they filmed "F Troop." He'd point out roads winding alongside the interstate that were parts of old Route 66. He had stories to tell about driving the old road.

Red took a nap, then while laying on his back with his feet on the ceiling, he started talking about what heaven was going to be like. He wondered if he'd have all his broken bones replaced. He'd been run over during a truck hi-jacking in California ten years back. Someone monkey wrenched him and drove over him while they took off with his truck.

The Arizona state line looked like a toll booth in the middle of the desert. They didn't hold us up very long. Red and Slim had everything in order. When we got to Flagstaff, Red woke up while we were riding over some railroad tracks. He was growling about something, and Slim turned to him. The car in front of us stopped while Slim wasn't looking. When Slim turned back and saw the situation he reached up and popped buttons, pulled a handle, applied the brakes and stopped about three inches off the car's back bumper. I was impressed.

In Kingman, Nevada we stopped for supper. Mark must've given me some money 'cause I bought a roast beef dinner and a post card. I dropped my family a line. A sign somewhere along the road said, "Las Vagas 5 miles." I saw the fires in California and some pretty steep hills, then I woke up to the sight of lights—blue, orange, white, and green—spread out in lines or squares as far as I could see. Red was driving and told me it was the San Bernadino Valley. We were about fifty miles out and that was as far as they'd go. He said to wait around, and he would try to get me a ride to the bus station downtown. It took a half an hour to get a ride over. A man came through yelling for everyone wanting to go to the bus stop. As I got in his car I saw Red limping around his truck, checking tires, in the same parking lot where he had gotten mugged ten years ago.

The bus stop was a couple of miles away. It was about one o'clock in the morning. I stood there with four other guys, taking it in, wondering why the station was closed. I could feel the dampness of the ocean. The temperature was warm again.

The next bus was leaving at seven o'clock in the morning, so I sat my knapsack against the wall and threw my duffle bag down next to it. A little conversation started. We found out from a local yokel that we didn't have enough money between us for a bus ticket to L.A. Well, I had my banjo and started playing. I'd never done this before. I'd learned to tune it from a book in Denver. I played some of Bob Dylan's songs that used a basic three-chord pattern. I'd learned Mr. Bojangles in the key of C, and I played a little John Denver.

It didn't take very long for a crowd to start gathering. I started having fun. A pool hustler came by and sat next to me. I continued to play while I answered his questions. "Where are you from? Where are you going?" He told me, "You'll be going further than that if you keep playing like that." I was on the right track, I was doing things right!! I told him we were waiting for a bus at seven o'clock and that we didn't have enough money to get everyone on. He gave me ten dollars and showed me forty more. He said, "I'll take this money into the next town and turn it into two or three hundred." A friend of his came by, and they decided it was coffee time. They invited me along. The cops had circled the block a couple of times already, so I asked the others to watch my stuff and went with them.

We sat in a little restaurant with a counter running the whole length of the place and with high-back wooden booths along the wall behind it. We talked about our seven-second trips to Venus and back (the record was three and one-half), and how the whole earth was nothing more than a thin layer of solid mass floating around a molten firey core. Normal things people talk about over a cup of coffee, and I was digging it. I could see by the wonder in their eyes that they were talking about things they really believed in. I could almost believe in them myself.

On the way back to the bus station we met a couple of fellows who followed along with us. I sat down next to my duffle bag, leaned on my knapsack, and started playing again. The crowd grew to about twenty people. A big woman, really dirty, sat down on my duffle bag. I was playing Red River valley. She started talking to me in a drunk, sad way. While I played she told me she had a son about my age in Hawaii, serving in the Air Force. My heart went out to this fat, pock-faced, smelly old woman. I realized she was a mother who really missed her son, and as she sat there crying, she made me think of my mom and I wondered if she was thinking of me.

Before too long I was checking out my crowd of people. The two who followed us back from the restaurant were holding hands, talking with two other men as they leaned against the building. My pool hustling friend had a man and woman passing time in conversation. The lady was dressed in a short black dress with ear rings, nylons, and high heeled shoes; her man was in a suit. The three of them walked off after a while as did the four guys, with their hands in each other's hip pockets. Mom was still sitting there and the police were making a regular patrol around the block.

Between the time the crowd dispersed and the station opened, we rested. I made seventeen dollars and some change, more than enough to get us on the bus. I had two dollars left as we rolled toward Los Angeles. When we got into the city I looked everywhere I could at the buildings, people, and cars. I jumped from one seat to another as the bus twisted through downtown. I saw a man that looked like John Lennon standing on a corner. That was about the time they let the Beatles back in the U.S.A. on the west coast, so it could've been him. He looked like the picture of Lennon on the Abby Road album.

When I got off the bus I asked for directions to the nearest beach. It wasn't far, only a few blocks. Highway 1 ran along the beach, but it didn't look any different than any other city street. The beach was only one block to the west of it. There was a big, round auditorium just west of the highway, right next to the sand. The Doors were playing there that day.

I dug the beach with its yellow sand and big waves constantly rolling in. It was not nearly as crowded as I expected. Salt spray filled the air and the sky was as blue as a baby's eyes. I'd seen the Pacific Ocean four or five times, but this scene reminded of a cartoon, and I expected Pluto or Mickey Mouse to come strolling up any time.

It was time to get back to the basics. I hadn't eaten since Kingman, and I was hungry. I asked a local derelict where the soup line was. I'd never eaten in one before, but it was time to start. He told me the only soup line was at the Salvation Army and pointed north on Highway 1 away from the auditorium. I found the Salvation Army with no trouble. I sat through a service before supper and found a place in the supper line. I was carrying all my things, and a guy in line asked if I knew how to play "Dueling Banjos," from the show *Deliverance*. I set my things down and started playing it. I was close to the door and the music drifted into the chapel. Somebody, a sergeant or a colonel, came out and said they didn't allow that kind of music to be played around there. I had to leave. I tried "ifs," "and," and "buts," but I had to leave. I was proud and ornery, so I left as if I had wanted to go anyway. Those potatoes and that ham didn't smell that good after all. And those biscuits . . .

I walked north and back to the beach. I walked over to the Long Beach Pier and checked out the bar at the end of it. A few years later I saw it on the news after a tidal wave hit it. It looked pretty wet.

It was getting dark when I headed into town. I talked with a guy riding a bike about where I could get something to eat. He said Redondo Beach was a good place and told me where it was. The big buildings of Los Angeles were behind me when the sun came up the next morning. I found a beach and followed the fence between the beach and the hotels. I found a little hole through the fence into the bushes. It was early. I couldn't see anyone, so I threw my bags through it and crawled in after them. There were two rows of cedar-like bushes with a path down the middle of them. I crawled through till I hit the fence separating the hotels. A sharp left turn brought me close to the buildings, into a little cove where I could sit up. There was room for my bags. I could sleep there without worrying about anyone on the beach seeing me, and hotel guests would have to look straight down from their windows to see me.

I slept till around noon. I heard people walking by, couples talking, children down on the water front. I wondered if I could get out of there without getting spotted. I took only my banjo and crawled to my opening. There were only a few kids and their parents out there, playing in the water or looking the other way. I climbed out. I was free. I was also hungry.

A quarter of a mile to the north I could see tent tops, like a carnival. I headed for them. It was the Redondo Beach Pier. There were food stands set up along it. A big canopy let the lunchers sit at picnic tables and eat hamburgers, pizzas, pop corn, tortillas, cotton candy, hot dogs, and a variety of other snacks. I noticed that no one cleared up after himself, so I grabbed a napkin and started cleaning tables. There was a part of a hamburger here, some French fries there. It turned out to be quite a meal. I ate lunch and supper that day, and lunch and supper the next day too. Once I tried to stop a lady from throwing away a full hamburger that her kid wouldn't eat. "Excuse me ma'm, could I have that hamburger?"

"You certainly cannot. Buy your own food!" she said as she jammed it into the receptacle. I hadn't eaten out of trash cans yet, so I consoled myself with another half hour of cleaning tables.

I'd been playing my banjo along the beach between meals. I made about two dollars in two days but everything was all right, I had my place to sleep. I was eating, and I was swimming in the ocean to stay clean. I'd struck up a couple of conservations that led me to parties with drugs and alcohol, so I was getting high also, for free. Life couldn't get any better for a 1960s hippie. Not much free love yet, but I was sure I was on the right road.

■ *Karl Smithson*

Karl Smithson has been a homeless activist for many years, almost a walking conscience on homeless issues for Nashville politicians and voters. He is an occasional guest columnist for the local newspapers and a frequent subject of their stories.

I AM A MAN

My name is Karl Knox Smithson. I am forty-eight years old. I am unemployed, impoverished, chemically mentally ill, disabled, and sometimes homeless. I want to tell you my story. And I want to tell you about my dream and about my vision.

I was born in Nashville, Tennessee on August 23, 1948. My father had a degree in engineering from Vanderbilt University, and when I was eight years old we moved to Tullahoma, Tennessee where he worked as a project engineer at the largest wind tunnel facility in the world.

And it was in Tullahoma that patterns were formed that I have repeated throughout my life. I have always been the outsider, the misfit, the foreigner, the loner.

I graduated from Tullahoma High School in 1966. That fall I entered college at Middle Tennessee State University (M.T.S.U.) in Murfreesboro. After one semester I quit and went to work at a shoe factory in Tullahoma. They worked us very hard for very little pay. I knew I did not want to do that for the rest of my life.

In the fall of 1967 I reentered M.T.S.U. And that fall I was first committed to a state mental hospital. It is hard for me to remember all the events that led to my incarceration, but I do remember that I was always speaking out in class and asking questions and challenging the professors. My best memory from my first commitment to Central State was that two of my professors thought enough of me to visit me.

I received ten weeks of shock treatments in the spring of 1968. The purpose of shock treatments is to bring about loss of memory which is then supposed to break the depression. I believe shock treatments are evil. I believe shock treatments are punishment, not treatment, that are administered to people who refuse to adjust to what the powers to be in this evil, corrupt, immoral world define and declare to be reality. I refuse to adjust to an evil, immoral, and corrupt society. I pray and hope that I will always be given the strength to remain creatively maladjusted. The Good Book tells us not to be conformed to this world, but be transformed (Romans 12:2).

Martin Luther King, Jr. tells us in *The Strength to Love*, "The salvation of the world from impending doom lies in the hands of the creatively maladjusted."

Just a little over three years after my shock treatments—in 1970—I was teaching a class at M.T.S.U. where they had previously kicked me out.

～

I graduated from Middle Tennessee State University in 1971. I received the award for outstanding student in political science. I also received an award for having a 4.0 average as a history major. From fall 1971 through spring 1972 I taught two classes of American History for two semesters as a teaching graduate assistant.

I completed almost all my course work for a master's degree, but I never wrote my thesis. Instead, I dropped out and went to work. For four months I worked eighty hours a week. I lived in Murfreesboro and drove to Nashville where I worked as a motel clerk afternoons and evenings from 3 P.M. to 11 P.M. And then I worked as a parking lot attendant from midnight until 8 A.M. Why did I do this?

On June 1, 1969 I was married. My wife was a native of Murfreesboro. She was also a graduate student at M.T.S.U. in 1971-72. One night she very nearly died when she took all of her sleeping pills after drinking heavily. She told me what she did. She hugged me. And then she laid down on the bed and was unconscious within minutes. I got her to the hospital as quick as I could.

She lay virtually lifeless on her bed in the intensive care unit. Her skin was blue, and she felt stone cold. She was more dead than alive. I was later told that a doctor said he wouldn't give a dime for her chances of living. But she did live.

I had not been a good husband. Basically all I did was study, but seeing your wife more dead than alive does get your attention. For the first time in our marriage I put her first in my life. She became my number one priority. I decided that I would do whatever it took to help bring my wife back to life with a new beginning and new hope. And I did it.

Her psychologist said I helped her more than he did. And I did. I learned to listen to her. I spent hours and hours listening to her. It was the greatest experience of my life seeing my wife come alive, blossom, and flourish. And it was also very, very powerful, for we reached a point where the stronger she got, the weaker I became.

In December 1972 my wife received her master's degree in psychology from M.T.S.U. At the time I was working as a juvenile probation counselor over a four-county area in Middle Tennessee. I continued to get weaker and weaker as my wife got stronger and stronger. Something had to change. My wife had outgrown me. I agreed that she should leave me.

She had become my whole world. When she left, my whole world ended. I had no reason or purpose to live. I tried to kill myself and ended up committed to the state mental hospital for the second time in the spring of 1973.

The usual procedure for committing someone to a state mental hospital is for a parent, relative, or friend to sign a petition asking for a judge to issue the order for incarceration. Tennessee law requires an examination by two medical doctors. And then the petition is presented to the county judge.

Formerly in rural Tennessee, the county judge usually did not have a law degree. That a citizen of Tennessee could be deprived of his liberty by a so-called judge who did not have any legal training was a gross injustice. The Tennessee state legislature eventually changed the law, so that today all judges who have the power to incarcerate must have a law degree.

When my wife deserted me, she called up my parents and told them I was their problem now. She washed her hands of me and started a new life and treated me as if I had never existed. She became a therapist in the Nashville mental health system.

In his book, *The Myth of Mental Illness*, Dr. Thomas Sazz defines a mental patient as a loser in a family dispute.

⌒

I spent most of that year living at Central State Hospital in Nashville. It was a very good experience for me. I was very fortunate.

My psychologist, Ron Check, became my friend. I met with him for therapy twice a week for the next two years. I can still picture Ron with tears in his eyes as he listened to my story. It was Dr. Ron Check (who tragically committed suicide eighteen years later) who taught me something I believe with all my heart: that the solution for people in crisis is not more programs but personal relationship with people who have the courage to care and open their hearts to the suffering of others, who respond to their pain by sharing it and taking concrete action to get rid of it.

And it was also while I was incarcerated in the admissions ward at Central State that I learned a very important lesson that I try to practice today: that to become free you must be willing to take a stand and put your life on the line.

His name was Herschel Brown. He trained walking horses in Shelbyville, Tennessee, the Walking Horse Capital of the World. Like Big, Bad Leroy Brown, he was originally from the South Side of Chicago. He was also a former Golden Gloves Boxing Champion.

I was told that when Herschel Brown threw a "fit" that it literally took dozens of aids from all the various buildings to come and handle him. On a locked admissions ward of a mental hospital, you get a rare opportunity to see how the pecking order is established. In our world of the hospital ward, Herschel Brown was number one. Whatever Herschel wanted, Herschel got.

One day Herschel decided he wanted my red shirt. He told me my shirt was his shirt, and he took it. I am, I confess, basically a coward. But there comes a time in all men's lives in which you must take a stand. My time had come.

I told Herschel it was my shirt. He could have it, but it was my shirt. Herschel invited me to fight him. I politely declined the invitation and then did not move a muscle. And there I stood. All alone.

Whenever a fight occurred everyone cleared out. The aides would lock themselves up in the office until the smoke cleared.

I let the boxing champion take the first swing at me. I never swung back. And I won. And I gained my freedom.

Fortunately I had some aides in the locked admissions ward who liked me. They immediately switched me to an open ward before Herschel killed me. The next morning Herschel was like a walking zombie, full of injected thorazine.

You must take a stand to become free. You must be willing to die.

⌒

I consider myself a revolutionary. I have been at war against the state for almost thirty years.

When I was in college I took courses on the American Revolution, the French Revolution, the Russian Revolution, the Protestant Revolution, etc.

One time I read a trilogy of books about Lenin, Stalin, and Trotsky. In the preface the author printed a poem by Robert Frost, which has had a major impact on my life.

In the "Masque of Reason" God told Job:

"Society can never think things out,
They have to see them acted out by actors,
Devoted actors at a sacrifice,
The ablest actors I can lay my hands on."

As I studied the lives of revolutionaries, I learned that there was usually one event which radicalized the person's life. My event occurred on February 27, 1975 in Manchester, Tennessee, the county seat of Coffee County. His name was John Ray. He was the county judge. In my opinion, he had committed me illegally to the state hospital twice.

I had been working at a factory in Tullahoma in 1974 and 1975. There was a recession, and I lost my job. I was living with my parents. My father had always told me that I would have a home with them. His only requirement was that I love and obey both him and my mother. And I would like to think that I did so.

Of course I was a major disappointment to my father. He told me that all he ever expected out of me was that I would be able to keep a roof over my head. Losing my job indicated to me that my hopes becoming financially independent were not going to happen. Most everyone incarcerated at a state mental hospital comes to have a very negative self-image. I came to the conclusion that my life was over. I came to believe that it was cruel and unusual punishment to place a person in a state mental hospital. To commit a person to a state mental hospital was to doom that person to a LIVING HELL for the rest of his life. I decided this time I would let my father see how he liked Central State. And that is why I tried to have my father committed. In my eyes and in my rage I wanted him to have a taste of the LIVING HELL that he had given me as my inheritance.

I went to see Judge Ray. It was time I take a stand again. I was fighting for my freedom, with life and death seriousness. I lost.

Judge Ray's face turn totally pale. He ran around his desk like a chicken with its head cut off. He called up the sheriff. They put me in the drunk tank. Ron Check drove down from Nashville to explain me to the judge. As Deputy Conn drove me to Nashville, I asked him, "Aren't I supposed to have a trial before the judge?" The deputy replied: "He never wants to see you again."

But there was one small problem. Judge Ray had signed commitment papers stating that he had given me a trial as required by law. Of course he did not give me a trial. *He lied.* Judge John Ray grossly violated my constitutional rights as a citizen, and he violated my human rights as a child of God. Ever since that event of February 27, 1975, I have been seeking JUSTICE for myself and for people like me.

When I reached the state hospital in Nashville, I told them there was nothing wrong with me. I told them I was a political prisoner. They said, "Sure, sure. Come in and stay awhile." A few months later, those same hospital officials were asking me when I was going to leave. I told them, "Look, I may be crazy, but I'm not dumb. It is a mean, cruel world out there. I like it here. I don't want to leave." I fought them as long as I could, but by Christmas time, 1975, they finally got me to leave. And that has been the story of my life. Taking stands. Fighting for freedom. And seeking justice.

You can look it up in the law books. All the lawyers in Nashville told me I couldn't sue the county judge because he had judicial immunity.

I had always dreamed of being a lawyer. I twice entered the Y.M.C.A. Night Law School in Nashville but never lasted more than a few weeks. But even though I never became a lawyer, I can think like a lawyer. And that is what is important. To all lawyers in Nashville I said, "You are wrong. I am right. Yes, I can sue the county judge."

And there it is in the Federal Case Law: SMITHSON V. RAY (427 F. Supp 11 (1976). On May 3, 1976 Federal District Judge Neese ruled "that the judge was not entitled to judicial immunity for any acts beyond his jurisdiction." And it was because of SMITHSON V. RAY that I became HOMELESS as of July 17, 1990. That summer I became energized again. I came to sincerely believe that God wanted me to move to Nashville into the Union Rescue Mission and become homeless.

I became homeless voluntarily. I was not forced to move out from my parents' house. We were now getting along okay. I made the move because I sincerely felt I was being led by the Spirit of God. I sincerely felt the Spirit of the Lord was upon me. I still do. Even more so today than ever.

The first thing I did after getting off the Greyhound bus on July 17, 1990 that brought me from Tullahoma to Nashville was to buy a bus ticket to Bristol, Tennessee. And then I moved into the Union Rescue Mission where I was basically to reside for the next seven months. As soon as I got settled in and adjusted to my "home," I visited the Davidson County Courthouse on July 31, 1990 where I filed a pro se complaint against the State of Tennessee and the Honorable Ned Ray McWherter, Governor. While living in Tullahoma in the early 1980s, an office of the federally funded legal Services Corporation was opened. I asked the lawyers there to help me gain justice for the violations of my rights I had suffered. They turned down my request. But I appealed their denial and was finally assigned a lawyer.

Kathleen Maloz went to court for me, and she got court orders to have the records of the 1975 commitment expunged and sealed.

Now that I had official documents and court papers proving that my rights had been violated, I now sought punitive damages for all the harm and injury and suffering that had been inflicted on me by the State of Tennessee. And that was why I filed my pro se complaint on July 31, 1990. In my own mind I was declaring war against the state of Tennessee and its leader, the governor.

1990 was an election year. I planned to enter the election as an independent candidate for governor and carry the war against the state to the electorate. That was why I bought that bus ticket to Bristol, Tennessee. I was going to walk across the state like Lamar Alexander did in his successful campaign for governor in 1978.

I had spent a day with Lamar during that campaign. I ate breakfast with him in Tullahoma. Then me and Lamar and my boss drove to Murfreesboro where we ate lunch, after we first stopped and walked around the square in Manchester. And then we walked out the road to Franklin. I didn't see Lamar do anything that day that I couldn't do as well if not better.

But I had a problem. The campaign T-shirt that I was going to wear as I walked across the state said on the back: "Karl Smithson for Mayor." So I decided to run for mayor of Nashville in 1991 and postponed my campaign for governor.

(The reason I had that T-shirt was explained by a front page story that appeared in the *Tullahoma News* on November 16, 1983. The headline on the front page read: SMITHSON PLANS MAYORAL RACE.)

When people ask me why I want to run for mayor and for governor when I have absolutely no chance of getting elected, I think of what my friend the Rev. Bill Friskis-Warren told *The Tennessean*: "Karl has done more to humanize homelessness, to put a face on the issue than almost anyone else in our community."

And almost exactly one year after I became homeless and moved into the mission, that Karl Smithson for Mayor T-shirt appeared on the front page of the *Nashville Banner* of July 26, 1991. Ten days before that, on July 16, 1991, my picture appeared on the front page of *The Tennessean*, along with the other three candidates in a mayoral debate.

And that has been the story of my life: homeless one year, and the next I'm on the front page twice in ten days.

∽

I now have a new T-shirt. On the back it reads "Karl Smithson for Governor." My shirt was created by my good friend Anne Brose who was selected by the Mayor's Committee on Disability as 1996 Artist of the Year.

I consider myself to be an expert on public opinion, the political process, and revolution. For the last twenty-five years, I have been learning in the School of Hard Knocks what I learned in theory in college.

I know from personal experience that that great promise from the Hebrew prophet Isaiah is true and real: "For God gives power to the tired and worn out and strength to the weak. And they that rail upon the Lord shall have their strength renewed. They shall mount up with wings like eagles ... "

As I write, by the grace of God, I'm soaring higher and higher. How high will I fly? Only time will tell.

I came to Nashville, the city of my birth, and became homeless in order to make my last stand.

On Monday, October 28, 1996, *The Nashville Banner's* religion editor Francis Meeker had this to say about me: "Karl Smithson, 48, likes to think he can make a difference in the world .... Because he suffers from bouts of severe depression, Smithson is unable to work and draws a monthly disability check of $470. He lives in Parthenon Homes, a low-rent housing complex in the West End for the elderly and people with disabilities."

Why was the religion editor writing about Karl Smithson? Because I gave $1,000 in an attempt to save a Black Institute at the Vanderbilt Divinity School.

About two weeks later on November 13, 1996, religion editor Ray Waddle wrote a front page article in *The Tennessean* about a retreat for the homeless that I sponsored and financed. Once again my picture appeared on the front page. And I was quoted: "When people learn you're homeless, they stop listening. Politicians don't listen because the homeless don't vote. We need an advocate, someone the public will listen to."

Here I am, Lord. I'll go. Send me.

In my Here I Stand campaign I will be calling for a new policy of the SPIRIT where the number one requirement is the courage to care through sacrificial love. And this is my story. It is my SONG.

■ *Jim Mince*

At the time I knew him at MATTHEW 25, Jim Mince was a day laborer and Willie Nelson look-alike who also played guitar, wrote songs, and sang. He talked with a Texas accent and spelt phonetically. I left his spelling intact to give readers an idea of his speech.

THE BEGENNING OF THE END

In China recently there was supposed to be a gathering of students and scollars. They gathered to protest the way the government was being run. They wonted to see a better government. They were for democracy.

The government let them have the meeting, then when things were in full swing, the government sent troops in, killing and mutulating hundreads. They had obsurvers, so that later they could round up the ring leaders. Education is good, but this is what they ment when they said a little nollage can be dangerous.

I have been in Nashville little over a year. I came here to see what I could do with my songs. Shortley after I arrived my truck was stolen along with ever thing else I owned. So I was forced to live on the street. Being a construction worker and having a good traid, most of what I had saw in life was the good life. I never saw people haf to stand in doorways to stay out of the rain, or sleep under vidock's on hard concreat, some time with cordbord under them to keep the cold of the concreat from coming through. Get up at five in the morning to go to the mission for breekfest and by six go to the labor sourse to be sent out on all sorts of jobs from carring sheat rock to shingles at a meager wage of three thirty-five. And then only three to four days a week. How in heaven's name dose suciety expect these people to get off the street? They don't. This world is ruled by five percent.

When I grew up, times were good. If you would work it didn't take long to get ahead. And I have been up and down the hill a couple times so I can't complain. I look around and see the drunks on Broadway and from time to time I've found myself down there. Now these people in the barrooms, that I talk to, some run a scam while others tell the trooth.

I beleave in God and Christ and from the turn of events that put me on the street I beleave I was ment to see theas things. And I try my best to stand for what is right.

I am now fifty years old and God has been good to me. Hard work and persurverance has kept me strong, and on my fiftieth birthday I climbed over the peek of the Ryman Auditorium. And I'm grateful to God to feel this good.

But what I've seen and hurd since I hit Nashville hurts a body way down deep inside. I was drinking beer one night at Nashburl last fall when a man I never met came up to me. He told me how he had contracted agent orange while in Viet Naum and that he was dying.

I bought him a drink and stood up and drank to him. As we left the bar a cop car came up. And two cops jumped out. He was only about eight to ten feet ahead of me and before I knew it they had his hands behind him and had hit him on the right side of the fore head three times.

At this I stepped up and told the cops that I had just gotten out of jail an didn't wont go back again. But if they hit him one moor time they were going to give me a reason to do so. I also told them if that be the case they had better call for some back up.

At that they arested him and took him to the hospital. Another man that was with us let me sleep in the back of his pick up that night. And when I woke up the next day he brought me back to town. I went up to the mission and there I met the man who had been beet up. And he invitet me out to his brothers house, gave me a sheep skin vest and three pair of cordoroy britches. I had a nice hot bath, and a large soft bed to sleep in that night.

And shortley after that the cops beet a man so suverely that he died in the hospital that night, so I was told. I talked to men on the street who said that the cops had his hands behind his back before they ever started beating him. It don't take much to figure out who was right.

So one week after New Yeres I walked up to the mission some time shortley after ten. I had been drinking and the adminestrator told me I was bared for life. I've been back since so I guess that waren't true. I had saw men come in to the mission with a countinance that gload. A smile and how you doing coming from them. And they stay a month or to for meager wages. I'm talking five bucks a week or less.

Then they hit Broadway one night for a laff or two. Well they mess up, and the mission kicks them out. Theas same men I've saw mope around like zombies.

So when I was told that I was barred for life I said, Then I might as well nock your head off. I went through the door and hit the man in the nose.

At that a large black man who I had no quarrel with came at me. Not really wanting to hurt him, for I knew he didn't know the reason, I through a punch and hit him in the chest. He picked me up and through me through the door. And as I hit the wall on the other side I saw three cop cars pull up. I scrambled to my feet and hit the side walk. Two cops stood three feet in frunt of me.

They had there sticks helt high and were waring green wool sweaters. The one on my left said run for it. At that I replied I'm not running. But I knew at the best I was in for a whopping. And I said the hell I won't and headed down the hill.

When I got to where the red cross sign was across from salvacion army I turned a bit to find out where they were. A club hit me across the throat and well I hit the ground. They hit me across the throat one moor time.

I balled up and prayed Lord forgive then for they don't know what they do. Thinking they had done there job, they put there hand cuffs on me. And then I lay in jail tell the next morning.

The charge was short and simple. I was charged with staggering outside the mission. And a man came by the drunk tank and said plead guilty and youl be releasead. Thinking what they might do if I spent a week in there I pleadead guilty to the charge.

Now I'm a working man and I eurn my money. I don't steel and I don't cheat. But I had goten off from work at the Ryman. And as I started up the hill at Fift and Broadway I met a friend who said let's have a beer. We were setting in the Turf just he and I. At a table right next to the door. At six thirty a cop came in placed his self about twenty feet from where I sat and comminsed to stare at me. Well I stared back. And after a few seconds he pointed toward the door.

Well he arrested me. No rights did he read. So I set in a van on Broadway for a while. Now I don't thank the cop was bad, but I was mad so I pissed right in his van down on Broadway. They took us all to jail. And he said he still like me. Even though I pissed right in his van.

It was turist season and he had his orders. Arrest any one that looks supicious. Now how high up theas orders came I do not know. But the charges all seem to be the same thing, drunk.

The next day was a work day and I should have been at work by seven. Scared I might loose my job I pleadead guilty. They releasead me. And I was back down at the job by ten.

Now the night of the Summer Lights came around. And I was staying with some frinds at Tooter Inn. And they had all took off earley. And I was by my self.

So I desidead to check out the Summer Lights. I had barely got up town. And I started across the street when a car hit me in the left leg just below the crouch. It threw me across the hood onto the windshield. And I rolled on to the side walk on my back. It seamed like just seconds tell the ambulance arrived and the cops were standing over me. The driver was a young man with his girlfriend. From the way he shook, I knew that he was scared.

So I checked out all my limbs and I knew that they weren't broken. And I told the cops to let him go, it was my falt.

So instead of letting me go they wontead to arrest me. So I said take me to the hospittle. When I arrived at the hospittal I was met by theas same cops, who said with a smurk, You mean you took up an ambulance when some one could have been dying. When they get done with you, well get you yet.

I gave the reseptionest my name. And when she went in to the back I looked around and they were gone. So I got outside the door. And the closest thing I saw where I could hide was a dompster. So I spent the night in there and walked back to town the next day.

I didn't work Monday or Tuesday. For I was in no shape to clime the hights.

This land was built on freedom and liberty and justice for all. Like the people over in China, I wonder where it went when so few can tell so menny what to do.

If a person's doing rong then arrest him. But don't arrest a man cause he wares a red bandanna, or because of what you think that he might do. He must do the crime before he dose the time, or let me ask you, is this little China?

The last thing I have to say is about a friend of mine I asked to hold a couple hundread bucks. He went out to find some grass and they cought him with a couple of dime bags. Now he had my money and two week's wages of his owne. So he spent two weeks in jail on suspission of dealing.

Now he has to go to court to prove his innosence of a charge that should not have been to begin with. Let liberty prevail. And keep us out of jail and who know we might be suciety to.

Commentary: Can We Find Our Way Home?

Shortly after starting work at MATTHEW 25, I got into an argument with an acquaintance who claimed that most of the homeless were mentally ill. He had no firsthand knowledge of the matter, but had read it somewhere. I argued on the basis of my limited experience that many were just the victims of bad breaks, such as divorce and job layoffs. At the time that was pretty much the case—at least at MATTHEW 25.

My feelings were probably shared by those who had created the MATTHEW 25 program. To enter, a man had to have a job. Once there, he had to bank three-quarters of his weekly salary, attend AA or NA meetings once or twice a week, and attend evening shelter discussions on topics such as how to hold a job. The men could stay for two months; in some circumstances, three. The idea was that when they left they would have a job and enough money for a down payment on an apartment and have their problems under control.

I kept in touch with many of the men long after they left MATTHEW 25, and after working there a year began to notice that many who had left with hope and determination, eventually ended up back on the streets. They got into arguments with their bosses and walked off the job or got fired. Sometimes they shared apartments or motel rooms with other alcoholics and drug addicts. One or more might not pay his share of the rent and all would be thrown out. One way or another, most managed to work their way back onto the streets.

At the same time more and more men and women were being pumped onto the streets. And many, I was to find out, were mentally ill. But how many others in the country were seeing psychiatrists and psychologists, let alone taking anti-depressants? Why was the United States churning out so many alcoholics, drug addicts, and depressed and/or mentally ill persons? Clearly enormous numbers of people were using drugs and alcohol to escape from their individual purgatories and hells. It became clear that the little reeducation that we were doing at the shelters was insufficient to effect any revolution in the lives of the homeless. Their problems, whatever they were, were too deeply ingrained for our attempts to make a difference.

I remembered Robert Bolt's introduction to his play, *A Man for All Seasons*, in which he said that people of former times had models by which to pattern their lives—Stoic Philosopher, Saint, Rational Gentleman—but that we had none. Well, we do have at least one, the Consumer, and it is widely shared and destructive. We have other reductionist models—some claim we are a collocation of atoms or molecules, a bundle of reflexes, a vehicle for genes, or naked apes—and though they are not models for behavior, they unfortunately influence it. Materialist explanations of human behavior deny higher functions (e.g., intellectual intuition) or explain them in terms of lower ones (as when behavioral psychologist John B. Watson reduced thought to a series of laryngeal twitches), and once the population has come to accept these explanations, it accepts its own devaluation. As others have remarked, once you believe that you are a naked ape you begin to act like one, and it becomes easier for you to accept a dehumanized environment.

I began to think that having no shared and adequate idea of full humanity that we had created institutions, including workplaces and schools, that were deforming us. And that it was this deformation, caused when basic needs are thwarted, that was creating so much deviant behavior. Consider what has happened to work and education, and the results their degradation have produced.

Beginning with work, we note that prior to the industrial revolution artisans used their skills to make utilitarian objects things of beauty. Afterwards, as more and more objects came to be made by machine, the craftsman became a machine tender, a servo-mechanism. The dehumanization of nineteenth-century industrial work has been fully documented; the documentation of the contemporary dehumanized workplace is underway. In both centuries, work is seen merely as remunerative toil, not necessary for full human development. Stripped of art, it has become labor. Today, for example, we have ample descriptions not only of minimum wage workers struggling without pensions and hospitalization, but of corporate managers who live in fear of being fired because top management believes fear motivates employees better than job security and trust. To cite one example, a 1997 article by David Dorsey in *Fast Company* magazine discusses the work of two men trying to change the contemporary office with a program that classifies the emotions that spur motivation as 'red' or 'green.' "People are motivated by either 'red' emotions—anger, fear, greed—or 'green' emotions—genuine enthusiasm and confidence. Either sort of fuel gets results. Yet one set of emotions gets results as it slowly destroys people; the other can actually improve people's quality of life."

Add to this that Wall Street investors encourage drastic reduction of a company's work force or the relocation of its plant(s) to decrease labor costs, and that more and more jobs are part time and / or temporary. Corporate gurus are telling us that white collar and blue collar workers alike must be prepared to have four or more careers in a lifetime and that most work will be on a contract basis. Probably none of these futurists have asked themselves what the social costs will be. Probably none has recognized that such a system will induce such anxiety and poverty that rates of alcoholism, drug abuse, and violence—not to mention divorce—will soar even higher. Yet workers and managers are told that, like it or not, this is the future and they had better adjust to it.

Education is just as ill. Consider, first of all, that the function of schools is to help perpetuate a culture. Curricula are shaped to produce a type or types of individuals needed to lead and preserve the culture. Aristocratic cultures create a knightly education. Young men in Homeric times were trained in music and gymnastics: music for the cultivation of the soul and gymnastics for the body. In ancient Rome, where full citizenship demanded that men enter public life and oratory was important, training focused upon rhetoric. Later, in medieval times, colleges and universities taught the liberal arts, which originally included the mathematical as well as the language arts, as a preparation for the study of philosophy and theology. In time the rigor of studies abated, and the introduction of the elective system by Harvard in the nineteenth century paved the way for the general elimination—beginning in the late 1800s—of mathematics and classical languages from the prescribed syllabus. The loss of rigor has proceeded apace, until in our time there are few mandatory courses and the resulting smorgasbord of studies at American colleges is, according to a 1986 report by the Carnegie Foundation for the Advancement of Teaching, intended to appeal to the student as buyer. The study noted that American students are trained to respond well on tests and to master details in a special field. "But technical skill, of whatever kind," the report noted, "leaves open essential questions: Education for what purpose? Competence to what end?"

The students themselves tell us they are in college to get well-paying jobs after graduation. And what the "liberal arts" colleges tell us or used to tell us in their catalogs, was that they were preparing free men. But the "curricula" or "course of studies" at these schools are, of course, without purpose or end. The humanities are in disarray. The physical, biological, and computer sciences fare much better: at least they can prepare students for work. But colleges have no vision of the kind of people they want to shape or of the kind of society we should have. Such talk was abandoned long before it became politically incorrect. Such colleges cannot perpetuate let alone resurrect a vital and healthy culture because they have no vision of a culture beyond what the major corporations have created. An educational smorgasbord not only fails to provide direction to the young, but adds to their confusion and thwarts an integrated understanding of things, which great curricula provide. Humanities without vision and narrowly focused into disparate fields deadens curiosity and intellectuality. They kill the desire to know, and thereby kill an essential part of the human being. Today's colleges are without curricula because those driving this society are, as a class, antiintellectual and unimaginative. The best such leaders can provide is narrow vocational training.

⌇

When it became clear to me that our inadequate and partial ideas on the nature of the human being were at the root of the modern crisis, I decided to investigate what traditional civilizations said constituted full humanity. One thing I knew: that full humanity, according to the ancients, was not conferred at birth, but was hard won. I wanted to make this investigation a public quest, bringing together the homeless and non-homeless, those with power face to face with those who lacked it. On the other hand, I wanted the people with power—legislators, journalists, direct care providers and others—to realize that homelessness is a systemic problem and that modernism is its root. I approached the Tennessee Humanities Council with the idea of a seminar, suggesting thirteen weeks of the Confucian classics, thirteen weeks of Greek texts, followed by thirteen weeks of medieval texts. They were enthusiastic and we got our funding.

The seminar was to be run on the Socratic model. I wanted to be able to identify at least one homeless individual who would emerge from these discussions as a public figure. He or she would be cognizant of traditional thought and modernity's divergence from it. From the readings and discussions of the books, and from the arguments, I hoped to sharpen this person's analytic and speaking abilities. I wanted this person honed for public debate with politicians and bureaucrats.

We had two sessions with a different group at each, one at noon with brown bag lunches, the other in the evening. The first noon session had twenty-five people, at least; the evening session almost as many. The numbers soon dwindled, but those that remained were loyal to the process. I had, as one of the homeless care providers said, created a kind of church. Over the length of the thirty-nine weeks we had not only direct care providers attending, but bankers, Vanderbilt and Fisk University professors, artists, a Hollywood script writer and producer, aspiring song writers, several journalists, and others. With them were men and women living under bridges or in shacks along the Cumberland River or in shelters.

The seminars were occasionally explosive, as the two times that mentally ill members attacked newcomers and drove them off. Sometimes the sessions lacked spark, but many times the discussions were penetrating. One of the most characteristic things about the discussions was the reaction many had against the texts. Traditional ideas were scoffed at, particularly by the academics. One Vanderbilt University professor, for example, described Socrates as a "wild eyed fanatic who sat on rocks staring into space" and claimed that Plato was a fascist with an iron fist concealed inside a velvet glove.

The first set of readings focused on the idea of vocational classes and their mutual responsibilities within a hierarchically ordered society. The interconnection of these ideas was not the complete answer from any of the traditions as to what constituted full humanity, but they gave us part of it. I began with five short readings, each from a different culture and illustrating the traditional idea that each of us has a vocation and belongs to a distinct natural—not social—caste. The Hindu and medieval Christian cultures had both illustrated the idea with the image of a body whose parts represent the different castes or classes. The brahmins or priestly caste are represented by the head, indicating the primacy of contemplation over action; the knights and nobility are represented by the arms, whose duty is to execute the orders of the head. The legs represent the peasantry, upon whom all stand. What our medieval Christian writer, John of Salisbury made explicit, and our Hindu text, the *Brahma Sutra*, left implicit, is the necessity for and interdependence of all parts.

While there is, according to tradition, a hierarchy to gifts, all are necessary for the full functioning of society. In chapter XII of I *Corinthians*, St. Paul had talked of that with respect to the church. "And God hath set some in the church, first apostles, secondarily prophets, thirdly teachers, after that miracles, then gifts of healings, helps, governments, diversities of tongues." The church needs all spiritual gifts, Paul stressed, just as the human body needs all its parts.

For the same session we read the opening hundred lines of the *Iliad* and saw the mutual interdependence of men and gods, and their responsibilities towards each other.

With these readings it became clear that since each person's gifts are needed, the exercise of one's vocation is a duty, a responsibility. These readings also made clear that traditional peoples, living in hierarchical societies of natural castes, and within a cosmos structured by a hierarchy of forms, knew their position within the cosmos and within their societies. Furthermore, each traditional culture viewed its land as the center of the world, and the center of their land as sacred. Add to that that the hearth was the sacred center of the home, and the column of smoke from the tepee or hut the equivalent of the world axis, and it is clear that traditional peoples were framed by a concentric ring of symbols that positioned them squarely at the center of the world. Such people were truly at home in the world, even the nomads, whose wanderings were dictated by the rising and setting of stars.

After reading the selections for the first session, I asked the participants whether democracy offered us a set of mutual responsibilities and a sense of interdependence. The groups were silent. That, as Steven Meinbresse noted, was because we had none. For all of our anti-traditionalist complaints and railings against castes and classes, we have no theory of duties and responsibilities. We talk endlessly about our rights and go to court for them, but are silent about our responsibilities.

As a freshman reading *The Odyssey* at St. John's College, the great books school, our seminar tutors would ask us, what is Home? They had no answer, they were genuinely intrigued. Why does Odysseus want to return to Ithaca? He has to endure incredible hardships to get there. He is attacked by men and gods and monsters, buffeted by furious waters. His companions are murdered. So why does he endure it? He could have called an end to his troubles when the goddess Calypso offered him her bed and immortality, but instead Odysseus keeps plunging onward, for ten years. His travels, at first, are motivated by the search for plunder and knowledge; later he learns from the shade of Teiresias the prophet that his palace is overrun by suitors who seek his wife's hand. Ithaca is in disorder.

It is in disorder because he is not there, and it is his duty, as king of Ithaca, to restore order. His home is a particular place, this one island, but it is also his place within a particular society. But he is not only king of Ithaca but *a* king. And a king cannot spend his years adventuring around the world without dire consequences for himself and others. Home is a particular place but it is also determined by our place within society and the cosmos, among the men and gods.

The responsibility of following one's vocation is a major theme of Plato's *Republic*. In it, Plato argues that the just man is one who minds his own business, which means he attends to his own work, follows his own vocation. That is one's duty. The just society is one in which all classes attend to their proper work, that which they do best. We could liken the just society to a well-tuned instrument: when the strings (classes) are tuned (tend to their proper duties), the proper intervals between them are maintained and harmony prevails. The result of not minding one's business brings about disorder. It is what happens when the cobbler displaces the captain of the ship, or the butcher decides he is a horse trainer, or worse yet, when the ambitious lout becomes a politician or a merchant achieves a position of power.

Having destroyed the idea of natural castes and their interdependence and having jettisoned teleology and hierarchy in nature, and above all, having replaced a symbolical mode of thinking with an empirical mode, we wrote ourselves out of the picture: we became alien entities within the cosmos, accidents of nature. We were no longer at home within the world, and certainly not at its center.

$\backsim$

I think that having alienated ourselves and having lost knowledge of our Home that we have affected our hearts. A part of our alienation as a society comes from the fact that the majority of us live in great urban centers far distanced from the land and participation in natural processes. We think that we can control nature and try doing so in various deviant ways, most conspicuously through genetic manipulation. We are afraid of death and try to sustain our lives at all costs, since length of years is more important than quality of time. As an urban people and as materialists we have, somehow, become sentimental and yet cruel. For all these reasons we have come to treat all things as commodities (mechanized dairy farming, for example, treats cows as milking machines; the cosmetics and drug industries use rats, monkeys, and rabbits as product testers), and from there it has been but a small step to treat people as commodities (a baby is conceived to provide bone marrow for an older sibling; raising a corporation's stock value and the wealth of a few justifies firing many hundreds of employees). Once people are a means to gratify us and not an end in themselves, the homeless become more than a nuisance, they become detritus.

That is the view of the enormously popular radio commentator Rush Limbaugh, who in the early nineties repeatedly referred to the homeless as "human debris." He had weekly "homeless updates," in which the homeless would be mocked. One day Limbaugh—a self-professed Christian—took great pleasure in gleefully telling his audience about a homeless woman who had taken shelter one night in a dumpster and had been compacted with the trash the next morning. Since his callers are screened to prevent opposing viewing being aired, we will never know how many people objected not only to this story but to his obscene characterization of the homeless. It is to the shame of media and cultural critics that his words were not loudly and forcefully condemned. The fact that Limbaugh's ratings remained extraordinarily high says volumes about his listeners.

In 1994 writer Michael Ventura reported that Los Angeles radio talk-show host Emiliano Lamon said, "If homeless people cannot survive on their own, why shouldn't they be put to sleep?" Many callers approved of his solution. To those who objected, Lamon retorted, "Do you have a better solution? Do you have a better solution?" As Ventura noted, the fact that Lamon could say this publicly without shame means that he had the support of a significant majority in Los Angeles. Such people are, as Ventura wrote, "dead of heart." They are far, indeed, from fully functioning people, no longer seeing neighbors and fellow citizens as beings endowed with Spirit but as detestable objects.

The creation of a society where all have a home and are at Home is presently beyond our means, for it would require as a first step our spiritual restoration, which given the many conditions now constricting us, is not an immediate likelihood.

RURAL
AMERICA:
THE
MIDWEST

Introduction

The essays and stories in this section were taken from *Heartland Portrait*, a book that grew out of three years of work in rural Iowa, three years of running writing workshops for farm families and residents of rural towns. *Heartland Portrait* itself is a compilation of earlier books, the first of which, *Voices from the Land*, received national attention with a feature on National Public Radio's "Morning Edition" and an Associated Press story that ran in almost every major daily in the country. From the sales and letters that the writers and I received from people across America, I became convinced that there was a great hunger in this land for things rural.

Buoyed in part, I suppose, by this response, we continued for a second year, and kept producing books. *Simple Times*, the second in the series, was written by the now-deceased Clara Leppert, who was then 84 years old. *Simple Times* recounted her life from 1909 to roughly 1950.

Then came *More Voices from the Land*, another anthology, which focused on the ongoing farm crisis. During the same period I began running workshops in northeast Iowa towns, whose purpose was to produce self-portraits of those towns. Stories from three of those books, Independence, Iowa, Clermont, Iowa, and Village Voices: Stories from the Amana Colonies are included in this volume.

But these essays are far more than an account of northeast Iowa, for what happens here is happening everywhere in rural America, a fact that cannot be overemphasized. Even those who do not live in rural America know that rural towns have a disproportionately high population of the elderly, that the family farm is fast disappearing, that rural America lacks an industrial base, and that poverty is widespread.

There is more reason than nostalgia for urbanites to read these stories. There is a deep interconnection between the country and the city, deeper than the connection of food producer to consumer, and it has to do with quantitative methodologies and the growth of centralized power and collectives that govern all our lives. The growth of production efficient methods (which put small farmers out of business) and powerful corporations (which monopolize farm profits) and the state and national legislatures (which tell us, wisely or not, how to use our land) have left many rural Americans poor and powerless. Wealth, concentrated in the cities, continues flowing to the cities, and there is nothing that rural Americans have been able to do about it. It is that powerlessness in the face of the great collectives that has led so many rural Americans to see the federal government as their oppressor and to rise of right-wing groups, including militias.

These stories describe, sometimes explicitly and sometimes indirectly, the impact of technology on farming practices, the land, and community. In the course of my work in Iowa I have found that what is true for rural Iowa is true for the rest of rural America. Those of us who live in the countryside—whether in Ohio, Kentucky, Mississippi, Iowa, Kansas, or in any of a dozen other states—share the same problems. These stories describe rural problems in the words of rural residents, but they also describe possible solutions.

I spent several years contemplating how one could go about rebuilding regional economies which had once flourished in the United States and several of the commentaries tell how I think the rebuilding might proceed, from the redirection of the individual to the rebuilding of towns, and finally to the coalescence of area towns into regional cities, and regional cities into a larger regional economy.

My conversations with people here on the need for a self-sufficient regional economy have awakened me to the divisions within and between rural towns, divisions perhaps too deep ever to repair. Fragmentation, I have often thought, is the driving force of our time, far more powerful than any integrating force. Thus it often seems that any integrating ideas that might emerge, no matter whose, will not be acted on. There is envy here, as elsewhere, and rural towns—like urban areas—may be far too divided ever to unite. Perhaps, after further dissolution, after a time of many years when our state and federal governments will have been reduced to a pro forma existence, then perhaps communities will emerge.

FARM STORIES

Introduction

The farm books grew out of a writing workshop that first met in the farmhouse of Bill and Esther Welsh, organic farmers and neighbors who first helped me recruit and organize the workshop. Bruce Carlson, the Lansing dentist, told me about them and suggested that I contact Bill. Later, when the local paper announced that the Welsh Family Organic Farm was hosting a tour of their operation, I realized that this was my opportunity to begin recruiting.

As we were escorted around the buildings I met another of my neighbors, Bob Leppert, who was the first in our area to adopt organic farming methods. I talked to Bob about a workshop as we trudged around, explaining that the book would offer farmers the opportunity to say to the public what they wanted about the ongoing farm crisis. I explained the success we'd had in getting national attention for the homeless books, and Bob was interested.

The same day, after the tour, we all sat inside the Welsh's garage on folding chairs and socialized. I talked to Bill Welsh and to Greg, his eldest son, who at once realized that the book represented an opportunity to present so much of rural life, including the emerging organic revolution.

A few nights later I spent three or four hours talking with Bob Leppert until midnight, an intense conversation I can recall to this day: the kind of passionate conversation young college students generally have, full of conviction and ranging over many subjects.

Shortly after that, Bob and I visited the Welshes again, drawing up a list of possible participants. Three months later, when we finally met on a Monday night around the Welshes' twelve-foot dining table, there were seven of us, three farming couples: Bill and Esther Welsh, Bob and Barb Leppert, Danny and Frances Cole, and myself. Danny dropped out but Clara Leppert, Bob's mother, Bruce Carlson, the Lansing dentist, and Greg Welsh joined us. Others came by briefly, among them Dorothy and Richard Sandry.

We began meeting shortly before Christmas 1991, and met every Monday after evening chores, rotating from one farmhouse to another, until spring planting. For me it provided community; perhaps for the others too. Certainly they anticipated each week's meeting, not only for the writing and the reading and the reactions they got to their work, but for the socializing afterwards, when the hosts would bring out tea and coffee, sandwich makings or desserts. They called it lunch.

Over food and coffee we would discuss the loss of community, the decline of the national economy, the problems of the family farm, and ways to counteract the dissolution we saw everywhere. And I would think to myself, "If only some of my city friends could hear these conversations!" Without being there, they would find it hard to believe the level of sophistication.

Most of us had separate agendas for the project. I had told the farmers that once each of them had finished a piece that we would give public readings with discussion afterwards in which they would be able to engage the urban audiences, and that those discussions would be the heart of the project.

I anticipated that my neighbors would impress urban audiences, and they did. After their reading in La Crosse, Wisconsin, a college professor remarked, "I thought people like that died out forty years ago!"

I am extremely fortunate to live among them. Having resided in ten states, among all sorts and conditions of people, I have seldom met their like. They live the agrarian ideal that Jefferson wanted for this country: they are the virtuous citizens that he dreamed would fill the continent. Their writings are record of a community that once existed here, of the growing costs and instability of farming, of the love of the land. It is a record that will endure.

■ *Richard Sandry*

Richard Sandry retired from farming several years after the workshop closed, tried several other occupations and is now back farming. He has a natural gift with words and since the workshop occasionally writes a story.

MEMORIES

It stands alone now and largely unnoticed by the numbers of people who pass by it every day of their busy lives. Like a giant old oak tree that is removed from the scene, it would not really be missed, unless for some reason, one day, the building would be gone. Officially it was known as Lansing No. 3, but to most it was known as the Churchtown School.

Its life has been stripped from its interior: the students' desks, the teacher's desk, the recitation bench, and all the material that set it aside as a place of learning for those first wonderful eight years of elementary education. Its bell having rung to call the children to its doors for the last time some thirty-five years ago, its only purpose now is to serve as a monument of brick and mortar to by-gone days. Days of a slower pace of life, when terms like 'substance abuse,' 'AIDS,' 'government programs,' 'government deficits,' 'welfare programs,' and 'abortion' had not yet come into being.

Built in 1875 on the highest spot in the nearby area, it commands a panoramic view of the hills and valleys dotted by farms and homes. Some of the farms are now empty and their buildings mostly abandoned because, due to the government's cheap food policy, their owners could not make enough money to support their families and had to move on. These same farms in earlier times were prospering and sending sometimes six or seven children to school, all at the same time.

Due to the lack of records we have to use our imagination and fantasize that maybe the builders of the school somehow stored away a spirit in her. Maybe in the belfry or perhaps behind her two large blackboards. What stories she could tell of nature's elements beating against her walls like so many armies trying to knock down the walls of a fortress. For nearly one hundred and seventeen years she has won every battle, and stands as sound as the day of her completion.

She would remember her first teacher telling the students about then-President Ulysses Grant and of the Civil War and President Lincoln's assassination just ten years before.

She also heard firsthand of current events like the Spanish-American War, the sinking of the Titanic, the first automobile, the first airplane, World War I, the great depression, World War II, and the Korean War. The time span of fifteen presidents from Grant to Eisenhower.

I wonder if she would remember that first day of school in the late summer of 1941 when a shy, black-haired boy entered her door for the first time to begin his eight years of education. He soon learned the advantage of being the first one to school on those opening days in succeeding years, not because he was so anxious to begin the year, but because that usually gave him the pick of his desk for the year. The best one being the one by the window, where if the teacher didn't notice, he could look out of the window to see which neighbor was passing by with their team of horses or which one was going by with their new Farmall H or M or John Deere A or B tractor.

The old building would surely remember the students preparing for the Christmas programs for weeks before the big evening arrived. That evening all the parents and many others of the community would come to see the program of "pieces" and plays. The final instruction being to speak loud and clear so the people in back could hear. This was all followed by a gift-exchange and a two-week vacation.

She would remember the row of bicycles parked by her wall in the spring and fall and the coaster sleds in the winter time. Also the row of dinner buckets ranked in the hall waiting to be opened at noon and sometimes their contents traded or bartered for something in someone else's bucket. Also the large water cooler, which was filled every morning by two of the older boys going to the creamery with a can and bringing back the day's supply of drinking water. This was an enjoyable twenty-minute trip.

When nature called, the procedure was to raise one's hand and ask, "Teacher, may I leave the room?" Permission granted meant a trip of about forty yards to the outdoor toilet. Funny, but nature always seemed to call more often in the nice days of the spring and fall than it did when it was thirty below zero in the winter time.

Heat was furnished by the one large register in the middle of the floor, which also necessitated an outside trip to the side door to stoke the old furnace with coal. The last day of school in the spring was also a big occasion, as that day all of the mothers would pack the picnic basket with goodies and the fathers would stop their work long enough to come to school so everyone could enjoy the picnic dinner. After a few games were played, the parents would take the children home with them to begin the summer vacation. That day brought talk (with mixed emotions) of whether there would be a new teacher for next year.

Now back to reality. Fifty years have passed since that day in forty-one. The boy has grown to be a man, the black hair has mostly turned grey, and as he drives past the old school he looks into that same window, smiles, and says to himself, "Old school, thanks for the memories."

■ *Richard Sandry*

THRESHING

When you are ten years old and can be along with the men on the threshing crew, it can make you feel pretty grown up. The threshing ring then consisted of about twelve neighboring farmers.

Sometime in July when the oats fields were all a golden yellow, it was time to cut and shock the grain. The grain binder was brought out from its year of rest in the machine shed and was pulled by five strong horses, or in later years by a tractor. The fields then turned from yellow to a shade of green as the oats were cut, tied in small bundles, and deposited in rows on the ground by the binder. Usually this was done on some of the hottest days of the summer.

The oats bundles then had to be picked up by hand and shocked. A shock was usually six bundles set on the ground with one bundle laying horizontally on top, called the cap. Many farmers liked to do the shocking in the cool of the evenings, sometimes keeping on until midnight. For the next two weeks, the shocks went through a sweat, or drying time.

It was then time to begin threshing. Each farmer would bring his team of horses and his "basket rack," which was a large wagon box to hold the bundles. Some had tractors hitched to the wagons. It was necessary to move along the rows of shocks to load the wagon. This is where I came in as a tractor driver. This was a big help to the man who was loading the wagon, as he did not have to crawl continually on and off the tractor. To be able to drive those early tractors was quite a thrill for a young boy.

The bundle wagons were then brought, one on each side of the threshing machine, and the bundles pitched into the machine, one bundle at a time. The machine separated the oats from the straw, the oats coming out of a spout and put into sacks. The sacks of grain were then hauled to the granary where they were emptied. The straw was blown onto a pile which was called the straw stack.

Dinner was always something to look forward to. Three or four of the farm wives would go together and cook the noon meal. It was served family style with all of the men sitting around the table. When the men were eating, there was plenty of kidding and telling of tall tales, which really held my attention. I'm sure my dad did not share my enthusiasm for the threshing, as for him it meant a lot of hard and sweaty work, but for a ten-year-old boy it was the big event of the summer.

■ *Clara Leppert*

Clara Leppert was one of the most beloved people in our area of northeast Iowa, and when she died in 1996 at the age of 87, she left a huge gap that will never be replaced. She and her husband, Clarence, farmed and had three sons and a daughter. Her book, Simple Times, *recounted her life from 1909 to around 1950.*

MEALS FOR THRESHERS

When the grain was ripe it was put in shocks, most people placing six bundles together and a bundle on top to keep the rain from soaking in. The grain was usually oats, sometimes it was barley, which was scratchy and made us itch. Afterwards, the dry grain was put in the huge threshing machine, which separated the kernels of grain from the straw. We expected sixteen to eighteen men when we threshed, and they worked from sunrise to sunset.

For many years Marie Fritz and I helped each other cooking meals. In the morning we would put a bench outside, and place two wash tubs of water on it, two or three basins, a couple of combs, and a mirror.

Some people gave lunch both forenoon and afternoon, the women taking it to the field. We took lunch only afternoons. We would take sandwiches, cookies or doughnuts, coffee and real homemade lemonade. Two or three days before threshing, we would bake two or three batches of cookies. Threshing day we usually had a big beef roast, mashed potatoes and gravy, two or three vegetables, cheese, and always two kinds of pie.

For supper we usually had meat balls, meat loaf, baloney or wieners, escalloped potatoes or potato salad, vegetables, cake, cookies, and sauce.

One time when Clarence was helping thresh at a neighbor's, they were served delicious clover blossom wine. It tasted like flavored sugar water, but after a little, the table began to go around; pretty soon it was going around so fast, it was hard to catch the food when it went by. After awhile, all was well again.

The next big group of men worked on silo filling, then corn shredding. As it got cold, the men got together again to saw wood. If one neighbor worked for another five days and the other one worked two days, there was never anything said about one owing the other.

■ *Frances Cole*

Francis Cole, another of our neighbors, raises sheep and beef cattle with her husband Danny. In her late seventies, Francis still tends the animals and, up until a few years ago, went on an annual wagon train ride in the Dakotas and traveled widely, including once to Australia.

THE TORNADO

May 22, 1962 is one of the days in my life I will never forget. It started like any other day with our morning chores. It was corn planting time, and my husband went to plant early that morning on one of our far back farms about two miles from home. Around noon the weather became very hazy and sultry and very still. We all kept working at our daily chores, but my mother said, "Start your chores and milking early, something bad is coming out of this weather." She was always afraid of us being in the barn when it was storming.

Well I, my aunt, and the man who was working for us got done and were out of the barn by 6:30 P.M. The sky was threatening and so dark and hazy. We all went to the house for supper. My husband was home from corn planting by then.

Well, after supper we done up the dishes and about 9:00 P.M. everybody was heading for bed but me. I had a bowl of gold fish and started cleaning them. I went outside to throw out the bowl of water and rain drops like spoonfuls and very hot were coming down, and it was so dark you could not see the hand before your face. I hurried inside, and just as I came through the door a gust of wind blew dirt right behind me. I rushed to the stairs and called to the folks to run for the cellar, something was going to happen. Well, we did. I was the last one down the stairs and could see through a window. Everything got real bright and it sounded like a freight train was going through the yard. Well, that is when it struck, then all got deathly quiet.

We finally went upstairs and rain was coming down the back stairway, a window was blew out and we got a big piece of cardboard to nail over it. Well, then mother looked out of her bedroom window, and that is when the nightmare began. Everything looked bare outside. We could see lights we never could see before.

I and my husband went outside and had to walk through the front yard as all the electric wires lay in the yard. The windmill lay only a foot from hitting the house. Our red barn was flat, tree limbs all over, pigs were squealing and calves were bellowing. The only light we had was in the house, all the others were out. Mother called some of the neighbors and one came over. We worked with the power saw freeing calves and two Angus bulls we had just bought. One had his leg injured and had to be sold, five calves were dead, as well as one sow and many young pigs. A sheep had a foot cut off and some geese were killed.

Well, when daylight came we found we had lost seven buildings. Our sheep shed we never did find. And everything had damage to some extent, except our tool shed and two brood coops full of young chickens. Seems crazy, but by 11:00 P.M. the stars were out. It was a beautiful night. Next day, lot of folks helped salvage things from the wreckage. Our milk cows got so frightened they took out a section of cowyard fence and we didn't find them until the next day. A system to milk them was set up in the old barn and we struggled with that all summer. By August a new barn was up and slowly we got back to normal, but no one knows what cleaning up after a tornado is like until they go through it. I know I will never forget.

■ *Barb Mitchell*

Barb Mitchell is married to David Mitchell, another workshop writer. She works in a Lansing, Iowa nursing home. A talented writer, she and David have participated in other Free River Press workshops. They have two daughters and two sons.

APRONS

I remember when aprons were important to all women. Everyone wore them, including my mother.

A few years ago I went to a birthday party with my sisters, cousins, and aunts. There was a table full of aprons, and we were told to pick one out and wear it. We were to think about it, and at the end of the party tell a story of what kind of an apron it was. It was interesting what came out of it.

Also to help us think we played a game of writing down the uses of an apron. Can you think of any uses for one? My mother answered that question many times over the years, and I had to think.

Mom's apron served many purposes. They kept her dresses clean, covered up missing buttons, or a dirty dress. There was always a clean one handy in case someone drove in the yard. At times she had several on. They brought garden stuff into the house, held eggs gathered from the chicken coop and more.

As little kids we often got an "owie." An owie is when we got a finger or an arm, a toe or a knee hurt somehow. Mom's aprons were always big enough to cover it or wrap it up and hold it close to her. It always got better. The grandchildren often came to her for something.

There was always a pocket, and in it were many things. A button found laying some place, a hanky for anyone's nose or cut. Often there was something for the grandchildren to reach in and take out. They loved it.

She played peek-a-boo with many babies with her apron.

If it was a bad day she threw it over her face to cry, and no one would know it. It wiped many tears from all of us. Sundays brought out good ones as company often came back then. My aunts would come visit with one on.

Mom had a wringer washer back then. I often watched and later used one myself. The apron strings often got caught in the wringer. Round and round they would go before Mom popped open the wringer to free them.

It was my job to take down the washing from the lines after school. Have you watched the wind blow the apron strings? It was as if they were constantly trying to free themselves or to reach further. Sometimes they were around the clothes line and had to be unwound in order to take them down. Back then they were ironed and folded just right. I'd always run my finger over the string to unwind it again.

There were many different kinds of them—full ones, gathered ones, fancy ones, and more. A long one always came up to the chest with a loop over the head. It was tied at the waist like gathered ones. A gathered one was usually gingham and covered the bottom half of their dresses. Other kinds of aprons were used too. Waitress at weddings wore fancy ones. Now you see them in restaurants. Cooks wear them, butchers wear them.

Maybe you can think of more uses or kinds of aprons. My girls enjoyed playing house with them. At kindergarten the kids paint with one on. So there are still some uses for aprons today. But with automatic washers and dryers it is easier to take care of them. Can you remember Mom or Grandma with one on?

■ *Barb Leppert*

Barb Leppert was a respected fourth grade teacher for 35 years in the Lansing elementary school, until her retirement in 1996. She and her husband, Bob, recently sold their dairy farm to their son. Still, twice a day Barb feeds the calves, helps with milking and cleaning up.

THE COMING OF MACHINERY

With the coming of the age of machinery came long hours in the fields and consequently the loss of yet another old and valued tradition . . . that of visiting neighbors.

When there were only horses to pull the machinery, farmers could only work just so many hours, and then the horses had to be rested. The chores were done at the same time every night, and that left ample time after supper to go visit a close neighbor for the evening to play cards or whatever. It was fun. You never knew when someone would pop in, but it seemed like you always had some fixin's in the refrigerator for lunch.

Now when the field work starts you might see your husband at mealtime, unless he decides to take a sandwich and an apple along to the field with him, in which case you will only see him for five minutes when he comes in, washes up, and falls into bed exhausted. He falls asleep two minutes after his head hits the pillow, so if you have anything you want to talk over with him, you'd better talk fast.

This ritual goes on during the planting, cultivating, and harvesting seasons. Then one day you come home from work and he's sitting on the steps with a big smile on his face and he says. "I'm done with the first crop hay. Let's celebrate and go out to eat. Why don't you call Betty and Curt and Donald and Eleanora and see if they want to go along?"

That's about as close to the old time visits as we get anymore. But that's the price we pay for progress!

■ *Dan Byrnes*

A tall, lanky young man with glasses, Dan Byrnes looks like a well-turned out graduate student of an Ivy League school rather than an Iowa cattle grower. After college he worked in Minneapolis, but eventually decided to join his father on the family farm.

THE SILO

In the 1920s my grandfather, John Byrnes, built a silo thirty feet tall, fourteen feet in diameter. The construction method was very similar to the method used today: cement staves one foot wide, two feet long, and two inches thick are set side by side in a circle. Metal rods or bands are then wrapped around the outside to support the structure. The inside is covered with plaster to keep the silo airtight. At the bottom of the silo, where there is more pressure from the stored silage, there are more rings. On my grandfather's silo the rings near the bottom were spaced two feet apart, and near the top, three feet.

The silo was located next to the barn. Each year the unit was filled with chopped corn silage. The filling was done by neighborhood crews. Corn plants were cut by hand, loaded on flat wagons, and then fed into a machine at the silo that chopped the plants up and blew them through a pipe. The corn silage was then fed to the cows during the winter. Each day someone would climb up in the silo and use a fork to throw down the needed amount. The silage was carried to the cows with a basket. In the dead of winter the silage would freeze to the sides, so an axe was used to chop it out. The silo worked well for about forty years. As farming changed, the silo became too small.

In 1961 my father and uncle built another silo, located about fifty feet from the old one. In 1971 another silo was built, this time sixteen by sixty. In 1979 a fourth silo went up. Sometime in the seventies they quit filling the small silo. Too much labor for too little capacity. The wooden doors rotted out, and the staves began to crack. Near the top a few staves were ready to fall out. My cattle loaf beside the silo, and in order to prevent an accident we decided to tear it down.

At the Barn Restaurant in Prairie du Chien there is a series of photos of a man knocking out staves with a maul until the silo toppled. Another man from Viroqua, Wisconsin won ten thousand dollars from "America's Funniest Home Videos"—one hit from a maul and his silo came crashing down.

I have absolutely no experience in tearing down a silo, but on Thursday night at 7:00 P.M. we started, my father and I. We decided to knock out a stave on each side, thread a cable through it, and then pull with a tractor. My dad is in his seventies and does not swing a maul much; he does drive a tractor. We went out to the silo with cables, chains, a tractor, and an eight-pound maul. The top staves looked like they could fall at any minute. What would happen if I hit a lower stave? Would the vibration cause an upper stave to fall? My dad said he would watch above, and if he yelled, to get the hell back. I beat a hole in each side, threaded the cable, and hooked up to the skid loader. My dad drove forward, and the tires spun on the cement. Two big black marks were left. We went for another tractor, the sixty-five-horsepower loader tractor. It left bigger marks than the skid loader. The silo did not budge. Next we hooked up the one-hundred-horsepower International tractor. More black marks. My dad backed up and took a run at it. The silo did not budge. Maybe after seventy years here the silo had learned the Byrnes' trait of stubbornness.

Time for a new plan. My idea was to cut one of the metal rings. My dad got the skid loader, loaded the oxyacetylene torch, and parked safely inside the barn next to the silo. I stood next to the silo with the torch. The band exploded with a bang as I completed the cut. Again my dad pulled and again the tractor just spun. We cut another band. This time I was prepared for the band to explode out, and I ran away after the cut was complete. My dad pulled again. This time the staves on the south side started to move. We wanted an even pull so the structure would fall between the fence and the barn, not on them. I took the maul and beat out the staves on the north. The remainder of the staves pulled out easily, but the silo still stood. With a four-foot hole in the side going halfway around, it looked like a monster ready to bite into anything that came near it, or at least smash a skinny farmer who was foolish enough to go near it.

Then my dad thought up a plan: go up and knock out a stave behind the third band up, and then hook up the cable.

Unsafe? Yeah, but most of farming is unsafe. I walked up, took a swing and then ran back, out of the way. Then I hooked up the cable. My dad got in the tractor, I stood way back. The silo came down with a crash. Dust and rocks flew like a bomb had just exploded. In a few minutes the dust settled, and the silo was now just a pile of broken cement and iron. At 8:30 P.M. we quit for the night.

All of the material from the silo will be re-used. The staves will be used as base material under new cement, and the metal bands will be used for concrete reinforcing bars.

The silo project is just one of a long string of facility repairs that we have done since I started to farm in 1987. My dad and I are builders. Many evenings are devoted to fixing facilities. We are proud of the fences we have built, the buildings we have fixed, and the concrete yards we have made. The sense of accomplishment after building something is great, and the facilities make our livestock work easier.

My grandfather would probably not recognize the farm today, but I hope that he would approve of the changes.

■ *Bob Leppert*

Bob Leppert was one of the first organic farmers in Allamakee County. Most farmers resisted the idea of the workshop, but Bob, open to new ideas, found it intriguing. Having retired from farming several years ago, he now spends much of his time studying herbs and natural medicines.

FARMING

The first farming I was able to do when I was growing up was to help take care of the chickens: feed them, get the eggs, and at night make sure they were all in the coop with the screen door closed so foxes couldn't get them. I was too small to harness the horses because the horses were so big. My brother was three years older than I and he could get them on by himself. Everything, the plowing, discing, and planting, was done by horses. We had our W-30 McCormick Deering tractor, but it was only used for providing power to grind feed, thresh grain, and shred corn because we had all horse machinery at that time.

I can remember when planting corn I would help move the planting wire for the planter. It had buttons on it and would be stretched all the way across the field to be planted. The planter had a guide to hold this wire while going across the field, and each one of the buttons would trip the planter to drop the corn in the ground, so that when we cultivated the corn, we could cultivate it the long way and also go across the field to help control the weeds.

Chemical fertilizers, herbicides, and insecticides weren't available yet. About this time, hybrid corn became available and would be standing in the fall when it was time to harvest. This was unreal, because the open pollinated corn seemed always to be laying on the ground. My hands would be so cold when we had to pick the ears out of the snow. I would keep asking if it was time to start chores so I could get to the house and warm up.

About this time we got our first rubber tire tractor, a two-cylinder John Deere B, with a brake for each rear wheel, which was really an improvement to help it turn in loose soil. This tractor would run on power fuel, which was similar to kerosene. The tractor had two fuel tanks, a small one to put gasoline in and a large tank to hold power fuel. When the tractor was cold it had to be started on gasoline and switched to power fuel when it was warmed up. I can remember the fuel man filling our fifty-five gallon tanks in the shed. There were no pumps on the truck and he filled five gallon cans and carried them in and emptied them in the tanks, each time moving a lever with numbers on the rear of the truck to keep track of the total amount of fuel delivered.

As each year went by, Howard and I would pester Dad to cut the horse tongues off the implements so we could use the tractor on them. Also, we kept buying more machinery as it became available after the end of World War II. In 1946 we purchased a new John Deere A tractor with a two-bottom plow and cultivator for $810.00. Then came the fifties and with it, chemical fertilizer, herbicides, and insecticides. I remember the first year we used a herbicide: the instructions were not followed correctly and we had corn that year, no weeds, but it was four years before anything else grew on it. We never did use any pesticides because we only had corn one year in a field, then it would be rotated to oats and then hay for the next two years.

In the fifties we purchased our first diesel powered tractor and a four-row corn planter and cultivator. During this time, the popular statement was, if you are having financial problems, get bigger. My brother and I would buy every calf and pig we could afford and then some. We would rent farmland even if we had to drive five miles to get to it. We worked day and night to get all the work done. We did this all through the fifties and sixties. By the time we got into the seventies we were so big we were having serious problems getting money to keep going. We had passed the limit at our local bank and were getting money through them from two other banks in the cities.

About this time we had grown with our cow-calf operation to two hundred and twenty cows. Then two farms we had been renting were put up to auction and we figured we couldn't afford to purchase them. The next year the State Conservation Commission notified us that it was terminating the leases on the land used to pasture our cattle. We were very disgusted and in the spring of '72 we took a hundred and fifty of the cows to the sale barn. As I look back now, it was the best thing that could have happened to us. The cattle sold good and we were able to lower the amount we had borrowed quite substantially at the bank. This was the first time we were able to pay off rather than borrow. We changed our cattle operation around and sold yearling calves rather than finish them out to fat cattle for slaughter. We found as we got smaller that our profits increased. Better efficiency meant less interest to pay at the bank.

About 1976 I got invited to a dinner meeting put on by the Wonder Life Corporation and got introduced to organic farming.

There were a couple of farmers there who had been farming this way for years, but I couldn't believe that this could work, even though I thought it was a good way to farm. So I had to try it. My brother, Howard, was not very interested in the idea, but we decided to try it on fifteen acres.

The Wonder Life Company had a program and recommended that a chisel plow be used instead of a regular moldboard plow and that a soil inoculant be used, which helped get the soil back in condition. The first spring after we had used the soil inoculant we noticed lots of angle worms again. The way we had been farming, using the chemical fertilizers, few could be found, even though we never had used any insecticides.

We kept increasing the number of acres cropped with this new program, even though my brother was not too interested. Our yields were not as big as we when we used chemical fertilizers, but out costs were lower. The soil improved in texture, too, and became more like a sponge, taking less power to till. As a result, the farm ponds around the edge of the fields in the pasture started to dry up because the rains would soak in, rather than run off.

One drawback we discovered was when chopping corn in the fall to fill silo, we could only fill the wagons half full because they would sink into the mellow soil and we would be stuck. My son, Andy, was big enough by this time to pull loads to the silo, and when he came home one evening from helping our neighbor fill silo, I asked him if he had problems pulling in the loads of silage. He replied, "Dad, their fields are just like concrete. Never got stuck once." Our neighbors had been using lots of fertilizers, herbicides, and insecticides, and the wagon tires only made prints on the soil.

About this time my brother Howard's two boys were out of high school, and we decided to divide the partnership. When we divided up the farmland, I got one hundred and eighty acres next to the home farm, and got to rent the home farm, which is three hundred and fifty-five acres. The farm is owned by my brother, sister, and me.

For the next six years I didn't use any chemical fertilizer or herbicides, and I had good crops. Once while I was getting the strips evened out to the same number of acres, I did something I was told not to do. I put one strip back to corn for the second year. It was a failure. The corn didn't grow good and the weeds came. I chopped it for silage, but there wasn't a good ear of corn in the field. Since that time, I have used some organic fertilizer, which helps get the corn up and out of the ground sooner so I can cultivate. I do use a small amount of herbicide if we get a rainy spring, and I can't get out to cultivate.

All the new equipment and devices to make work easier on the farm have a price tag attached. As I look to the future with my farming operation, I can see the day when I will have to decide either to borrow huge sums of money to purchase replacements for worn-out equipment, or quit farming altogether. I've been getting along by purchasing used equipment and repairing it, but even this old used equipment is getting scarce and the price is getting higher because of the high cost of new equipment.

My 4020 John Deere that I purchased new in 1964 has ninety-five horse power and cost $4,700. Today a new John Deere tractor with the same horse power costs $42,000. My round hay baler cost $3,100 in 1972; the same baler today has a price tag of $26,000. The field chopper which cost $1,800 new in 1956, costs $26,000 today.

I have been getting along with my old equipment because I have a small farm, and I make most of the parts for this old machinery when it breaks. I have to, because most repair parts are not available any more from the machinery dealer.

If I could only get a fair price for all the food I produce, I could make some machinery purchases which would help the hometown people and would put many people back to work in the factories again.

■ *Esther Welsh*

Esther Welsh and her husband, Bill, now run the business side of the Welsh Family Organic Farms in rural Lansing. Before that, she worked twelve years as an LPN. Esther and Bill raised three sons and five daughters.

GETTING STARTED

As our farming career was about to begin, I saw that our major assets were our hopes, our dreams, our faith in God, a lot of ambition, and family support. Bill's only possession was a 1953 Chevy, and I had nothing but a small savings account. I was working in the office of a local factory, and Bill was working in a gas station just to get by until we could start farming.

Bill used his free time to go to farm sales, hoping to find the bargains and buy some of the essential farm equipment we would need. Then moving day came. Our household furnishings consisted of wedding gifts, family extras, and a new refrigerator—one with a foot pedal to open the door. Our local implement-appliance dealer said it hadn't been a big seller, so we got a bargain. A big, rusty, round oak stove, standing near the back entrance was to provide our heat. As the March winds blew through the house and water began to freeze in the kitchen sink, we came to realize that we needed another source of heat. We merely mentioned to my dad that our water pipes had frozen and that we even had ice in the dish pan. Soon we had an oil burner that they weren't using. Oh, how nice it was to be warm again!

For early spring field work we borrowed a tractor, a plow, a disc, and a planter, either from Bill's family or mine. We planted a garden, but I know we harvested more out of our parents' gardens than we did our own, and much of it came in jars.

Money was always in short supply and the cupboards were often pretty bare. Oatmeal was our staple. We didn't have a lot, but we didn't have much debt, either. When our first load of pigs was ready for market, we planned our first celebration. We invited Bill's brother, Dan, and his wife, Sarah, to have supper with us. All four of us squeezed into the cab of the pickup and took the pigs to market, then went to buy groceries for our celebration. We bought a chicken, potatoes for french fries, and bakery bread. We all worked together to cook supper. It was a fabulous meal. I can taste it yet.

In time, the rented farm where we began our career was sold, so we moved to the farm where we live today. This farm was owned by my uncle, Bill, and he had been renting the farm because of failing health. Now that we had more land, we bought more cows, and more feed. A brand new John Deere 60 tractor was delivered, which cost us $2,215.00. To us that was a lot of money at that time, a major debt, but this past year a major tractor repair cost over $5,000. By the time we bought the cattle, the feed, and the tractor, we were well indoctrinated into the process and need to borrow money. When I would get nervous and wonder how we were ever going to pay that money back, Bill would re-assure me by saying, "You can't start farming without borrowing money." Oh, how true that was and still is!

Our record keeping was simple those first years. Unlike my uncle, who kept his receipts in a shoe box and recorded checks and deposits on a long stick and merely got another when the first one got filled, we tried to keep a record of all farming and household income and expenses. We find those records interesting yet today. For example, in 1955 we paid $193.80 for a new foot pedal refrigerator, $25.80 for a used wringer washing machine, and $9.15 for a pair of bib overalls for Bill—the same brand that cost $21 to $23 today. That same year, market pigs brought $15 per hundred weight; today we are getting $40 to $43 per hundred weight. Prices have increased, but so have costs, so it seems we merely handle more money.

As time goes by, our hopes and dreams may change a bit, our ambition may fade, but we continue to see God in the things we do and in the people we meet, and we know that we all need one another.

■ *Esther Welsh*

CHOICES

My husband, Bill, and I have shared over thirty years of farming experiences. During each of those years our plans and ideas have changed frequently. We dreamed of the good life, we planned, we studied, and we worked. We looked to our elected officials, to the universities, and to the Extension Service for information and advice and sometimes were misled.

We consulted nutritionists and feed dealers to help us develop rations for our livestock to get the best rate of gain. We depended on seed dealers and fertilizer salesmen to recommend products and amounts that would produce the best quality and highest yields. There were so many things to consider. Then we had to weigh the information and make the best choice possible and yes, we made some mistakes. Mistakes that often became more obvious and more serious over time.

Our farming operation grew bigger and bigger. We rented more land. We tried new products as they were introduced. With more land and more work, it was essential that we find ways to cut corners. There was no time to cultivate the corn three times. There was no time to study the needs of the land or the livestock. There was no time for family fun.

And then came the eighties. For many farm families and small businesses those years will be remembered as truly hard times. The value of our land, our equipment, and farm production slid to a devastating low, while farming input costs increased and interest rates climbed to a high of twenty-two percent. Those same capital investments that we had planned for, and that appeared sound to us only months before, had now become unmanageable debt.

Financial difficulties and forced decisions are painful. Feelings of defeat, depression, and desperation cast a cover of gloom over farm families and farming communities. At the time, we were raising beef cattle and pigs and sliding backward financially at an accelerating speed. When the cattle and pigs went to market, they were scarcely bringing enough to cover our cost of production. There was no profit, yet there were bills to be paid.

There was work to be done but there was little enthusiasm. Our minds were struggling with choices; our hearts were aching over forced decisions. Everyone in the family was feeling the tension. We were all willing to work hard and long. We were even willing to do without, to ask for less, but who in their right mind wanted to work ten to eighteen hours a day and still fall short on payday? We needed to find alternatives. We had to make changes. If we thought that things were bad we were soon to realize that it was only going to get worse.

We were completing some definite plans to cut back on land, inventory, and work load. At the same time we were making giant strides toward changing our farming operation from conventional to chemical free. We had a confirmed order for twenty-five hundred chickens if we could raise them without using antibiotics and without hormones to hasten their growth. We had always raised chickens for our own use, but this was a sizeable difference. We were confident that we could do it. We were excited about the opportunity. Finally our plans were coming together.

Then one day early in March, my husband, Bill, suddenly began to complain of a tight feeling in his chest and of shortness of breath. He was anxious and restless. He was rushed to the hospital where he was to remain for three days. After extensive testing, he was told that he could go home and do what he felt like doing, that he was as healthy as a twenty-nine year old.

Three days went by, and all was well. Our niece and nephew had come to spend a few days. Our daughter, Jeanne, a nursing student, was home from college, so we invited friends to come for supper. I was just putting the finishing touches on our meal when again Bill began to complain of tightness in his chest and shortness of breath. He said, "Just get me some oxygen, and I'll feel better." Our son Gary had the car running, and we convinced Bill that there was no time to waste. We went back to the hospital.

This time the diagnosis was heart attack, and was followed by three weeks of hospitalization and more tests. Finally on April 3, his birthday, Bill was released from the hospital with orders to rest, not to lift over five pounds, and to eliminate stress.

That was sound advice to insure recovery, yet it seemed like unrealistic advice for a farmer in the spring of the year, but again there were no choices.

Our son Gary managed to seed the oats, and planted the corn that spring too. Under different circumstances he might not have been allowed such an important responsibility. This was Gary's big chance to prove himself capable. There were many offers of help and support, a real benefit of living and working in a small community.

Not all the decisions we made throughout the years were well planned. Some were made in an instant, but at the time we felt we were making the best choice possible. Our farm and farming is important to us and to our family. We consider it a privilege to produce food, a basic need for all mankind. We are proud and excited to tell the world that we can and are producing crops and livestock without using synthetic chemicals and antibiotics. We are confident that the choices we have made so far will help to preserve and protect our land, our water, and our environment for our own use and for generations to come.

■ Greg Welsh

Greg Welsh, son of Bill and Esther Welsh, is a graduate of Loras College in Dubuque, Iowa. Greg certifies organic farms in Wisconsin and Iowa for Oregon Tilthe. Before that he traveled for Iowa State University's extension services, advising farmers on how to make the transition from chemical to organic farming.

FORCED AUCTIONS

They gathered at the auction, harmless buzzards, strangers, neighbors, friends, relatives, patiently waiting, watching as the farmer's lifelong collection is sold.

"All right boys, what do ya want to give for it boys?" the auctioneer spouted, as the disc, plow, wagons, and tools sold to the highest bidders. Children wandered about, oblivious to the liquidation of their future.

Forced auctions, like an Irish wake, finality on the one hand, a neighborly respect to those passing on the other. No one asks why. It hurts too much. No one denies, it wouldn't be right.

■ *Richard Sandry*

STORM CLOUDS

It is a nice warm June afternoon. The sky is a robin's egg blue with the white cumulus clouds lazily drifting on their way to their rendezvous with the horizon. A gentle breeze ripples my short-sleeved shirt as I gaze out over the cornfield. Knee-high already and the deepest dark green you can imagine. I think about all of the money we borrowed and all of the planning and time it took to get that crop to where it is now.

My son comes to my side. Now my mind drifts back to when I was his age and I stood beside my father looking at the results of his toil those years before. Then I think, is this the end of the line? I think of how farming has changed over my lifetime, of how we have progressed to where profits are practically nonexistent. What has he to look forward to should he wish to farm? I am filled with a deep sadness and fear for his future, as I have seen an interest in raising livestock and working with the soil being nurtured in him, maybe even bred right into him. "Let's go to lunch, Dad," he says.

This brings me back to reality, and for the moment I forget the future and the past. I look to the west and see the dark ominous storm clouds rapidly moving upon us. "We had better hurry," I tell him, "or we are going to get wet." In the back of my mind I remember something being said on the radio this morning about storms coming this way.

We finally get home and just as we come into the house, the rain begins to fall. Shortly the full fury of the storm is upon us. As I watch, looking out through the window, I think of how the days of

my life go. How the clouds on the horizon of my sunrises sometimes, later in the day, turn into the black clouds of fear, of despair,
of anger, of uncertainty, and of depression.

As suddenly as it began the storm ends. The corn is bent but not
broken. Soon the sun will come out and the corn will straighten and
begin to grow again. I think how a turnaround in the farm economy
would revive the farmers, make them refreshed with that spirit and
vigor that has always been a farmer's attribute.

Tonight I will thank the Lord for seeing me through today and
ask for guidance for tomorrow. With spirits bent but not broken.

■ David Mitchell

*David Mitchell joined the farm writing workshop the second winter
of its existence, during which time he made his decision to retire from
farming and began this diary. Five years later he is finishing hogs on contract and working for a masonry company.*

DIARY

Monday, February 15, 1993

Not much time left before the sale. Damn phone, I feel like taking it
off the hook. Every time I sit down, it rings. See, it's ringing again.
This time it's our daughter, Donna, from Ames. She's excited about
having a teaching interview in Farnam, Nebraska. She wants me to
look it up in the encyclopedia to locate the town.

After looking at the road atlas, and not finding it, I tell her that
I will look it up in the encyclopedia like she asked me to, and call
her back. Explaining the location, and encouraging her to go, I tell
her I wish the farm sale was over so I could drive her there. We talk
some more about the distance and whether Mom will be able to
rearrange her work schedule and drive to Ames and take her over. I
say, "I'll check and have her call tomorrow."

As we say our good-byes my mind goes back to the farm and the sale, especially the accomplishments and failures of the last twenty-seven years that we farmed. Sure glad I have the record books for all twenty-seven years.

I spend the rest of the evening adding some of the totals. I want to know how many pigs we had finished for market in those twenty-seven years, so I go through each account book, one for each year, '66 through '92, and add the totals. Approximately twenty-two thousand. I feel proud of myself for that.

Now for the bad part, the interest paid. One hundred eighty-one thousand dollars for twenty-seven years. Then I break it down to the eighteen years that my brother Jerry and I were in partnership together, and the last nine, when I farmed alone. Thirty thousand dollars for the eighteen years in partnership, one hundred fifty-one thousand dollars for the nine years alone.

Tuesday, February 16, 1993

Our daughter, Lisa, came over from Viroqua today to help us get things ready for the sale. Her daughter, Kelly, was with her. She sure is growing fast.

I got Lisa busy with cleaning the small addition we call the mud room. We plan to use it for the checking of the sale.

When Lisa was done with the mud room, I asked her to clean the combine windows and the inside of the cab; there's plenty of dirt and dust in it. It hadn't been cleaned since before we combined the oats in July. There is oats chives still on the floor. She done a wonderful job with both tasks.

A lot of people were still calling to ask about this or that piece of machinery, so I did a lot of running back and forth to get my jobs accomplished for the day.

I had no idea that there would be that many people calling, if any, to ask about the machinery or the cattle. I had never done it myself when I went to other farm sales to buy some item we needed.

We were learning many new things about a farm sale, by our firsthand experience. I knew there was a lot of work to prepare for it, but the task seemed to get bigger, and it seemed I wasn't gaining much ground.

Wednesday, February 17, 1993

More phone calls asking about the machinery. Sure am glad there are a lot of people interested.

Dan Cole came over today to help get machinery out and lined up. I took the tractor and blade and bladed the snow off the field below the buildings, the only somewhat level area on the farm. Hard to blade the snow into windrows, because of the volume of snow we have. That reminds me, they are talking about more snow for the weekend. Dan and I started putting the pieces of machinery in two rows in the field. I really enjoyed working with Dan. A lot of machinery was frozen to the ground. I was afraid we might break something getting it loose.

Barb called us in for dinner. More phone calls. I took it off the hook for awhile so I could finish my dinner.

I know that I made some wrong moves, buying some of the machinery too soon or not figuring what it would cost to own it per acre of use. I guess my desire to own things or the greed got carried away somewhat.

The pain to own these things or the extra work to service the debt was getting too much. I see now that the writing workshop was the power or the people I needed to help to come to grips with my situation.

Thursday, February 18, 1993

Dan came again today to help. James Moore and John Gibbs, two other neighbors, came too. My brother Billy came out from town.

There was some repair work I needed to get done on the corn

planter. It took a lot of our time. Jim made a trip to Eitzen for parts. It was a busy day getting more equipment to the field, even with all the help. But it keeps my mind from all the worry. Thank you, God, for neighbors.

Friday, February 19, 1993

I went to Eitzen after chores, for oil filters for the 8010 and stopped at the vet's office to check on test results for the cows. I was kind of worried. Three of the cattle did not test clean the first time, so the vet retested them about a week ago. Thank God they tested clean.

After supper I spent some time answering the telephone again. A man from Wisconsin called about one of the D17 tractors. As we talked I sensed he needed someone to talk to him, so I did. There sure are a lot of stressed farmers. Lord, what do we do to help?

Saturday, February 20, 1993

More people came throughout the day to look at the machinery. It really kept me busy with taking time to talk with them and getting the work done. Jeff Sweeney came later in the afternoon and helped a little. He also helped write up a contract for renting the pasture.

Sunday, February 21, 1993

We went to church and to breakfast this morning. Laid all the things that were bothering me before the Lord. It's great to know him and have a place to go when things get too much for us.

Lots of new snow today. The weather man says it's going to keep coming. I'll spend most of the day pushing it around and grading it off our driveway, which is one-half mile long. These next two days are going to go fast with the extra work that the snow makes.

More people came and called again today. I'm starting to feel I'll be glad when it's over. I think I'm starting to burn out again.

Monday, February 22, 1993

Lots of new snow. There must be at least fourteen inches. Dan and Billy came out to help again today.

The county sent a man with a maintainer to widen the snow on the driveway and plow snow off the field north of where the machinery is lined up. The windrows of snow are six feet high in some places. It was quite a job even for the maintainer.

I really worried about Dennis Weymiller's sale that was scehuduled for today. Lord, sometimes the crosses are more than we can bear. My nerves are beginning to bother me, and I'm getting grumpy.

Barb went to the bank for us today to get the titles for a couple of the vehicles we're selling.

Tuesday, February 23, 1993 *Sale Day*

I'm up early for once, for one of the biggest days of our lives. It seems there is a week's work left to do before the sale.

Really glad it's going to be over soon. Most of the days I felt I was running around like a zombie, rushing and stopping to greet someone, now and then.

It looks like it's going to be a great sale. Lots and lots of people, hope there's going to be enough parking for them.

Doug, Eddie, and their hired man, Paul, came. The swatter wouldn't start. Paul got it running just before the sale started. It's damn cold. We got the last of the tractors and self-propelled equipment started so it would be warmed up for the sale.

It was good to see a lot of people out from town too.

I was really glad when it was over. Some things could of brought more, and others brought more than I expected.

Sunday, January 2, 1994

Wow! Almost a year has gone by since the sale. Not all sunshine, but some roses—you know they have thorns.

Some of our farmer friends are calling me lucky for not being in farming during the '93 planting, growing, and harvest seasons. I keep telling them someone had to pay the rent.

We didn't sell the farm, we rented it out. The land that we didn't rent out to the taxpayers through the CRP program we rented out to neighbors.

We still have our income tax to pay for '93. Hopefully we can refinance the farm to pay that.

It's like they say, the longer I've been away from full-time farming the less I want to go back to it and be a slave to machinery and other things. I've tried sales and learned a lot about it. I will probably do some of it in the future. I presently deliver bulk propane.

■ *Bruce Carlson*

Bruce Carlson is a dentist who works conscientiously on local community projects. In his free time, depending on the season, he gardens, bikes, skates, or skis. He also practices zazen, or Zen meditation.

SOIL

I was not raised on a farm, but farming and the soil have been a part of my life. Living on the world's largest fertile plain has had an impact on me. The texture and feel of soil in my hands has been a powerful connection to the environment for me since I was a boy working in my parents' garden.

I was raised in Ames, Iowa, home of Iowa State University, one of the original land grant colleges. These institutions have shaped farming practices for over a hundred years. In the late sixties and early seventies, when our society was in turmoil, the government and these agricultural institutions felt the need to expand U.S. agricultural exports to feed the world and bolster our economy. Farming techniques that had been evolving for centuries were put aside and the genetic engineering of seeds and the heavy use of chemicals became the way.

Looking back, if we would have developed sustainable agricultural technologies for export, the world's food supply would be light years ahead of where it is today.

To save and build the soils we have left, is what organic farming is about. There were a few farmers who followed their instincts and never left crop rotations, wind breaks, and the many practices that farming fence-to-fence with lots of chemicals and big equipment seemed to make passé. It must be hard to be a sustainable farmer and see the majority of your colleagues throwing chemicals everywhere and reaping short-term profits from exploiting the land.

The turmoil between generations that the sixties produced was very evident in organic farming. It seemed that organic farmers were hippies with long, dirty hair living in a commune. This image was promoted to the point where it would have been un-American to see any value in anything these people believed in.

If the universities had promoted the values of the Aldo Leopold Center for Sustainable Agriculture, instead of following the advice of pro-chemical lobbyists, like the former Secretary of Agriculture Earl Butz, the hippies would have only been on the fringe for their lifestyles, not their farming practices.

To see the corruption and greed of corporate America creep into our soils has been hard for me. When I watch soil run thick as chocolate down an erosion rill, I am sickened. Taking for granted and abusing this precious ingredient to life is a sin. I find it hard to believe that even a hundred years ago, when soils were so thick it seemed they could not be depleted, that a farmer would not have been saddened to see the destruction of his fields from the power of one rain storm.

We speak of tolerable soil loss. Why do we farm on a limited and depletable medium and speak of its demise as tolerable? Why do we tolerate non-sustainable agriculture?

I have lived on the banks of the Mississippi River for fourteen years. The power that a river is, the energy in moving water, may be why I love this ecosystem so much. The soils from the hills that surround this mother of all rivers have literally been choking the life out of the water.

The realization that farming practices are the reason for the river's demise has been hard for me. I've always felt the Corps of Engineers was the dirty culprit by diverting as much water as possible away from the backwaters into the main channel. To see chemically laden silt choking these backwaters is wrong, yet we have done almost nothing to stop the practice of tolerable soil loss that has led to the depletion of life within this river's ecosystem.

I feel the way we treat our soil is so indicative of how we feel about our planet and the ecosystem we live in. Could it be that if we changed our thinking about soil loss not being tolerable, air and water pollution not being tolerable, human suffering and corporate greed not being tolerable, that all life on earth would be sustainable?

■ *Bill Welsh*

Bill Welsh has been prominent in the organic farming movement for years and now serves on the National Organic Standards Board. He and his wife Esther, along with their son Gary and his family, run the Welsh Family Organic Farm.

THE DAY THE WELSH FAMILY FARM TURNED AROUND

Friday, May 10th, 1981, is a day that I will always remember. My day started at sunup. It was corn planting time in Iowa, which means long days in the fields. We started with chores at the home place and figured out how we could make the best use of the day. A bit of anxiety was pushing us because the following day, at noon, we were to leave for Dubuque to attend the college graduation ceremonies for our eldest son, Greg. We decided that I would start planting, while Gary went to the other farm, "Pat's," as it was called, to feed the cows.

I had just pulled into the field with the corn planter when I saw Gary racing to the field where I was working. I knew as soon as I saw him coming that something was very wrong. When he got to where I was, he jumped out of the pickup and hollered, "Come quick, the cows at Pat's are crazy!" We rushed to get over there, stopping at the house only long enough to call the vet.

As we arrived at Pat's, the first thing I saw was one cow lying dead. As I walked into the lot where the cows were, one of my favorite cows took after me and chased me over the fence. I remember thinking, what in the world is wrong with her! She was always such a gentle animal. Then we noticed three more dead cows piled on top of one another in the corner of the fence and the others running, as hard as they could, around the lot. Soon the vet arrived and he immediately said, "They are being poisoned by something."

A search began to find the source. We looked, we thought, and we looked some more. We found nothing. Soon four other veterinarians arrived to help. Brothers and neighbors were called to help, and in less than an hour the yard was full of cars. The search continued for a cause, but nothing was found.

The veterinarians decided we just had to start getting the cows into a catch chute so they could be injected with an antidote. Someone went to get the chute, others went after gates to make a runway to guide the cattle into the chute. At the same time, it was decided that one of the dead cows should be sent to a diagnostic lab. The nearest lab was contacted, and they said they would be glad to do the testing, but due to the fact that it was Friday, they could not get at it until Monday. Nevertheless, my brother Bernard was chosen for that task. Someone else went to get a manure loader to hoist the cow into the back of his pickup. Bernard immediately left for Madison, Wisconsin with a dead cow lying in the back of his pickup with all four feet in the air.

Bernard tells the story that when he got to Madison, he wasn't sure how to get to the laboratory. He saw two young men standing on the street corner, so decided to ask them for directions. As he approached them he decided it would be more fun to ask, "Where's the closest McDonald's?"

At Pat's, the job of putting the cows into the chute began. We were told that this would have to be done every four hours for at least forty-eight to seventy-two hours, maybe longer. Plans started developing on who was going to help with each succeeding shift so that we would have enough help to get through the night. The cows moved into the chute fairly easy the first trip, but each succeeding time it became more and more difficult, until at last, we were literally carrying some of them. Each time we put them through the chute, more had died.

Sometime in the afternoon, between "chute jobs," I was sitting on the fence, still trying to figure out what had happened. Then I remembered, there was a bale of hay that the cows were not eating. I had told Gary the day before that he should not give them more new hay until they had cleaned that bale up. I started wondering where that bale had come from and Gary remembered exactly, because there were very few bales left in the shed. We all went to the hay shed and soon found the problem. We found parts of a decomposed paper Dyfonate bag (an insecticide used for rootworm control) laying on the floor where that bale had been. Going back to the feeder where the refused hay bale was, we found parts of the same Dyfonate bag. The mystery was solved.

We continued to give the cows their antidote shots every four hours. Between each exhausting session, I felt very troubled about whether or not to try and go to Greg's graduation the following day. The decision was tearing my guts out. I had often dreamed about the day Greg would graduate from college, now would I even be able to go?

I spent the night in the barn, getting only a few minutes of sleep while lying on a bale of straw. This was probably the longest night of my life. By morning, the decision to go to graduation seemed much easier, probably because I was too tired to argue with my son, Gary, my brothers, and my neighbors, who had been telling me all along that they would take care of things.

At noon we left for Dubuque. I still wondered if I was doing the right thing. The time spent in Dubuque seems hazy. All I really remember was how proud I was of Greg for accomplishing something I had never been able to do.

When we returned home Sunday evening, I went straight to Pat's to check on the cows. By now thirteen had died. Soon the vet arrived again. They had decided at noon that day to discontinue the antidote shots because they really weren't sure if the last cows had died from the poison or from the antidote. The vet and I sat on the fence that evening and talked for a long time. He told me that a tablespoon of the insecticide, Dyfonate, spread evenly enough throughout the bale, could have killed all those cows and that if we used five pounds of it per acre for twenty years that we would have one hundred pounds of it somewhere in our environment. It might be dispersed, washed away by rains into nearby ponds, creeks, rivers, and eventually into the ocean, but it would always be somewhere. It is not biodegradable. It was in this discussion that I first realized that the chemicals we were using in farming were the same ones used in chemical warfare that I had learned about years before as an instructor in atomic, biological, and chemical warfare during my tour of duty in the Air Force. Frankly, that scared the hell out of me. I vowed that Sunday evening that never again would I use that product or anything like it on any land that I owned.

That is when the search for ways to farm without chemicals began. We didn't know where or how to start, but were convinced that we had to find a way. Planting time, 1982, became a real nightmare. We were unsure of what to plant where, or what to try first, but we were positively sure we would not use any more insecticide. Some of our crops that year were not that great, but we were learning and became confident we could do better next year.

■ *Greg Welsh*

THE WAY BACK

*Sometimes you have to go a long distance out of your way to come back a
short distance correctly.* —Edward Albee

I grew up on a farm in northeast Iowa, the eldest son of eight children, nurtured by my father's pride and embraced by the land. But
eventually everyone needs something of his own, a sense of who he
is. Trying to find mine, I rejected a proud father and the vulnerable
land, and I learned a lot about selfishness, anger, loneliness, before
my search brought me back to where I started. I don't know if I'll
ever find that elusive self I was after, but I may have found a crucial
part of it in what I tried to leave behind.

My first eight years on the farm were magical. Each day brought
with it its own adventure, the fascination at the birth of a calf, a new
corner of the hay barn to explore in awe. And the crazy yearning, the
consuming hunger to operate the machinery. I remember how my
brother, Gary, and I planned for weeks the best way to ask Dad if we
could drive the tractor in third gear. After a fairly extensive safety
speech, he, miraculously, said yes. You've never seen two happier
boys.

But few idylls last forever, and never those that begin when we're
young. Third gear advanced to road gear, and I began a spiral of personal disillusion and dissatisfaction about the same time Earl Butz
began in earnest his assault on the land and the American family
farm. Expansion, yield, fence-row to fence-row production, "feed
the world."

We rented more land, poured on fertilizer and pesticides, tried
for that ultimate yield. Chores now were done with syringe in hand.
Dead livestock no longer phased me at all. It seemed normal. The
veterinarian almost lived with us. He sent us his bill as we buried the
animals. We were farming by the book, and it was tearing our family apart.

It was a question both of "too much" and "too little." Too much productivity that meant too much work, too much debt, too much anger, with too little return, too little communication, too little time for love. I was old enough to know there was more than one right way, and I had ideas of my own. But my father didn't seem capable of listening. He only seemed capable of working hard. I hated him for working so stubbornly hard.

In contrast, town kids had made it. No chores to speak of. They could play baseball whenever they wanted. Often I would stay overnight with friends in town, but seldom asked friends to come to the farm. I told my mother they wouldn't have any fun. I was in high school, and I was ashamed of the farm, my family, my life.

I longed, vaguely but completely, to make a difference, and it seemed clear that I couldn't do so at home. So I dreamed of escape: to college, to law school, to a time when I could exist on my own terms, without the stigma of where I'd come from and who I'd been.

In college I got to be a town kid. I missed calving in the spring, the planting, the field work. I missed harvest. I would go back to the farm gladly on vacation. But the romance was short-lived each time, and I was equally glad to leave again. I never gave a thought to returning for good to the embrace the land held me in as a child.

While I was in college, nothing every really replaced my love for my family. But that love did take some curious turns. Naively, I pictured myself a successful lawyer with enough money to help them out of their mounting debt. I pictured them loving me finally for what I'd made of myself. I pictured myself recognized. But I never pictured myself sharing my life with them steadily, completely, as I had before and as many rural families still do.

As for my father, I felt sorry for him. Because he was still on the farm. Because he was still working hard. Because he still didn't know what I already was sure of.

My world expanded with each new possibility, each new friend, each new bit of knowledge I acquired, even as it shrank from the lack of intimacy with the people and things that formed my heart as I grew up. After a close college friend met my parents at graduation, he turned and said to me, "I didn't know you came from a farm." Somehow I'd forgotten to tell him. Somehow I'd forgotten.

Then, in the spring of 1981, an incident occurred which I see now as the beginning of my gradual return to the love of both my father and the land, love I had always needed and will never outgrow. A year earlier, at planting time, an empty bag of Dyfonate insecticide had been overlooked and left on the floor of our hay shed. A little later, the shed was filled with large, round bales of hay, which during the year we fed to our cattle.

Now, after a whole year, the bale of hay that had been on top of the empty Dyfonate bag had absorbed enough residual pesticide to poison forty full-grown pregnant cows. Thirteen eventually died. It didn't take a college education to realize there was something incredibly wrong with what had happened. I was outraged. Why were we permitted to buy such toxic products? Why were they allowed to be on the market in the first place? And what about the six to ten pounds per acre of Dyfonate that we and a large percentage of farmers like us used each year to control rootworms? What had it already done, what was it still doing, to our soil, our water, our food, ourselves?

The experience shattered my father's rigid views of farming. He swore he'd never use chemicals again. He found a reason to fight, to believe, a reason for more than stubborn work. He opened, grew, rediscovered discovery. He became approachable. I saw that he could see me, hear me again. I saw there could be a way.

But I wasn't ready. For four years I had pursued other dreams, had tested other environments, and they weren't so easily abandoned. I spent the winter working in Corpus Christi, Texas. I kept in touch with my professors, applied to law schools. I knew what I wanted.

In Texas I developed a condition I convinced myself was cancer. And why not cancer? Look at what the Dyfonate had done to our cattle. I remembered how, in high school, the daughter of a neighboring farmer was diagnosed with cancer. Cancer seemed to me the logical, horrifying inheritance of farm families, the deadly bequest of chemical agriculture.

Suddenly my life seemed so very short, my accomplishments so very few. I'd made no difference, I would never make a difference. I was angry, frightened, lonely. I was dying.

I went home.

It took about two months for the official verdict to come in. Expecting the worst, I cried all the way to the doctor. But I did not have cancer. I had a serious infection, but it could be cured completely and fairly quickly with antibiotics. I had gotten a stay of execution. The relief was amazing. So was the feeling of stupidity. My imagination surprised me.

Nothing really changed. And everything did. If my cancer wasn't real, the threat of cancer to myself, my family, my neighbors still was. The economics of overproductive agribusiness threatened a whole way of life, my way of life, despite the years I tried to deny it. And the chemical dependency at the heart of that economics threatened not only the lives of farm families, but of anyone eating the food farms produced, or drinking water from contaminated aquifers.

I, too, rediscovered discovery.

Of course transformations are never really instantaneous. After every turning point there are residues left of our former selves that only patience can eradicate. For a while I became a self-righteous environmentalist, the most righteous environmentalist in the country for sure. I was intolerant of the sheer blockheadedness of many farmers in the light of my new found truth. There were still heated arguments with my father, despite our similar views.

It was clear to me that the natural, organic life of the soil was a slow, dynamic process never to be completed. But it took much longer for me to see that the inner lives of men and women, my father's and my own included, are similar processes.

It seems to me now the true quality of both the soil and the spirit, of all life, should not be judged on what it is at any given moment, like a finished product, but should be loved for the emergent things they are. It seems to me now that all things are continually making themselves and each other. And there seems little need for amends. Everything—the crops, the laughter in my father's eyes—is reconciliation.

I am always amazed at the amount of life in the soil, at the resiliency of it, and I am convinced we should do nothing to destroy its creative ability. And I am amazed, too, at the life, love, and resiliency in my father's heart and, to my surprise, in my own. I'm amazed and afraid, and I pray I will soon cease doing anything that might endanger that creativity.

■ *Linda and Michael Nash*

Linda and Michael Nash came to Iowa via Colorado. Both have graduate degrees from the Eastman School of Music. Linda was a professional harpist until four years ago and Michael a professional conductor until about age 42. Michael also holds an MFA in photography and has worked as a graphic designer. They now run a Community Supported Agriculture farm (CSA) outside Postville, Iowa.

DO YOU KNOW WHO GROWS YOUR FOOD?

Do you know who grows your food? It is a simple but important question, and one that has always been of great interest to us. Who grew this food and where did it come from? California? Mexico? Florida? There are many political, environmental, and health issues tied to food production and consumption. What chemicals are used on the soil and on the food? What means are used to extend shelf life during shipping and sale? Does the food retain its nutritional value?

When my husband and I were able to realize a long time dream of owning a farm, we immediately began discussing how the farm would be run, and how we would market our farm's bounty. There were two things we knew for sure: everything would be grown organically, and we would plant a high volume of vegetables and fruit for human (not animal) consumption. We were not interested in producing large amounts of commodities, but large amounts of high quality, organic food.

Why do we grow organically? Because the use of pesticides and herbicides by American factory farms is an increasing health problem of huge proportions. The process of using more and more fertilizer to make up for declining soil quality cannot continue indefinitely. When we bought our farm, we had the well water tested, and it failed every single test for potability. It was totally unsafe to drink. In fact, it was dangerous to drink, and the problems in our well can be traced directly to runoff from field chemical applications and animal manure. On the other hand, sustainable farming practices, such as crop rotation, the use of composted manure, and planting cover crops such as rye grass or clover, which are later tilled back into the soil as green manure, build the soil safely and protect against erosion. Organic agriculture keeps chemicals out of the soil, out of the water supply, and off your plate, and this is very important to us and to a growing number of people.

In planning for the future of our small family farm, we also knew we wanted to be more involved in the local food system than just making deliveries to a distributor or retail outlet, and so we decided to start our area's very first Community Supported Agriculture (CSA). Under this plan, we sell shares to members at the beginning of the season. For an agreed upon price, the shareholders receive a weekly delivery of produce throughout the summer months and into the fall. By this method, farm community members share the risks of farming and weather, and the bounty of the fields. Eliminating the usually wide gap between farmers and consumers builds interest in the farm and its success. This was brought home to us one day when a member was visiting the farm during one of our shareholder get-togethers. He stood out in the field and said with a smile, "Just checking out my sweet corn." This strong connection between us as farmers, and the CSA shareholders we deliver to, is very meaningful to us, and our members have let us know that it is meaningful to them as well.

We take the word "community" in CSA very seriously. Recently we started a program to solicit donations from businesses and individuals to pay for CSA shares for Opportunity Homes and Martin Luther Homes. These are local group homes for developmentally and physically challenged adults living with varying degrees of supervision. We felt strongly that income levels or the ability to decipher a brochure should not exclude anyone who might benefit from a CSA share. We have received a lot of support for the program, including donated work time from CSA members who want to help out. The group home residents have enjoyed visits to the farm, and we have had the satisfaction of reaching out to the community.

One CSA member donating work time is Mike, who was diagnosed with severe multiple sclerosis several years ago. By making changes to his diet and lifestyle, and by eating organically grown food as much as possible, he has been able to greatly lessen the effects of the disease. As a strong proponent of organic agriculture, Mike was glad to find out about our place, and glad to put himself to work to support the CSA, the group homes, and organics in general. We're grateful for his time commitment, and are always grateful when we find another person in our area who supports organic agriculture. We have in fact found many people in our area who are interested in organics, and so all of the food we grow is used within a 25 mile radius of the farm. When there is a strong connection between growers and eaters, the benefits on both sides are enormous.

But what if you don't know the grower? What if there isn't a CSA in your area? What about out-of-season items? Then we depend on finding certified produce and other products in our local stores. When something is certified organic, it means an independent inspector has come to the farm to review the field histories and to inspect the crops. The inspection must be done after planting, because it is the crop that will be certified, not the farm or field. The inspector views records going back five years. The previous three years must be clear of disallowed chemicals, and must show how the farm works to build the soil. The inspector then reports to the third party certification organization of the farmer's choice, which decides if the crops can be certified organic.

Recently, the USDA proposed a set of national organic standards meant to replace the varying standards currently used by the many different third party organizations. At first look, consistent government standards seem like a good idea, because, in theory, they would enable consumers to know exactly what the word "organic" means. But . . .

The USDA did not show an interest in the development of the organic industry until large corporations began to see that there was money being made in the field, especially with organic grains in international markets. If the USDA introduces standards which are universally recognized, markets open and production increases. This all sounds good on the surface. But . . .

The increasing demand for organic produce will pressure growers to produce more and to do it easier and quicker, producing a more consistent product. This leads back to large corporations controlling the organic industry and lobbying to ease standards to fit more efficient production. USDA research has not focused on innovative, sustainable organic practices, although they blow the "sustainable horn," when it serves their purposes. Only .08% of the entire research budget of the USDA has been spent on organic practices. So what does this mean?

This means that "organic" could come to mean what those who lobby the government and the USDA want it to mean. Certainly, large corporations see that "organic" printed on their labels will sell products, and they will do what is necessary to get it there. But, they have no interest in maintaining the integrity that the organic industry has built over the years. If these corporations see a way to make money by "adjusting" the government organic standards, they will spend the money to lobby until it gets done. "Organic," then, becomes the next buzz word for mass-produced products which fit the watered-down, lobbied version of the word.

The standards that were proposed this year by the USDA included the use of irradiation, sewage sludge, the feeding of rendered animal by-products, and the use of genetically modified organisms. These are commercial farming practices that have never been allowed by any organic certifying organization, and yet would be allowed by the new national standards. The National Organic Standards Board has been working on the standards for years. They requested and received input from the organics industry, but their recommendations were largely ignored by the USDA when the USDA wrote the standards. Because of the huge public outcry against these proposed standards, they have been withdrawn for the moment, but it seems unlikely that they will ever be as strict as the current rules used by most third party certifiers. It is inevitable that the organic industry will grow to include mass-produced food, international buyers, and that the industry will change to meet these new situations. It is not, however, desirable that the industry accept less demanding standards.

Because of this, we will continue to market our produce locally, supporting our own area economy, and continuing to connect with people who feel as strongly about organics as we do. We have chosen not to certify our produce, although we qualify and have the necessary records. If one of our farm community members has a question about our farming practices, they can come out and see for themselves, or just ask us. So we have not felt the need to go through the certification process, which is expensive and time-consuming. However, when we go to buy groceries at our local stores, we buy only certified organic products, because as consumers, it is very important to us that the crop has been inspected. We see both sides of this issue, and do not rule out certification for our farm in the future. In the meantime, we don't plan to let the government tell us how to run our farm.

No matter the outcome of all these issues, it will not affect our primary goals: grow organically, market locally, and build connections with our farm community members. The most important standards are the ones we have set for ourselves.

■ *Don and Mary Klauke*

Don and Mary Klauke have multiple responsibilities. In addition to running their own organic vegetable farm and raising sheep, they are marriage counselors. Don is also Rural Life Director for the Dubuque Archdiocese.

VERTICAL INTEGRATION IN AGRICULTURE

Think of it! We used to worry about communism. We called it "Big Brother" and said that left unchecked it would take over the world. But maybe Big Brother will not be a political philosophy. Perhaps it will be multi-national corporate greed which controls the world through total vertical integration of its food supply.

One of the most understandable definitions of vertical integration we ever heard was uttered by a farmer friend of ours. He described it very succinctly as "a conglomerate that owns everything from the genes in the plant or animal to the space on the supermarket shelf."

What's so bad about that? some people ask. After all, agricultural departments of state universities, their local outreach (County Extension facilities), and agribusiness have long preached "efficiency" as the key to good business. Efficiency is a key to the explanation of the structure of much current agriculture. Central control of all the steps of a product results in greater efficiency and greater economic gain to the one in control of the most. If you have a number of people, each taking care of a piece of the product, you have a lot of input and a lot of diversity. But if one entity controls all aspects, you don't have the difficulties associated with discussion and decision-making, but you have also lost diversity, individual control, and local accountability. Big Brother?

Why does society seem so eager to look at all of agriculture through one narrow knot-hole? "Bottom line" is becoming the mantra chanted in every boardroom, research facility, and farmstead across the country. All judgments are made in terms of money, not people or communities, not land or water, just present, not future.

Four companies now control most of the world's food supply through this type of monetary structure called "vertical integration." Let's take a top pork producing firm as an example of how vertical integration works. This firm controls the genetic make-up to develop pigs designed for total uniformity in production and in packing. They raise the breeding stock used in their farrowing operations where newborns live with their mothers until being sent to nurseries a few days later. The corporation owns the feed mill, the pigs, the packing house. There is no need for the traditional auction house or buying station where independent producers used to sell pigs that were ready for market. In the system in which the corporations operate, prices are set, not by open bidding, but by contracts written before the pigs are born.

That same corporation controls the grain which it stores and mills in its own facilities. This grain is used for its hog feed, and for flour and cereal grains for human consumption. This corporation owns pharmaceutical companies that produce the antibiotics and other drugs used to promote growth, alleviate animal illness and the stress of shipping. At the same time another branch produces drugs for human medicinal needs.

The multinational pork producer may also have the genetic material and the seed companies to provide the grain used in all their operations, and controls the herbicide and pesticide that they insist needs to be used in the "manufacturing" of their products.

The multiple entities listed in this pared down description of the process don't all fall under the same name. It is extremely hard to tie the realities together because of the constant buying and selling, merging and amalgamating within the corporate structure. A small example made this very clear to us when we ordered seed from a well-known seed company several years ago. The order was confirmed by a former Midwest family nursery and, within six weeks, was shipped by a pharmaceutical company. In terms of hog production, typically a small corporation formed, let's say, by a local feed company with a landowner/producer, and using money from outside investors, will have one name. The same kind of contractual relationship between another neighboring landowner and the same feed company will have another name, making it nearly impossible for members in a community to know who owns what, who their neighbors are, and who is responsible for what happens.

The wealth generated in the money-making maze does not find equal distribution among the producers and caretakers of the animals and land, or even the workers in packing and distribution. It ends up paying a CEO and assuring high dividends to investors.

It is touted that jobs are being created and the rural economy developed, but at what price? Production contracts are eagerly grasped with little thought to the liabilities incurred. While the corporation provides assistance putting up facilities and owns the hogs, the local land owner/producer, who contracts with the corporation to raise the hogs, bears the financial burden and the liability for these buildings and the manure generated in them. The buildings will be serviceable for a few years, hopefully long enough for the producer to pay the financing costs. Many of them, however, will need major repairs or be unsuitable for use and become a major financial and environmental liability before they are paid for, causing some farmers to lose the land they were trying to save by building them.

Many of the landowners we have seen entering into these production contracts do so out of fear—fear that they will lose their farm as so many others have done; fear that they will lose the market for their hogs because processing plants now control their own supply source and local buying stations are closing, or fear that the feed dealers will force them into bankruptcy because they have bills past due.

What kind of freedom do people have when they act out of fear? Fear has limited their ability to seek information, to look at alternatives and to weigh consequences. It has encouraged them to take advice from those who have some kind of power over them—those who control the money for putting in crops or feeding the livestock. Their source of information is advertising—what public relations officers of corporations want them to hear—certainly not unbiased. Commodity groups, such as the Pork Producers Association, use funds taken from producers at market time to further an agenda heavily influenced by big corporations, corporations motivated by making fast money for their stockholders, not concern for the people, the land or the future. The president of one such group said it very clearly on a radio talk show when asked about the possibility of technologies which use less water for raising hogs and may be better for the environment: "We have this technology,"—current confinement facilities—"we will use it" was his cursory reply.

People think that having the manure contained in earthen pits or even lined pits or slurry stores [metal containers] will keep it from damaging the ground water, but most of the problems we have had in this area have occurred when the manure is applied to the land. Problems can arise because of runoff or because too much manure was applied. Applying it as a solid, instead of having so much water mixed with it, would be much better for the environment, but that would mean a change in the whole technology. And what about looking for the best technologies? In the mind of a corporation (or an individual) looking only at a financial bottom line, the best technology is that which makes the most money in the shortest time, irrespective of the consequences. Who pays for devastating consequences to people, land and water? Is it even possible to undo the damage once it occurs?

What happens to communities when corporations do the farming? Neighbors are pitted against neighbor, brothers against brother. In one situation, a woman is losing the day-care business she has established in her home because her husband's brothers, with another investor, are putting a large scale hog confinement operation one-quarter mile from her house. All those who have invested in the operation live away from the site and do not personally bear the consequences of their action on the air, water and land. However, they will suffer the loss of peace in their family because of their lack of respect for their brother and his family. Community and family cannot survive where the desire for money is greater than the love and concern for people.

Many times local and state governments provide incentives in the form of tax abatements or forgivable loans if corporations will come into an area and create jobs. Rural jobs may be created with the new pork producing corporations moving into an area, but they are extremely low paying and offer little or no benefits. At the same time many more farmers are going out of business because traditional markets are no longer available to them. The corporations have no need for the business in the community. They bring in their own builders and supplies, and in some cases, their own concrete plants. They supply their own processors, so there are no buying stations. (The people who worked in the buying stations are jobless, as well as the farmers who are displaced.) Other local businesses lose as the money made from the production of food and fiber is leaving the community and going to the corporate investors. It seems to be a case of taking from the poor and giving to the rich.

What happens to food when corporations do the hog farming? Pork is grown in strictly controlled conditions for profit's sake, not for good taste or healthfulness. Antibiotics used on the animals (mostly to help them grow faster, not treat illness) are creating drug-resistant germs that are ingested by people in their food. But this is just one more hidden price we pay when we purchase completely prepared food from faceless, nameless people, thereby losing our relationship to food, to other gifts of creation and to the Creator.

When we began farming, back in the early eighties, some people said that we were running away from reality; isolating ourselves from the direction of society. They wanted us to focus our education and extensive experience on making money our number one goal; leave the farming to the "efficiencies" of agribusiness. Since that time, there has been a lot of pressure on farmers to follow corporate "wisdom." Many of us, however, have come to question what happened to the freedom to live according to the values formerly associated with the family farm—values such as neighborhood, cooperation, justice, simplicity, care of the environment. This is not just running away from inevitable progress or mere nostalgia. It is setting a priority on people and the future rather than on the bottom line and corporate profit. Which of these sets of values is the foundation that will provide a lasting support for mankind?

Commentary

■ *An Interview with Father Norman White*

Father Norm White was Rural Life Director for the Dubuque Archdiocese for many years. For several years before his death in 1997, he was probably the best known small farm advocate in Iowa. This article consists of excerpts from an interview conducted in May 1995.

DANIEL IN THE LION'S DEN

I became Rural Life Director in January of '83 on a part-time basis. I was pastor at Fayette and Hawkeye and continued on that way. And during that first year, 1993, I worked closely with the newly organized Land Stewardship Project out of St. Paul, working against soil erosion especially, setting up meetings in Iowa.

By December of '83, it was obvious that there was a need for more than legal advice and financial help, which we were providing. It was obvious that they needed spiritual help, too, and so I switched from working against soil erosion to concentrate on soul erosion. I got that terminology from Bishop Maurice Dingman when I first heard him talk to us Rural Life directors in Des Moines.

In the winter of early '84, in an attempt to help that soul erosion, we put on three retreats . . . Well, word got around the countryside that we were talking about the legal options for farmers as well as low input agriculture and that sort of thing. So a banker complained to an assistant bishop, who in turn told the archbishop and the archbishop in turn said to me, "By the way, a banker complained that you're bringing up legal things in these retreats."

I said, "Well, I'll talk to him, I'll call him. It's important that we understand that aspect."

I called him, he set up a meeting a few days later, and I said, "Who'll be there?"

He said, "Well, our loan officer, and our land bank director, because the land bank has an interest in a particular farm, and the extension director."

I asked who, and he told me. I said, "Oh? The regional director? Did you know he's the one who was quoted in *The Telegraph Herald* as referring to `Father White and that save the family farm shit?'"

He said, "It won't be Daniel in the lion's den."

I said, "It will too, but I'll come. I need to know how things are from your aspect."

So I get there, and not only were those people present but their lawyer, a man whom I taught in high school. I was his principal, I taught him speech. Also present was the pastor of the place, a man whom I taught when he was in seminary.

Their main concern was that Chapter 11 was being used by a particular farmer who had a loan with them, and they felt he should not do that. "If they feel they cannot make any more, they should go to Chapter 7, which is outright bankruptcy."

I said, "That means you're the first mortgage, you'll get everything that's left, and Main Street, the businesses, won't get anything."

"Yeah, but they (the businesses) are not going to get more than even ten percent if they file Chapter 11, the way you're recommending."

Twice during our conversation they brought out the portfolio of this one particular family that they were concerned about, and that we'd been working closely with. The first time they did this I said, "You have no right to even show me that portfolio. I know them well, I've been on their farm. I don't know their situation, and you have no business revealing, professionally, where they stand." When they showed it the second time I repeated that: "It is not right, it is not fair. To me it's immoral, it's unprofessional."

We went on for a couple of hours, and I had a list of questions, but then they all went back to work. I never did report this back to the archbishop. He never did ask me about it. I reported it back to the auxiliary bishop who had received the call in the first place and told him who was there. And he said, "Oh, you mean it was five against two?" I said, "No, it was six against one. This pastor didn't say much, but when he did he was obviously being pressured to take the bank's side."

It was some months later that Prairiefire (a coalition of farm organizations) wanted to have a meeting in eastern Iowa to talk to farmers about their rights and what we should be doing and can be doing.

And the young fellow who was helping me visit farm homes said he would contact this particular parish to see if they could use the church hall. It was the same town where this bank meeting took place. The pastor immediately said, "Yes, you can use the hall." Before the day was over he called the farmer back and said, "No, you can't use the church hall."

But that's only one example of parishes that we have found very non-cooperative. There's two pastors of a Protestant religion who wanted us there to do a retreat. So they arranged with one of the churches in town to have us there, but then, shortly afterwards they were informed by the leadership of that parish that the banker said, "That bunch is not meeting at our church." So they took us out to the fairgrounds.

There's another situation at a rather fundamentalist parish with a couple who worked with us a lot, trying to salvage some things. When they declared bankruptcy she was dismissed as a Sunday school teacher and he was dismissed as bus driver for their Sunday school, and then as they got into this thing further, they were dismissed from the parish, and they moved to another town.

The cruelty. It's part of this, "You have disgraced us by declaring bankruptcy." One of the problems I had out here was, why is it that business and industry can declare Chapter 7 and it's considered a wise move, good business, and when a farmer does it he's a bum?

Another woman who lost her farm, once they declared bankruptcy, did not receive the sign of peace from a member of her own choir for years. I don't know if she has yet.

I have never gotten very frank with the archbishop about the attitude of the Farm Bureau leadership in parishes because I'm sure they have gotten to him too. I'm positive of it.

I was to give two workshops for the Archdiocesan Council of Catholic Women, probably in 1986. One was in Waukon, and one was in the western part of the diocese. I went to the then president of the Dubuque county Farm Bureau. I went to his home and I said, "I am going to come out against your state leadership and national leadership in these workshops. I'm so sick and tired of Farm Bureau taking stances contrary to what the Catholic Church holds. Our bishops are talking about cooperation rather than competing." And he said to me, jabbing his finger, he said, "You're wrong! The Church is wrong! This is the United States! Here is the land of competition! Here we compete!" He said, "Furthermore, there's a first amendment to the constitution that separates church and state. You take care of church, I'll take care of agriculture!"

I said, "No way. It's not going to be that way. It's going to be a constant battle."

When the document "Strangers and Guests" was put together by the bishops of the Midwest in 1980, on land stewardship, land conservation, that sort of thing, the Farm Bureau fought that thing tooth and nail because of the things that were in there on conservation and the common good. They never use common good. It's MINE! The personal, individual rights thing.

The main architect of that document, John Hart from Carroll

College in Montana, just told me recently they're still sore, and they're still doing all they can to work against what the Catholic Church stands for in conservation stewardship.

One of the state conservationists in our diocese told me that he knows of a parish where the pastor is not allowed to preach on conservation. There's another parish where the retired pastor said to me, "When I first came to this parish the leadership told me, `Don't you ever let Father White preach in this pulpit.' "

⌁

I got my degree in U.S. History. I taught U.S. History, but I didn't know the rural story at all until I got this job, and people passed stuff to me. I probably had the job a few years before a NFO (National Farmers Organization) person gave me a copy of a report issued by the Committee of Economic Development in 1962. That document just really shook me. These were industrialists, and the closest thing to agriculture on that committee was someone who made ketchup. In there they said, "It's important that we get excess resources, people primarily, out of agriculture, off the land. We need to get rid of 2 million farmers." That was in '62. At that time we had 6.2 million farmers.

Towards the end of the document it said, "Now, of course, as more and more people leave the farm and come into the cities there will need to be a moderation of wages." Moderation which way? Flood the market with employees, then we can pay our price.

That committee on economic development apparently meets annually. It didn't meet again on agriculture until '74, twelve years later. They said, "We have succeeded in reducing the farm population by 2 million, we must need to decrease it even more. There are too many out there." And some time around there, too, there was a report put out by the young executives of the USDA talking about farm policies and what needs to be done. They said, "And of course if this was done it would result in the decrease in the number of farms, which we do not see as a bad thing."

And I'm convinced that the whole idea is that the fewer farmers you have the more coalition you can build, the more control you can have. And that's certainly the case now with the big farmers, the big land owners, they're not necessarily farmers themselves.

This was 1952. From 1942 to 1952 there was what's called the Steagall Amendment, calling for parity for farmers. Part of this was during the Second World War when there was a need for a lot of food, lot of markets, and during that ten-year period farmers were getting 110 percent of parity.

Parity is this: the price the farmer gets for his product is on a par with other elements of the economy, on a par with what he pays for things or on a par with what labor gets, or on a par with what manufacturing is making. The Steagall Amendment was not renewed when it expired in 1952. It was the intention of Congress at that time not to, because prices were for farmers. I'm sure that's the reason for it.

My dad became county treasurer in 1941. He remained county treasurer 18 years, and he told me that he could tell within a month after the Steagall Amendment expired that farmers were having more and more trouble paying their taxes because the price of their products started going down.

My brother, now on the farm, retired (he's eighty years old) considers himself a success because he convinced all of his sons not to farm for a living. Already in the sixties and seventies he said, "The government has a cheap food policy. It's not fair, we don't get a decent price for our product. We work, work, and work our tails off. It's not right because we're not getting the cost of production plus a profit."

The government's policy is a cheap food policy, and I compare it to the bread and circuses of Rome: keep the folks happy with cheap food. That's the bread, I'm not sure what the circuses are.

I feel that in the last ten years we have helped farmers go through pain. But at a hearing with our U.S. representative I said, "Unless you help us get better prices for the farmers, they're simply not going to make it." Then he said to me, "I think it's wonderful what you're doing to reach out to help the hurting farmers."

I said, "That's just a palliative, that's just to try to undo some of the damage."

So he talked on and on and finally I stopped him again. And he said, "It's great what you're doing."

I said, "I refuse to settle for being a pall bearer, helping the farmers bury their family farms. I just will not be a professional mourner, and only a professional mourner."

Well, I was that, I have been that. And we had quite a network of outreach to hurting farmers, and I don't think we've accomplished anything other than that.

౽

I've given up, I have really given up on trying to help keep middle and small farmers on the land through any kind of political process, and we failed miserably. My main concern now is food security world wide, including our own urban people. Because when a few people get control of the whole food supply, from the oink in the hoghouse to the wow! in the supermarket, then you'll know that something long lasting has happened to all consumers.

■ *Robert Wolf*

THE JEFFERSONIAN IDEAL

According to *The Des Moines Register*, Iowa lost one-quarter of its farmers in the farm crisis of the 1980s and will lose another quarter in the 1990s. But the devastating Midwestern floods the summer of 1993 made it clear that it would take less than a decade to force that next quarter off the land. Today the small Iowa farmer knows that his years are numbered, and he knows that his and other Midwestern farm lands are being transferred into the hands of fewer and fewer owners.

About the end of World War II this country saw the triumph of efficiency as the standard by which to judge agricultural techniques. After the war tractors replaced plows, mules, and horses. Herbicides and pesticides were soon introduced. All this meant that farming was getting "scientific," along with the rest of efficiently run businesses.

Tractors and chemicals obviously increased costs, but farmers were persuaded to accept them because they decreased labor and increased the chances for greater profits through greater yields. When you think about it, it seems remarkable that organic farming, which farmers had practiced for millennia worldwide, should have been wiped out in a matter of decades. And yet it was, partly no doubt because of the appeal for anything "scientific," and partly because of potential profits. But now one of these elements of "scientific and advanced" farming—the expensive machinery—has become a major contributor to the small farmer's demise.

Even before the effect of machinery's high cost began to take its toll, farmers were persuaded to get big, to buy more land, and to plant "fence row to fence row." In the 1970s FmHA loans were easy to get. So farmers got big. They bought more land, added to their herds, maybe built a new milking barn or added to their farrowing operation. Then in the late seventies, nobody knows quite why, loans were sometimes called in or rewritten, sometimes underhandedly. A farmer might be asked to sign an agreement that put him out of business.

By the mid-1980s more than a handful of farm families were living through the winters without heat, and with very little food. Many watched their herds die of starvation. The strain cracked many. Divorce increased. And then came the suicides.

All this continues to lead our country away from its rural roots, into an ever stranger and more complex future, far from the agrarian vision of Thomas Jefferson, who wanted America filled with farmers, because he believed that they are "the most virtuous and independent citizens."

Rather than see Americans divided in employment between manufacture and agriculture, Jefferson wanted to leave manufacturing to the Europeans, for the United States, he thought, could purchase needed goods from Europe in exchange for American food surpluses. One of the biggest arguments in favor of such an arrangement, he argued, was the physical and moral superiority "of the agricultural, over the manufacturing, man."

To John Jay he wrote: "We have now lands enough to employ an infinite number of people in their cultivation. Cultivators of the earth are the most valuable citizens. They are the most vigorous, & they are tied to their country & wedded to it's (sic) liberty & interests by the most lasting bonds. As long as they can find employment in this line I would not convert them into mariners, artisans or anything else."

But on the day Americans become too numerous for the land, then, Jefferson thought, "I should then perhaps wish to turn them to the sea in preference to manufacture, because comparing the characters of the two classes I find the former the most valuable citizens. I consider the class of artificers of a country as the panders of vice & the instruments by which the liberties of a country are generally overturned."

By "artificers" he means the makers of goods, artisans and manufacturers, those who employ themselves alone and those who employ hundreds. What is decisive for Jefferson is that manufacture breeds a demand for luxuries, and is opposed to frugality, a civic virtue. He had in mind the examples of the ancient world, particularly Rome, where a tough and free people acquired a wealth and luxury which corrupted them to the point where they abandoned their liberties for a dictatorship. Even in the early days of the republic, Jefferson considered "the extravagance which has seized them (Americans) as a more baneful evil then toryism was during the war." If Jefferson thought Americans were corrupted then by luxuries, what would he say to us today?

The framers of our constitution understood the intimate connection between economics and politics, between money and political power. "(Alexander) Hamilton and his school," historian Charles

Beard wrote, "deliberately sought to attach powerful interests to the Federal Government. Jefferson clung tenaciously to the proposition that freehold agriculture bore a vital relation to the independence of spirit essential to popular rule." Hence Jefferson's passionate desire to see America's lands filled with freehold farmers.

In 1821, not many years after Jefferson's presidency, American statesman Daniel Webster wrote: "It seems to me to be plain that, in the absence of military force, political power naturally and necessarily goes into the hands which hold the property." The early English settlers of New England, he wrote, "were themselves . . . nearly on a general level in respect to property. Their situation demanded a parcelling out and division of the lands, and it may be fairly said that this necessary act fixed the future and form of their government. The character of their political institutions was determined by the fundamental laws respecting property . . . . The consequence of all these causes has been a great subdivision of the soil and a great equality of condition; the true basis, most certainly, of popular government."

Webster, then, agreed with Jefferson that popular government rested upon the wide distribution of land among its citizens. Jefferson went further, wanting an agriculturally based economy for the country, because farmers were the best of all classes to uphold their liberty, first by their independence, and second by their lack of corruption. But the powerful and emerging mercantile, banking, and manufacturing interests in the developing country would eventually subvert that dream. Speaking on behalf of those interests, Alexander Hamilton wrote: "The prosperity of commerce is now perceived and acknowledged by all enlightened statesmen to be the most useful as well as the most productive source of national wealth . . ." By the 1920s commercial and financial interests had triumphed to the point where Calvin Coolidge could proclaim that "the business of America is business."

⌒

When we examine traditional civilizations, we find that one thinker after another warns us of the perils of commerce and finance. The argument, though, is from a different point of view than that of Jefferson, who is himself echoing the fears of Roman stoics. The stoics saw that wealth and luxury had corrupted the Roman people, but for Plato and others the argument against business revolved around its ability to corrupt the arts. For the Greeks and other traditional peoples, art was not confined to painting, sculpture, music, literature, and dance. The word 'art' itself is our clue to that, deriving as it does from the Latin word 'ars,' meaning skill, trade, or profession, as well as 'art' in our restricted sense. Thus in traditional societies anyone who made a thing was an artist. So were those who nurtured, such as physicians and farmers.

Underlying the very foundations of traditional societies was the knowledge that to lead a fully human existence a person must have an art that he follows all his life. The distinction between work and labor lies in the fact that work is imbued with art, shaped by it, and labor lacks art. Strip a person's livelihood of art, and you strip him of his humanity. A person stripped of his humanity eventually turns to violence, and much of the anger in this country comes from people working jobs that are better suited to robots than to human beings. As for farmers forced off the land, most are obliged to trade a complex art with multiple activities and skills, for low-skilled labor.

To understand how fully the deck is stacked against farmers you must understand that with few exceptions the only farmers who stand a chance of crawling out from under debt are those who can somehow market their own products directly to consumers. Otherwise they are locked into a price determined primarily by the five major international grain corporations, two of which are U.S. based. These multi-national corporations are the purveyors of wheat, corn, soybeans, rice, and other grains to governments around the world. Indirectly these company determine, here and abroad, the price of livestock and poultry, as well as bread, cereals, pasta, and other grain based produce. It is these companies, not the U.S. government, which sells U.S. wheat to Russia, Korea, and elsewhere.

In years when the sales of the multi-national grain corporations to foreign governments are relatively low, their influence is lessened, while that of the futures markets in Chicago, Minneapolis, and Kansas City is increased. But the major grain corporations have independent brokers buying and selling futures contracts for them at these markets. Considering the volume at which they buy and sell, their influence is considerable.

The prices on grain, pork, beef, and other commodities can vary widely within a day, affected by weather, scarcity, foreign sales and other factors. The middlemen, speculators, never actually see what they are buying or selling, and most fail to make a profit, but those who succeed can make a fortune. Such middlemen are unnecessary, and are symptomatic of a society whose driving force is avarice. As R. H. Trawney wrote in *Religion and the Rise of Capitalism*, medieval social theory condemned "the speculator or the middleman, who snatches private gain by the exploitation of public necessities."

Those farmers who are willing to play the very involved game of puts and calls on the commodities markets may protect themselves from loss. But the majority of farmers, nine out of ten, do not speculate on the market, and do not want to. It is not in their nature. Yet the politicians, the bureaucrats in the U.S. Department of Agriculture, and the bankers are expecting the farmer to become a "good manager," which means they expect him not only to use a computer to record his yields, profits, and losses, but to utilize the latest developments in biotechnology, and to operate successfully in the future markets. But the farmer is a special kind of artist, and to ask him to abandon his art and take up someone else's is to expect him to violate his nature.

This brings us to the very heart of this "civilization's" malaise: the denigration and abandonment of vocation, which is intimately connected to the idea of art. In traditional civilizations, all people had a vocation. A vocation is a calling to this or that kind of work, and this calling is determined by our aptitude, which directs our love. This is to say that we love what we do well or what we are called to do. But few remember the idea of vocation, or if they remember it, dismiss it, for we are a pragmatic people, and as pragmatists we can see no difference between work and labor.

Today the values of the commercial class are those that drive this society and its institutions. One outcome is that today, as in Plato's time, commerce has infected all the arts. Artists of various kinds, physicians, surgeons, and lawyers among them, confuse the art of making money with their own special arts. The small farmer has resisted, asking only for a fair price and the opportunity to continue farming.

But the pragmatist has no use for the small farmer, who is inefficient. He is inefficient because he is not a "good manager." And being inefficient, he is undesirable. As former Secretary of Agriculture Earl Butz has said repeatedly, "There are too many farmers." But what this society has yet to learn is that efficiency is a totally inappropriate standard by which to judge human beings and their work, though an appropriate one for robots.

To work backward, the farm crisis can be seen as the final clash between the urban forces of commerce and banking on the one hand, and agrarian, democratic interests on the other. The issue of the contest is not much in doubt, and when the farmer and his way of life pass on, the fiber on American democracy passes with him.

There is a beautiful book published several years ago, a forty year record on farm families in Jo Daviess County, Illinois. In this book, *Neighbors*, one of the farmers says. ". . . I love this land, all right. To me the land is my being. It's all I've got. It's my existence. I feel like I'm just a part of it. When you read in the Bible where it says God gave you this land to till it, to take care of it, to prosper, that's what it means to me. It's my duty to do this. I don't consider it a job exactly. It's a duty. A responsibility. This gives me happiness and satisfaction and a reason for being here."

How many of us would say that we have a responsibility to do our work beyond the responsibility to provide food and shelter for our families? For the vast majority of us, our work means nothing more than a paycheck. We have not found what the Buddhists call "right livelihood." We have not found our vocation, so do not know what it is we are supposed to do, have not found responsibility, and consequently remain irresponsible. But a society composed of people without duty and responsibility has no human centered course or direction. Without duty we are alienated, and that accounts, in part, for why so many of us are angry, why there is so much violence.

It is fitting to close with a passage from Thomas Jefferson, a passage from one of his letters to James Madison that has proved prophetic: "I think our governments will remain virtuous for many centuries; as long as they are chiefly agricultural; and this will be as long as there shall be vacant lands in any part of America. When they get piled upon one another in large cities, as in Europe, they will become corrupt as in Europe, and go to eating one another as they do there."

SMALL TOWNS

Introduction

All but two of the following stories are excerpted from *Independence, Iowa* and *Clermont, Iowa*, two Free River Press books written and published in 1994. Each was written on three consecutive Saturdays and the second on three consecutive days and to my knowledge they are the first books ever written about towns by the towns' citizens, sitting around a table and working in collaboration. Town histories have been written by several citizens working cooperatively, but this is not the same thing. These people, only one of whom at the time wrote professionally, are communicating experiences, sometimes very personal, which, snapshot by snapshot, build up a coherent picture of their respective communities.

I have found that every small town writing workshop I have organized since has also produced a collection of writings that reflect the idiosyncrasies of that town while communicating its underlying similarities with others. Independence, with a population of almost six thousand and a half-hour drive from an urban area, is more sophisticated than Clermont, and its writings (only two of which are included here) were more intricate, tending to detailed exposition and explanation of incidents. The Clermont stories, by contrast, were often descriptions of patterns of activity more typical of isolated small towns.

When I spoke to the organizers of both workshops, I specified that they should try to recruit as diverse a group as possible: old and young, male and female, professional, laborer, farmer, and student, so as to get as complete a picture as possible of community life given the limitations of workshop size and duration. *Independence, Iowa* was the idea of an Independence retailer, who soon got another local businessman to co-fund the project. The workshop had nineteen members, the most I had ever worked with at one time. Considering that an integral part of the workshop method is to have each participant tell at least one story and that the telling consumes much time, the process went extremely well. We had about half a dozen college freshmen, three high school students, a bank vice president, two teachers, a florist, a mental health worker, a saleswoman, a housewife, a journalist, and several retirees, including a former automobile dealer and an ex-teacher. Independence being the size it is, no one person knew everyone else, although several knew most of the others. Like all other small town workshops, it was convivial. At that time, Delores Martin, who wrote "The Flood of 1990" for the workshop, was a saleswoman. Her story so impressed the editor of the local newspaper (who also participated in the workshop), that she offered Delores the chance to write a weekly column. Four years later, Delores writes for the paper full-time.

Clermont, Iowa was made possible by the Clermont Community Club, which is a sizable and active group of residents and merchants. They enthusiastically endorsed the idea of the book. We had twenty writers in the workshop, but never all at one time. We followed the same general procedure that I used with the homeless, the farmers, and the Independence residents, with the addition of more individualized work on revisions. At least half the participants were farm couples; others included a health care worker, a housewife, a building supply dealer, a grade school girl, a college student, plus several teachers. That there were so few young people at the workshop was probably due to the fact that there are few young people in town— so few that Clermont, with two other area villages, is part of a consolidated school district.

In terms of size, Clermont conforms to the standard idea of a rural town; (it and its surrounding valley have a population of around nine hundred). In Clermont, as you might expect, most residents know each other. Judging from conversations I have heard and from the stories included here, it is a tightly knit community. But unlike most rural towns, which are usually conservative and resistant to change, Clermont is resilient, energetic, open to new ideas. All I can offer by way of explanation are the people themselves, who have the qualities that created this atmosphere. Why, I can't say, for Clermont's economic situation is no different from most towns its size, and most of its residents were born and raised there. But one happy outcome is that unlike some towns, where transplants are greeted warily and still considered outsiders after twenty years, Clermont welcomes new arrivals. The last lines of Jerry Kelly's essay, "A Changing Neighborhood," gives the Clermont perspective: "The next time you are on Highway 18 [which runs through Clermont] wave at the drivers of the cars you meet. One of them might be your new neighbor."

Writing workshops, I believe, should be a permanent part of every town. As in Independence and Clermont, they are a means of creating and maintaining community, enabling us to search for and discover the common notions that bind us together, making community possible.

■ *Khaki Nelson*

Khaki Nelson's given name is Gladys. She and her husband, William, farmed and sold Pioneer seeds in the Clermont area for thirty years.

SATURDAY NIGHTS IN CLERMONT

The sound of water pumping and the smell of a kerosene stove heating up. A large copper boiler is filled with water and put to heat on the stove. Mom and Dad lift the heated water into a round, galvanized tub. I stand back, watch and wonder how soon before I'm stripped of clothing and dunked in the tub. Lowered into the water, I shut my eyes tight as soap suds trickle over my head, down my face and body. I take a deep breath, hoping it's store soap and not homemade lye soap. I'm scrubbed to a shine, big sis is next. I scamper into my clothes—a pretty, starched print dress and patent leather shoes.

I shake my blond hair to get it dry, thinking, "I wish I was a teenager like my sis, with dark hair and beautiful." Mom and Dad are pretty fancy in their Saturday night attire. A change from Dad's bib overalls and Mom's feed sack dress and apron. I hop up and down singing, "Let's go to Clermont, I want to go to Clermont!"

The family scampers into the car and sighs with relief as the car starts and the four tires are full of air. At that moment there's a rumble of thunder and a big black cloud appears in the west. "Wait," my dad says, "if it's going to storm we can't start out. We have five miles to go and the road may get muddy." We file out of the car with heads hanging low, put our good clothes away, and wait for next Saturday night.

A week passes, same routine, a beautiful night, stars shining. We bounce down the road in the old car, anxious to see friends in town. The dolls, Shirley and Alice, are seated beside me, they will enjoy a night in town.

The lights show up distinctly as we near town and drive over the rumbly, rattly bridge. Clermont is alive and buzzing. Cars are everywhere, and streets are lined with people. What a sight! Oh, so exciting!

Dad says, "Hope we can find a place to park." The band is playing a peppy tune, and we immediately begin keeping time with our hands and feet to the beat of the drums and the wonderful brass horns. The aroma of freshly popped corn floats through the air from

Nora Halverson's popcorn stand. Five cents for a nice, big sack with plenty of real melted butter.

The stores are all open for business, three grocery stores to choose from. Tonight we get the week's supplies. We enter the grocery store, which seems so large and well stocked. I trail along behind my mom, hoping the storekeeper will notice me. Sometimes they give candy treats to the kids. Mom has a list of things she needs, tells the clerk, and proceeds to run here and there to gather up the things and bring them to the counter. She seems to know where everything is, and in a few minutes has it all together and sacked. We have sugar, yeast, oatmeal, raisins, flour (a very large sack), and wieners (they are hooked together and look like a chain of beads). The money received from selling the eggs down the street at the produce store will more than cover the bill. We are lucky we don't have to buy meat, milk, butter, lard, canned vegetables, or fruit. We have those things on the farm. We take the groceries to the car, and Mom meets with other ladies in front of Lubke's (five and dime). They visit about the week's happenings, upcoming marriages, and new babies born. With several aunts, cousins, and other relatives there it seems like a weekly family reunion.

The men congregate down the street at Pringle's, Gerner's, or the John Deere shop. The talk gets pretty lively, and sometimes heated about politics, crops, and prices. There is a barber shop near the John Deere shop with a neat red and white barber pole. The fellows think Saturday a good time for a haircut and some good conversation.

Meanwhile we kids gather around the water fountain on the corner by the grocery store. The boys get pretty wild with the water and splash it at ts. We giggle, laugh, and shout at the boys, "We'll tell on you." We enjoy strolling up and down the street. On one side the band is playing, across from the telephone office and Crowe's Drug Store. There is also romance in the air for the teenagers. A boy that's sweet on my sister brings her a box of cherry centers almost every Saturday night. I tease her, but she still shares those yummy chocolates with me.

A free movie is held several times during the summer. This is a very special treat, for we rarely go to a movie theater. It is set up outdoors between the old bank building and Gerner's. We sit on planks held up on nail kegs. My favorite movie is "The Little Rascals" with Spanky and Alfalfa.

After a great evening, Mom and Dad say, "It's time to go home. Tomorrow is Sunday, and we will be coming back to Clermont for church." Before going home sometimes we go to Peck's Ice Cream parlor for a treat, or better still, we take home a quart of ice cream and eat it before it melts.

Sleep comes over me driving home, but as we make the turn into the driveway our trusty watch dog barks and wakes me with a start. Sleepy as I am I won't miss out on eating that great tasting ice cream.

■ *Doris Martin*

Doris Martin taught in rural one-room schools for six years before becoming a fifth grade teacher. After twenty-nine years of teaching, she retired in 1990 but remains active in the elementary schools as a volunteer reader and story teller. Doris now lives in Clermont and was one of the organizers of that town's writing workshop.

BRICK CITY ICE CREAM

My parents and I moved to Elgin the summer of 1930 before my second birthday. My brothers Bob and Jack were born in 1930 and 1932. This was after the Depression, so money was very scarce, although I wasn't aware of that. I believe that children who are loved, fed, and cared for don't realize how poor their families may be.

We had no close relatives in the area, and my parents made friends slowly. My dad worked six days a week as a farmer, so he wanted to stay home on Sunday. My brothers and I played long, involved games that lasted for days, so we wanted to stay home too. My mother couldn't drive. She was always home working. Occasionally on Sunday after church Mom would say, "Let's go for a ride."

First she had to convince Dad, then get us away from our play. She would sweeten the offer with, "We'll stop in Brick City to get ice cream cones." That got our attention, we got very little ice cream.

The four mile ride to Brick City was long and boring but we were thrilled when we got there. We knew where it got its name—all those brick stores on Main Street and the brick homes around town.

We would park near Pringle's and Dad would go in. Jack was in front with Mom, Bob and I in the back. We would sit at the same side window to watch Dad go. It never occurred to us we might go in too.

Finally Dad would return with one of those pressed cardboard containers with five vanilla cones that probably cost a nickel apiece. We would sit in the car and eat those delicious treats.

Years later when I heard the name Clermont for the town my first reaction was, "No, that's Brick City, our ice cream town." Today I live in one of those brick houses, I walk to the Gas and Goods for delicious ice cream that costs fifty cents a dip. However, I don't think I have ever had ice cream that tasted better than those cones in that old car with my family.

■ *LaVerne Swenson*

LaVerne Swenson farms with his wife, Grace, and their children. He is working to establish an agricultural heritage museum near Clermont and is active with an eastern Iowa tourism project, Country Heritage Community.

SATURDAY NIGHTS

When Saturday night came we really looked forward to hearing something different and seeing something other than the mouth of a horse and the rear of a cow, the "udder" end. Movies were shown where the post office now stands, and later in the opera house. They cost a dime. We always got the news first, mostly war news.

In the early fifties we had outdoor band concerts. Cars would park around the blocks where the post office now stands, and people would sit in the cars and listen to the concerts. They didn't parallel park, but parked diagonally, so more cars could park close to the concert. After every song they'd blow their horns. The better the song, the more they blew. After the concert we'd get paid three pieces of paper. They each said five cents on them. Fifteen cents a concert, to be spent in town.

Really, the best Saturday nights came when I started enjoying the girl of my dreams. The band concerts lasted about an hour, and the folks liked to visit afterwards. I didn't have a car, so I'd have to hurry for maybe an hour visit with Grace. If luck was with us, we'd get to double date with someone who had a car. That was the beginning of our life forever together.

■ Mike Finnegan

A retired hog farmer, Mike Finnegan lives in Clermont where he is active in community affairs. A few years ago he won the Governor's Award for his community involvement, which included promoting the restoration of the mansion of former Iowa Governor Larabee. Mike was instrumental in organizing the Clermont writing workshop.

BURKHARD RIEGEL

Burkard Riegel is a legend. I remember well when I started farming in the late fifties. Riegel did many repair jobs for me, and if there wasn't a clear plan or method on the tip of his tongue, he would say, "Let me think about it!"

Everyone was always amazed at Burkard's method of bookkeeping. His system was immediate and accurate. He would often charge for his services with what seemed to me very little hesitation, anything from a nickel for a small job to a dollar for a big job.

Dad would ask, "How much today, Riegel?"

"Oh, gimme thirty-five cents."

Dad would hand him a dollar, and Burkard's hands would go into action, the quarter in one pocket, nickels and dimes in another. His bib overalls held the bills. Never examining or eyeballing the change, he would complete the transaction fast, and we would be on our way.

Burkard never liked to be bothered when he was busy at something, and he worked very early in the morning and late at night when farmers didn't come in to bother him. If he was deeply taken up with his work he often refused to look up when a farmer walked in to pick up his fixed piece. The finished jobs would be neatly stacked against the right wall as you walked in, and Burkard would quickly look up and nod in the direction of your fixed piece, and you were on your way knowing your bill was scribbled on some sort of crude but accurate account record.

■ *Lois Amundson*

Lois Amundson grew up near Elgin, Iowa and moved to Clermont after marrying her husband, Roger. They farmed east of Clermont until moving to town several years ago, where she now runs a bed and breakfast. Lois enjoys sewing and traveling.

PARTY LINE

Moving to Clermont as a shy young bride in 1955 brought many new experiences, one of them the old central telephone system and local operators. Having grown up in a neighboring community where we had converted to the dial telephone when I was six years old, this was a new experience. I learned to use the telephone by simply dialing the numbers I needed to reach friends or relatives.

Several days after moving into the old farmhouse, I happened to see my mother-in-law. She said she had been trying to reach me by telephone, but that I hadn't answered. Sure, I had heard the telephone ring many times, but we were on a big party line with eleven families and eleven different rings coming into the house. I couldn't differentiate three longs and one short (our ring) from three short or three long or one short and two long. As time went by I finally learned which ring was ours and answered the phone.

To make a call was also quite a challenge. It took perseverance. First you picked up the receiver and listened to hear if any one of the other families was using the phone, and quite often they were, so you waited. Next you gave the crank a ring to signal the operator you wanted to make a call. If the operator was busy with another call, you waited. If the party you were trying to call was already using the phone and the line was busy, you waited, and probably tried later. It took a lot of patience and endurance to accept this phone system.

Our particular phone had an extra button that had to be pushed and released before you could talk. If one of the neighbors was already using the phone, you could pick up the receiver and listen, and not release the button, and the neighbors couldn't tell you were listening, or "rubbering," as it was called. The extra button was not very common, but rubbering was. Of course, no one admitted they rubbered, but if there was any news in the neighborhood, it seemed that everyone knew it right away.

Calling a girlfriend for a date was a real trial for a young man. If he used his home phone, the whole community knew who the girl was, where they were going, etc. Worse yet, if the girl turned him down for the date, they knew the young man had been rejected and humiliated. So many a young gentleman made a trip to town and used the phone at the central office to do his wooing.

One fear or concern people had in using the party line was that the neighbors or the operators were listening so they chose their words very carefully, trying to get a message across, but not mentioning the specific topic. When a friend called she chatted a little before she asked me how the item that she had sent home with my husband had worked out. I was perplexed, I didn't remember any package or gift that Roger had brought home for me. I said I was sorry, but that I couldn't think of what he had brought home. I was not used to the guessing game yet. Really, I was very embarrassed, as someone had given me a gift, and I was so ungrateful that I couldn't remember what it was. She went on, describing it as long and part of that other gift. I was still blank. Finally the conversation ended, and she said she would tell me when she saw me.

As soon as Roger got home, I asked what gift or package he had brought the other day. He went over to the back of the truck and pulled out the handle to a dust mop. I had received a dust mop as a bridal gift, but as the handle was long and would have been hard to gift wrap, she waited and sent it over later. This was another tradition that I had to learn to accept.

I always smile when I remember Roger's grandmother, a very nice, older Norwegian lady. She figured she had out-foxed those telephone operators by always speaking Norwegian when she talked on the telephone to friends and relatives. I suppose she never gave it a thought that the operator might have been Norwegian too.

Eventually many communities got the dial telephone, eliminating the local operators. About 1965, the Clermont area got the dial system, but we still had eight families on our line. A great joy for me came later, in 1973, when we received our own private dial telephone, but I still find myself picking up the receiver and listening before I dial to hear if anyone is talking.

■ *Jennifer Olufsen*

Jennifer Olufsen grew up in New York State, lived in Africa, and now resides in Clermont. Trained in business economics, Jennifer works in the education department of Luther College in Decorah, Iowa. She has a daughter, Chantel.

MOVING FROM THE CITY TO CLERMONT IN 1992

The clock strides five, time to pick up my six-year-old daughter and head off to Clermont, Iowa. We have been driving up to northeast

Iowa every other weekend, hoping to relocate to Clermont. There are so many hurdles. It is yet another move, but for right now I just want to get on the road and not worry about all the problems. I drive past the crack house on the corner, and past the sign that marks the "Drug Free Zone," and it strengthens my resolve to make this move to Clermont work somehow!

It is starting to snow as we get on the interstate. The driving conditions are getting worse, but I have the same feeling that I used to have coming home from college at Christmas. Four long hours later, when we finally top the ridge overlooking the valley, it looks like a Christmas card. I have the feeling that we are coming home.

"Where is Clermont, and why do you want to move there?" my city friends asked. It is hard to describe. It is wanting a warm feeling of peace and security and belonging for my daughter, a sense of belonging and roots.

We came up for the first time for Threshing Days. Vernon Oakland had called me and asked if my daughter would like to ride on his threshing machine with his six-year-old son Kevin. I was going to have a table at the craft show, so I was busy while the parade was setting up. "Where is Chantel Marie?" I looked left and right and finally straight up. It is probably a good idea that I did not know what the threshing machine looked like ahead of time. At the end of the parade, Vernon set Kevin and Chantel off on the main street downtown. My husband was supposed to keep track of her. He came back and asked, "Have you seen Chantel?" I was frantic. ("Relax, this Clermont!") She had met up with Jeff Guyer, and he had taken her to Valhalla for a soda. That is why we live here. ("Relax. This is Clermont!!")

The pastor's wife—Clermont's unofficial welcome wagon hostess—said, "Welcome home" to us at church, as if we had only been away on a journey. The church, a different denomination than I had been attending, was filled with warm and friendly people and opened the doors to all who came through.

The K-12 school has modern facilities but still has a country school feel about it. Some of the teachers are going on their third generation of students.

My daughter always wakes up early in Clermont, although we often came in after 11:00 P.M. the night before. She woke up to the strange noises of birds and snowy quiet instead of sirens and traffic. "Mom, can I go outside?" It occurs to me that she is probably the only six year old in town whose mother thinks that she needs to be chaperoned to go outside. When we later moved here, it would take one full year to let her go alone to the barn, which is within eyesight of the house. The neighbors must have thought I was far too over-protective.

People greet us on the streets. My daughter has learned not to talk to strangers in the city, but this was so much nicer.

My daughter did a one and a half gainer off the swing set at school and needed to have her head sewn up. The school secretary called me at work, one hour away, and managed so well to tell me calmly that I had to come home. A good friend and very experienced Mom had picked her up and taken her to the local doctor. In the city I worked at a big hospital with the most updated equipment, and here the country doctor was going to sew her face up in his office! He was great. Gentle and calming, with hands as steady as a rock, he sewed up her forehead. For the next couple of weeks people whose names I could not always remember, came up to me and asked, "How is our girl?"

I have lived on three continents and in six different states. I did not move my family here because we were born here or because this is where the job is. We chose this town and are thankful for the privilege of living here. Clermontians are warm, caring, real people. They respect the work ethic and enjoy life with gusto. We live in a wonderful neighborhood. People here help each other out, and when you receive such good help, you look forward to pitching in and helping when you can. What a great place to live!

■ *Jerry Kelly*

Jerry Kelly, one of the organizers of the Clermont writing workshop,

*is a life-long resident of the town. He and his wife, Deborah, have two
daughters and a son. Jerry works in real estate; his hobbies are hiking,
hunting, and biking.*

A CHANGING NEIGHBORHOOD

Where do all these people driving down U.S. 18 come from? Where
are they headed? Have they passed through out little town before, or
will they come again? Think back to the last trip you took through
towns large and small, towns that you had never seen before. What
were the impressions that stayed with you, and why? Think about it.
Rewind that video tape in your mind and pay closer attention this
time. Why can one village stand out so much clearer in your mind
than all those other nameless, faceless ones? And which do you suppose our dear Clermont is to most of those passing through in that
constant, never-ending parade called U.S. 18?

Walk through St. Peter's cemetery and you'll see names on the
weathered, crumbling tombstones that you won't find in Clermont's
current phone book. Some family trees have run out of branches, or
have been transplanted to more fertile ground, or to climates more
to their liking. The dates on those monuments start with 1800-some-
thing, and list birth places in foreign continents. Those people came
to this valley with hopes and dreams, visions of the future for themselves and their families. Do you suppose they saw any come true?
We hope so, but in most cases we'll never know.

Wouldn't it be neat to be able to look back once into the eyes of
some of those forgotten people who called Clermont home? Do you
suppose their eyes carried the same sparkle that some of the kids on
the streets have today? Do you suppose the young fathers of today
go to the bank and tell stories of their hopes and dreams, with the
same conviction, the same determination, the same lust that these
nameless, forgotten brothers did, fifty, sixty, seventy-five years ago?
I bet they do!

I don't share the opinion that these are the worst times in fifty
years. Doom and gloom has been with us since Cain and Abel. And
we just keep going, don't we? I think that no matter how bad things

might seem, in twenty years these will be the good old days. In a few more years, the names on the stones will be worn away by the weather, and some think there won't even be anyone left to care or disagree. And the reason I disagree is very simple.

The next generation of people who migrate and settle here are the ones driving through town on U.S. 18 today. They won't be coming on a boat from some distant shore to flee famine or persecution. They are, this minute, drifting on the sea of uncertainty, in a ship called discontent. As long as we keep the light on in our lighthouse they will find us. I can give a very simple reason for my theory. There are some names in our phone book that weren't there twenty years ago. Times they are a-changing. The next time you are on Highway 18, wave at the drivers of the cars you meet. One of them might be your new neighbor.

■ *Delores Martin*

Delores Martin began her writing career as a result of the Independence writing workshop, where she was spotted by the local newspaper editor and asked to write a weekly column. She is now a staff writer for the Independence Bulletin.

THE FLOOD OF 1990

I looked out the upstairs window one more time at the bend in the Wapsipinicon River, a scant block away. All morning, this late August day in 1990, I had been monitoring its rise. Landmark after landmark slowly succumbed to the insidiously creeping water.

My house was beside the old Greenley Flour Mill, parallel with the dam, with nothing between it and the water except Veteran's Park. A flood was forecast, so here I was again running upstairs to get a good view and checking the river's impending rise.

This time, about 10:30 in the morning, the water was starting to trickle over the high bank and run down the street and through the park. My heart thudded in my chest. I had never seen the water this high. I looked again to make sure I was not imagining it. As I looked again it gained stature and looked as though a wall of water was heading straight for my house.

I rushed downstairs to tell my husband we had to get the cars out of the yard. We had my son's '65 Dodge and my cousin's '38 Chevy in the backyard, and of course no battery in either one at this time. My husband just looked up and said, "Don't get excited, there's plenty of time." After all, the intersection filled up with water and came up almost to our backyard every time we had a flood or a heavy rain, but never had reached the house, not even in the flood of '68.

I ran upstairs again and looked. This time it was a solid sheet of water pouring over the park, resembling the Mississippi rather than the Wapsi. I frantically ran back to my husband, urging him to hurry.

"It's coming up fast, we've got to move!" I screeched, sounding like a Blue Jay. "Everything is going under water!"

About ten minutes later he finally went out to see for himself. By then the water was ankle deep throughout our yard. We didn't have a chain to pull the cars, and by the time he went to call about borrowing one to move the cars, the water was waist deep, and it was useless. There was no way to get anything close enough to pull them out.

At that point we rushed to the basement to check on it. As we descended the stairs we heard the ominous sound of splashing, trickling water. This is okay out in the woods somewhere but has no business coming from my basement.

My basement is about one hundred years old and formed of limestone rocks stacked upon one another. The water level in the yard was so high that the water was seeping around the stones and creating miniature waterfalls in the basement.

The two of us formed a box brigade to start throwing things out of the basement. He was wading around grabbing boxes and throwing them up to me, as I stood halfway up the basement stairs. I then flung them out the basement door onto the lawn.

A very few minutes later the water was up to my husband's knees. I yelled at him, "Get out now, you'll be electrocuted!" I couldn't remember how high the furnace controls were, but I knew they were the lowest point at which water would make contact with electricity.

The water in the yard and basement had a different feel to it from the normal river water. Maybe it was just because it had invaded my domain, but it seemed slimy on my feet and legs. My hands slipped on the wet boxes my husband threw at me. The world had a dank, musty smell that had not been in my neighborhood before.

I looked at the furnace and then at the breaker box on the wall. "Oh my God!" I breathed. The water was going to cover the breaker box. I rushed up the stairs again and tried to look up the number of the light company. I knew we had to get the electricity shut off. Finally I called and had them shut off our service.

We left the rest of the stuff we owned in the basement as it started to float around like multicolored fishing bobbers, and looked out at the water-soaked world. We could no longer see any of the park, only the tops of the speed limit signs. Our neighborhood, our street, our yard were all a dark rolling mass of water. Even the huge cannon in the park had disappeared under a sheet of fast moving water.

We ran next door to the mill to check what was happening below the dam. I had never seen anything like it. The deafening sound of rushing water had entirely engulfed the dam, there was little to tell that it existed.

My adrenaline was pumping so fast I was almost giddy. There was nothing at all I could do. I was, for the first time in my life, entirely helpless. I watched the water creep up. It was now around three sides of my house.

Every few minutes I would run to the basement steps to see if it was going to come into the main floor of the house. I was like a barefoot bather walking onto a sun drenched beach on a first summer outing.

Now I had no lights and no radio or TV to get the current news. Was the river really still rising? It couldn't be, but the marks I had picked out on the street proved it was still going up.

We could not even decently clean up at home. The water heater as well as the washer, dryer, and furnace, all in the basement, were destroyed.

Night finally fell but there was no peacefulness to this sunset. The Main Street bridge had been closed because the water was still rising and roaring all about us. There was an unbelievable stream of onlookers and sightseers.

I was too frightened to even go in my house and rest. I passed through it to check the level of the water at each door, but could not relax with all that water gurgling beneath my feet in the basement.

The weather in late August here in Iowa can be horrid. I remember it was hot, and we didn't have a refrigerator to get a cool drink. I sat on my front porch in a sort of daze. I did not feel safe in my own house.

I kept imagining that if the water came around the fourth side of my house that meant it was over the main street and most of Independence would be inundated.

By Saturday evening and Sunday, I think half of Waterloo was driving slowly around our town looking at all the damage.

We who lived here, or rather, at this time survived here, could do nothing.

In the aftermath of the flood, life did not immediately get back to normal. Slowly, inch by painstaking inch, the waters receded. One day the river was back within its prescribed banks and the sump pump was furiously working in the basement.

As the waters receded down our street they left in their wake a slimy, smelly mass of mud and thousands of dead night crawlers. One day in the hot sun and the muck and dead worms wafted a very unappetizing aroma over the area.

In the park behind my house, the picnic tables were gone, as well as two of the bench seats that were cemented in along the river's edge.

As the sump pump finished its job, the heartbreaking work began. Every single thing that had been stored in the basement had to be carried out to the curb to be disposed of. I had a veritable mountain there awaiting the sanitation trucks.

My heart was heavy as I carried piles of leatherwork patterns and magazines to the curb. When I found a snapshot of my grandson as a baby that had been in my workshop, I sat down in the mud and cried. I knew what it had been, but the colors had run and streaked, so it was barely recognizable.

My husband got angry. "It's only a picture," he stormed.

"I know," I lamented, "but it reminds me of all things I can't replace."

After removing our belongings and carrying up the heavy, soaked, dripping carpets, we had the back-breaking job of shoveling up inches of mud into five-gallon buckets and carrying them out. It was a hot, heavy, stinking, sweating, seemingly never-ending job.

While this work was going on we were fed twice a day by the Red Cross truck, which came by till we got our electricity restored. It was something I never thought I would be doing, but I was very thankful for something hot to eat.

We added more water to the basement and hosed off the walls and floor. Then we disinfected all the surfaces.

The flood was not really over for me until I got my new furnace installed at the end of November. It was getting very cold, and we were thankful for it. Until then my kerosene had only kept us grudgingly warm.

To this day I still get very nervous when the weatherman advises we are in a flash flood watch.

■ *Hannah Chesmore*

Born and raised in Independence, Iowa, Hannah Chesmore is a junior at Iowa State University, majoring in English and Women's Studies. She hopes to go on to Writer's Workshop at the University of Iowa.

$4.65

I have worked at Dairy Queen for one year and four months. I plan to work there throughout my high school career. When I applied at

Dairy Queen, many of my casual acquaintances worked there. Since being hired, most of these acquaintances have become close friends.

When I lived in a small town, Rowley, just outside of Independence, going to Dairy Queen was a rare treat. Often my mom, my aunt Paula, and I would put on our pajamas and drive to Dairy Queen for a treat. I always got the same thing, a cherry dip cone. It amazed me. Why didn't the Dairy Queen fall off into the dip? I now know, from experience, that occasionally the Dairy Queen does fall into the dip.

Like all jobs, working at the DQ does get overbearing, but I don't complain too much. There's rarely a dull moment. Crying babies, cranky, worn-out mothers, picky ladies, people hard of hearing, little kids who can't make up their minds, the list goes on and on.

There's one man who comes through the DQ drive-through quite often. For awhile he always ordered a small vanilla shake. Just recently he changed his order to a small root beer.

"Hi. Welcome to Dairy Queen. May I help you?" I asked very routinely.

"Just a minute!" the man replied quickly.

"Go ahead and order whenever you're ready."

Then I waited for what seemed an eternity.

"Are you still there?" the man asked very rudely.

"Yes, are you ready to order?" I asked very pleasantly and politely.

"I want a small beer," he ordered.

"That was a small root beer? Will that be all?"

There was no answer.

"Thank you, please proceed to the window."

It never fails. He always has to be the smart guy. He has to make it tough on all of us. A small beer, we all thought that was pretty funny. When he approaches the window nobody wants to collect the money from him. He'll either complain about how much it costs or he'll make a pass at us. Hardly a turn on. Several times he has asked girls to marry him. However, I don't believe anyone has ever accepted. Sometimes I think minimum wage is good for a person my age, but on days like this a raise would be greatly appreciated.

It was the Fourth of July. The fireworks, which take place at the Mental Health Institute, had just gotten over. We had been swamped all night. However, after the fireworks it is always twice as busy. I was on drive-through with a friend of mine. The cars were backed up all the way through the DQ parking lot. We were mixing shakes and blizzards like mad. We always tried to be polite to the customers, but occasionally we slipped; they were usually understanding, *usually!*

One man came through and ordered two kid cones. He wanted us to give him cups to put his cones in. We politely explained to him that we weren't allowed to give out cups. He told us that was crazy, and that if we would just give him the cups he wouldn't tell. Like it mattered to us if he told anyone or not. We once again politely explained to him that we weren't able to do that. Then he started to get huffy and rude. Finally my friend went and got the man his cups. There were cars backed up, and we didn't have time to argue with him. She wasn't real pleasant when she gave him the cups. Big mistake! He threw a fit! He cussed and cussed at her. "You little smart *^*. Who the hell do you think you are?"

He wanted to know her name. He kept rambling on and on. We just shut the window and let him yell. He said he was going to call the owner. My friend cried. We all felt really bad for her. She didn't do anything wrong. Like I said before, sometimes minimum wage just isn't enough.

■ *Lisa Schmidt*

Lisa Schmidt was born and raised in Calmar, Iowa. She wrote this story during her senior year in high school. She is now finishing her freshman year at the University of Northern Iowa where she is majoring in English.

COLLEGE CHOICES

The rolling hills of northeast Iowa, the endless landscape of corn-fields, the sparsely populated towns that are few and far between, who would ever want to leave it? Plenty of people. Me, for instance. It's not that I don't like Iowa, because I really do. I'm very glad I got a chance to grow up in this land full of rich values and friendly people. Being able to say "Hi" to everyone you meet on the street somehow instills a more positive outlook on life into a person. It makes you more trusting of people in general and seems to give you a sense of morality that you can carry with you your entire life.

But when you live in an area like this your whole life, you begin to wonder what the rest of the world is like. For as long as I can remember, I've heard about the big cities on both coasts of the U.S. I've heard about the millions of people that live in them and the exciting things that happen there. Of course, I've also heard stories of the crime, the violence, the poverty, and the drugs that exist there, but to me, that's all they are stories. As horrible as they may seem, they are common in most areas of the world. Living in small town Iowa doesn't give you much of a chance to experience them, though it seems to me that Iowans are living a more sheltered life than the rest of the country. College is the first time a person can really take complete control over their own life, to chase their dreams and find their place in the world. I feel that if I don't get out and experience life then I will spend the rest of my life wondering what I missed. I've already been exposed to the Iowa way of life, now I want to see how the rest of the world lives. If the rest of the world lives in poverty and despair, then that is what I want to see. Choosing a college far away from here seems to be the only way to do that.

Gaining more life experience is not the only reason I have for wanting to study so far away, though. While growing up in such a small school system is basically a positive experience, there are certain drawbacks to it. Everyone knows everyone else in the school, and each person has a personality label (such as "cool," "unpopular," "shy," "smart," "stupid," "funny," "strange," or whatever else the creative student body can come up with). This label is with you for as long as you are around the same people day after day, so even though it may not accurately describe the person at all, that is all they will be known as throughout high school. Going to college in a different area of the country gives a person a chance to start all over with a clean slate and new friends, free from any label they had before. It gives you a chance to live life the way you think it should be lived.

My guess is that I'm not the only high school student in northeast Iowa who wants to get away from all the farms and surround myself with skyscrapers. I think deep down that everyone has the common dream to see the world and explore life at the same time. What better time to do that than during our college years? I realize that many adults (parents, teachers, community members, etc.) are against kids our age moving so far away from home. They view it as losing their children and loved ones to the bright city lights. This really shouldn't be a cause of concern for them, though. Very few of us are planning to stay away from Iowa forever. Don't think of it as losing a home grown citizen now, think of it as gaining a new, more experienced and fulfilled community member down the road.

■ *Patrick Kipp*

Patrick Kipp lives in Ft. Atkinson, Iowa and is a sophomore at Iowa State University majoring in graphic design.

WHERE DO YOU WANT TO BE?

Some of the better known television commercials are those made by credit card companies, most notably VISA. These advertisements always show some attractive vacation spot, ritzy restaurant, or location that appeals to different special interest enthusiasts. You will never see northeast Iowa in one of these commercials. One can almost imagine the introduction to such a commercial, if it did exist:

"There's a place in the Midwest where there's . . . well . . . a lot of farms and . . . well . . . that's about it. But hey, you might need to stop for gas or something, so be sure to bring your VISA card . . . ."

Depressing, isn't it? However, in many ways it is the truth, especially in the eyes of the local youths. Northeast Iowa has been described as "the most depressed part of the state." This is evident in the job opportunities, values, entertainments, and allure of the region.

First, let's talk about jobs. You can be a farmer, a factory worker, a nurse, or a tradesman of some sort, and that's about it. Almost everything is blue collar or "pink collar." There are very few openings for jobs that require college or university training. The few jobs that do require it are usually taken. Therefore, there is little reason why any college student would be attracted to the region.

Then there is the matter of things for young people to do. Football games, beer parties, and circling the high school with their cars are the local favorites. These activities are also about the only options, other than bowling or going to movies. In the line of entertainment, northeast Iowa leaves much to be desired.

For the youth of the region, it is often like growing up inside a gigantic bubble that separates you from the outside world, a world where exciting things happen. The term "Dullsville" might come to mind. There are no YMCAs, no discotheques, and no big name concerts. Boy and Girl Scouts are the best northeast Iowa has to offer in the line of youth organizations.

Other *legal* kinds of entertainment include high school sporting events, which are typical of the rural U.S. When those things don't suit your fancy, you can always rev your car engine or squeal your tires as you circle the school block. And there are drinking parties. In northeast Iowa, adolescent boys "prove" that they are "men" by determining how much noise they can make with their vehicles and how many beers they can down at a party. Other than that, the only entertainment that northeast Iowa youths have are the kinds that they create with their imaginations.

The subject of entertainment brings up another aspect of northeast Iowa values. This region is, without a doubt, primarily a conservative one. Few people want drastic changes. Many are against extensive government control. Many take conservative stances in areas such as religion, sex, and gender roles. In addition to this, a sizable number of the people in this white-dominated area take more conservative stances on the issue of race.

The conservative value system is further evident in the types of activities this region is willing to support. The people of northeast Iowa in general are very willing to support athletics, but are reluctant to support the arts. They will eagerly donate to the building of a new football field or baseball diamond, but will scream and holler about helping the art club get more paint or brushes. They will cheer for a star quarterback, but not for an All-State Speech contestant. The high school band just doesn't capture the public eye the way the high school basketball team does.

Children and teens share this attitude. Elementary students don't care what your favorite painting or play is, they want to know which NFL team you like the best. And among the most popular items of clothing for local adolescents are t-shirts that say "such-and-such a sport is life." Obviously, the next Ernest Hemingway or Gertrude Stein will not seek to reside in northeast Iowa for inspiration.

The final major thing that northeast Iowa lacks is allure. Young people want excitement, night life, things the big city has to offer. Chicago has the Museum of Science and Industry, northeast Iowa has the Vesterheim Norwegian-American Museum. Seattle has its well-known rock music scene, northeast Iowa offers polka and folk music. Hollywood easily outshines this region. Furthermore, young people want to shop in Chicago's Magnificent Mile, not in Norby's Farm & Fleet. And northeast Iowa doesn't have any night clubs, just restaurants and taverns.

All in all, northeast Iowa is not a youth magnet, due to the factors of employment, entertainment, value, and allure factors. It's "Hicksville," "Clod-hopper Central," "Old-timer Heaven," "Square Capital of the World," and so on. This region is not a place for young people looking for excitement, opportunity, and success. It's a back-country bubble, a depressed farming region that will never be on a credit card commercial.

Commentary: Small Town Economics

To understand small rural towns we have to understand their connection with the farm economy. Rural towns were created to provide services—smithies, grain and lumber mills, transportation connections, churches—for outlying farms, and so long as the country's farm economy thrived, small towns thrived. They thrived up into the 1970s, even though they ceased growing around 1900. Contrary to the common notion that small towns began to decline after the First World War (when an entire generation of young rural men saw cities for the first time), small towns reached their population peak around 1900. (It is interesting that 1900 is the year given by the federal government for the official Closing of the Frontier.) By that time the great rush for land was over, and restless wanderers who, like Laura Ingall Wilder's father, had farmed or kept shop in half a dozen locales, were for the most part settled. It was their children, from the turn of the century on, who began looking for opportunity in the cities.

It is that story, the search for opportunity, that governs the story of small towns. But before examining small towns today we need to see the activities that kept them vital for years. First, economics. Until the dominance of the centralized economy (which centers production in urban areas and relies upon advertising and mass distribution through the rail and trucking industries), America was comprised of largely self-sufficient regional economies. A high degree of self-sufficiency was needed, since small communities could not afford to import some necessities without exporting others in exchange. In 1860 the four-county area of northeast Iowa, for example, had 25 gristmills and 28 sawmills. In 1880 it had 80 flour mills. Beginning in 1855 one of its towns, Clermont, had a brickworks which for years supplied much of the region's building material. Limestone quarries throughout the area supplied some too. Logs cut in northern forests were strung together in rafts, floated down the Mississippi River and milled in Lansing, Iowa and sold throughout the area. Today the four-county area does not have one grist mill, flour mill, lumber mill, or brickworks. Since most area buildings are constructed of prefabricated metal sheets and posts, or of wood grown and milled elsewhere, local limestone quarries no longer provide building stone.

Farm families were likewise highly self-sufficient up to the 1940s, when the affordable goods offered by the centralized economy proved too alluring to resist. Prior to that time farm women made their families' clothes and baked bread, grew fruits and vegetables, made soap from the fat of slaughtered hogs. As long as regions also retained their small but important industries, they remained relatively self-sufficient until the advent of the Sears Roebuck catalog. A 1908 editorial in the Preston, Minnesota newspaper complained bitterly about the amount of money that the catalog was drawing from southeast Minnesota and urged locals to buy locally. It is an editorial that could be written today, in any of several thousand small towns, with only a change of names.

The economic part of the small town story is perhaps the basis for the rest, for once the economic patterns changed and new technologies were introduced, old social habits which insured vitality were eroded and destroyed. For example, up until the 1950s farm families came to town once a week, on Saturday nights, to sell eggs and buy groceries, to shop and socialize. The men would congregate in the taverns or on the sidewalks, discussing crops and politics. The women shopped, the youngsters played. Most towns had a band that performed on these occasions; later, after bands disappeared, movies were shown in the town square, on a sheet hung against a wall.

Now of course small town economies have been devastated. In the first place, the U.S. farm economy began going sour in the 1970s when federal agencies encouraged Midwest banks to extend large loans to farmers to expand their operations. Farmers took these loans but prices never caught up with costs, and a rash of farm and bank failures followed in the 1980s. Since then banks have stabilized and are once again earning profits, but farms are still going under. There are two formulas which claim to reflect the relation between farm failures and Main Street business. The ultimate source may have been one or more university studies, but now these formulas are quoted as common assumptions: one claims that for every seven farms that go under, one Main Street business fails; another claims that for every farm that fails, three small town employees lose their jobs. The point is that rural residents recognize that farm failures have a devastating impact on nearby towns.

Other factors account for the decline of small town economies. For one, in the last forty years improved tires have made automobile travel more reliable, and rural people now think nothing of driving thirty or forty miles to regional shopping hubs for better prices. As a result, small town retailers are disappearing in competition with the national chains such as Wal-Mart, while local cafes are trying to survive the competition from fast food franchises. Within a 900-square-mile area there is usually one regional shopping hub or mini-hub that draws most shoppers in the area. The homogenization of small town culture—its absorption first into the national economy and later into the global economy—has gone hand in hand with the destruction of small town society.

As noted, the outmigration of the young has been a major problem for small towns since 1900. The very lack of job opportunities in small towns means that the most talented high school and college graduates leave, for the jobs that small towns offer usually pay minimum wage or slightly better. Industries that locate in small towns generally call for unskilled labor. Youngsters, therefore, who want to study a profession or specialized trade, seldom find their way back to small towns once their education is completed. The State of Iowa, for example, expects that by the year 2020 its labor pool will be negligible.

Thus, with the most creative and brightest people having left, the pool available for problem solving consists of middle-aged or elderly persons usually opposed to change. Of the nine states which lead the nation in population of the very elderly (age 85 and over), seven are farm belt states—Iowa, North and South Dakota, Nebraska, Kansas, Missouri, and Minnesota. For that reason, many hundreds of small towns in these states are unable to alter the dynamic which is leading them to an ever smaller population and lower per capita income.

Not only are small town businesses fighting a rear-guard action, so are its schools. Dwindling rural populations mean that more and more schools in neighboring towns are consolidating, and with that consolidation often comes a loss of community identity, a blow more serious than the loss of yet another business. Declining populations also have states talking about consolidating county courthouses and their services.

As small towns find themselves shrinking in size and increasingly poor and powerless, they latch onto high school athletics as a means of maintaining a sense of community pride. Local sports teams are immensely important in small towns, and the high school sports heroes are town heroes. Academics and the arts are, in comparison, insignificant.

Small size and economic insecurity explain another aspect of small towns—their insularity. Today's small town residents are for the most part descendants of those who were living there in 1900. This gives residents a sense of solidarity, or at least a sense of Us and Them. That is one of the first things that any newcomer to most small towns notices. On the positive side, this gives small town residents an enormous sense of belonging, for their families' histories are intertwined for generations. Negatively, it means that children of parents who moved to such a town will always be outsiders.

From the beginning of settlement, rivalries between small towns have been great. In the nineteenth century, towns fought to be county seat, for the county seat was assured of county business and therefore, of survival. Across the Midwest, towns within a county frequently raided the county seat to steal its documents. Two towns in northeast Iowa stole documents back and forth two and three times. These rivalries have been carried into the present, at least once to the brink of violence. In one strange instance, the people of two other feuding towns say they just can't talk with each other. In recent years they have had a consolidated school district, which is amusing considering it is said that the feud goes back to a high school football game in the 1930s, when a player from one town kicked a player from the other. The practical outcome of so much rivalry is that most small towns have enormous resistance to regional cooperation, including cooperative projects that could reduce the cost of services. It also means that most small towns do not like to see a neighbor receive new industry.

Small towns are facing disintegration not only from dwindling population but from the presence of films and television, which have done much to destroy social intercourse. Until the advent of television, neighbors visited each other, and families—in towns and on farms—spent their evenings playing cards, talking, listening to the radio. Now with everyone living at a hectic pace, families are lucky to sit together for one meal a day. While this may not seem surprising considering the impact that mass communications and entertainment have had on urban populations, it is to some of us—at least at first glance—when we reflect that the very structure of small town life once prevented impersonal relationships. On further reflection, however, there appears no reason that rural America would remain immune to the disintegrating influence of mass entertainments, considering how swiftly traditional cultures in other parts of the world have collapsed when exposed to the values and images that they transmit.

Finally, worldliness has intruded into rural America to the extent that religion, which once formed an extremely important part of rural and small town culture, is on the wane. Youngsters attend church until confirmation, then are rarely seen again at services. Pastors say the church is no longer a body of discipline, for members are no longer willing to be disciplined.

Thus the major institutions holding civil life together—family, neighborhood, local school, county courthouse, the church—are in various stages of disintegration.

～

The social dynamic of small towns is baffling to urbanites. Used to speaking out on any issue, they find that small town residents are reticent when it comes to making themselves heard on public issues.

It has been said that you can't tell the truth in small towns. I was told that a visitor to one Iowa town asked a resident, "What problems do you have in Postville?" The visitor was told, "We don't have any problems." Small town residents do not want to rock the boat: they do not want to be seen as loud-mouthed critics or troublemakers.

As for standing out, it's not a good idea to take credit for initiating this or that project—better to allow a group to take credit. Fear of standing out extends to dress and hair styles. Dress is invariably informal, even for church and funerals. Rarely do men wear ties and jackets. The sometimes wonderful eccentricity of dress in urban areas—the strange hair styles, tattoos and piercings frequent there—is seldom if ever seen in small towns, even among the youth. In metropolitan areas individuals try to assert their individuality to avoid being lost in the mass, while in small towns the individual is known—everyone knows everyone else's business—and therefore seeks to play down his or her individuality.

On the surface small town life is pleasant and friendly. People passing on the sidewalk usually look at one another and say hello. In almost any small town you can leave your keys in your car without fear of theft. Volunteerism thrives. Ambulance and fire departments are usually voluntary, and quick to respond to calls. The image of small town life that millions of Americans harbor and long for— people living in a friendly, caring community, with no generational hassles—offers advertising copywriters a wealth of imagery, and some of it is true.

But small towns and rural America, in this story, are untouched by crime and drugs, untouched by the polluting and corrupting hand of corporations. But the fact is that drugs are making inroads. A few years ago in northeast Iowa, cocaine use was a problem among adults, now it's methamphetamine. In recent years teenage drinking and marijuana use have become more of a problem. As a student in one writing workshop reported, it is not unusual for high school students to come to school hung over and to fall asleep in class. Like their counterparts in the cities and suburbs, rural and small town youngsters cannot escape most influences of the national culture, its images, offerings, and pressures.

The future for most small towns is not good. If it lies within commuting distance of a large city, the small town is probably finding itself enveloped in metropolitan sprawl. The quaint towns along the Fox River Valley sixty or so miles from Chicago, for example, lie within a productive agricultural region of flat land and black earth that is now covered by tract housing. Farmers, unable to resist the offers of developers, have sold out. The new houses, often large, lie on unlandscaped and desolate acreage. They are generally ugly plywood affairs covered in aluminum siding, and very costly. Meanwhile, franchise operations and chain stores have opened up in strip malls. The once quaint areas with beautiful farmland and small towns with brick and stone buildings have been altered beyond recognition. Those who have moved in droves to the Fox River Valley in order to live in the country have found that their very presence has destroyed what they came to find. When we read or hear that an increasing number of urbanites are seeking solace in country living, this is what is usually meant.

Another group of small towns are those in farm and ranching states with small populations and semi-arid conditions, towns in Kansas, Nebraska, the Dakotas, Wyoming. These states are part of the Great Plains whose lands are far less hospitable than those of greener farm states, such as Iowa, Minnesota, or Wisconsin. Consequently, their populations never grew as large as those of the latter states. Further, the average Great Plains farm is now much larger than that of other states, and thus their farm and ranch economies cannot support populations of any consequence. Towns of two hundred and less succeed one another on the east-west roads across the plains— towns too small even to support one cafe. The state universities, county extension agents, everyone involved in agriculture sees that the trend has been and will continue to move towards larger and larger farms. For this reason alone most of these towns, I suspect, will disappear within twenty-five years.

There is a third kind of small town, however, which stands a chance of not only surviving but of thriving—prospering without growing much in size and therefore without losing character. These are towns outside the reach of commuters but still within a three hour drive of the city. There is much slower growth in these towns, but their long-term prospects are better. Many are in areas which are attracting urban refugees who can conduct their business outside the city. Unlike their counterparts moving to tract housing near urban centers, these people are intent upon preserving the character of their adopted homes.

COMMUNAL LIFE

Introduction

Lawrence Rettig

The story of Amana begins in the province of Hessen, Germany, in the year 1714. In that year the Pietistic Movement gained two enthusiastic new adherents: Eberhard Ludwig Gruber and Johann Friedrich Rock. They felt a deep dissatisfaction with the orthodox Lutheran faith and the clergy who expounded it. Like other Pietists, they believed implicitly in the divine inspiration of the Bible and felt that human spokesmen could still today reveal the divine will of God.

Together with others who shared their religious beliefs, Gruber and Rock founded a new sect based on the promise that God could and would reveal His wishes and guide His children by messages transmitted through inspired prophets. These prophets, called *Werkzeuge* (tools), were regarded as passive instruments, directed solely by the hands of God.

Calling themselves "Inspirationists," the sect began to preach their doctrine of divine inspiration throughout Germany and Switzerland. The movement had its ups and downs during the remainder of the century. In the early 1800s, the group experienced a revival. Paralleling this revival was an increase in the degree and incidence of persecution by various governmental bodies and the general populace. For their mutual protection, Inspirationists from all areas of Germany soon began to band together in the relatively tolerant province of Hessen. The group occupied much of the space in the Ronneburg Castle near Büdingen and in several other leased estates in the surrounding countryside.

Religious and political persecution became increasingly hard to bear and the cost of land to accommodate the influx of members became more and more exorbitant. Finally, through the divine testimony of Christian Metz, the charismatic new leader of the Inspirationists, it was made known that salvation lay across the sea to the west. In 1842, several community leaders set out for New York. They purchased a tract of land near Buffalo and by 1843, three small villages had been laid out and occupied by emigrating Inspirationists. The new community was organized as the Ebenezer Society.

Choosing to live communally, the Society became one of many other communal and utopian societies founded in the United States during the eighteenth and nineteenth centuries. During the 1800s alone, almost one hundred individual communitarian/utopian settlements took root in American soil. Many faltered, however, and disappeared from the scene within the span of a few years.

For nearly twenty years the Ebenezer Society grew and prospered. But in the end, the old problem of lack of land and the money to pay for it returned to haunt the colonists. In November of 1854 an inspection committee journeyed westward to the new state of Iowa. Of all the available lands they saw, a tract along the Iowa River approximately twenty miles west of Iowa City pleased them most. During the next ten years, the Ebenezer Society was gradually moved to Iowa, where its holdings increased to 26,000 acres.

The new community in Iowa was named the Amana Society and consisted of seven villages: Amana, East Amana, Middle Amana, High Amana, West Amana, South Amana, and Homestead. For over seventy years the Amana people lived a simple communal life of religious isolation. Their farms and factories prospered.

But a growing Amana soon wrought inevitable changes within the Society. William Miller, Society druggist at the time, summed up these changes with great insight when he observed that "the first generation has an idea and lives for that idea. The second generation perpetuates that idea for the sake of their fathers, but their hearts are not in it. The third generation openly rebels against the task of mere perpetuation of institutions founded by their grandfathers. It's always the same with people."

Strong influences from the outside were making serious inroads as well. The coming of the automobile, the telephone, the radio, and other modern agencies of communication made it impossible to maintain isolation.

On June 1, 1932, after eighty-nine years of communal life, the old religiously-oriented order came to an end. A new, far more secular society was born when over ninety percent of the members voted to form a joint stock corporation organized for profit. This event, known as the "Great Change," transformed Amana forever. The church no longer governed the secular affairs of the community and became known as the Amana Church Society to distinguish it from the newly-secularized Amana Society. Members over twenty-one years of age were issued shares of stock according to the number of years of service they had provided the old communal society. With these shares, members could purchase the homes they occupied and the other necessities required by a radically changed lifestyle. In addition, adult members received one Class A voting share, which entitled them not only to vote, but to free medical and dental care and covered all costs associated with burial.

New businesses not associated with the Amana Society began to spring up in the various villages, since the new order did not prohibit private enterprise. Perhaps the most well known of these businesses was and is Amana Refrigeration, Inc. Begun shortly after the Great Change by Amana native George Foerstner, it is currently a division of Raytheon, a large conglomerate based on the East Coast.

Today, the Amana Society is a successful corporation which issues revised shares of Class A stock that no longer provide medical, dental, and burial benefits. However, these new shares are available not only to Amana residents, but to all interested persons. The seven villages are populated by native Amana folk and "outsiders" alike. Church Society membership has been opened to "outsiders" as well. The church continues to evolve as new generations and new ideas take hold. Services on Sunday mornings are conducted in both English and German. They retain such original practices as acapella hymn singing, lay preachers, and the separation of men and women in the sanctuary.

~

■ Marie Calihan

Marie Calihan was born in Davenport, Iowa in 1914. At the age of eight, she and her family moved to the village of Amana, where she lived and worked until she was eighteen. She has since returned to Amana, where she has made her home for the last sixteen years.

COMMUNAL KITCHENS

It was 1928, and I was fourteen years old. I had graduated from eighth grade in the spring and had been assigned to cook in a communal kitchen in Middle Amana, where I lived. There were nine kitchens in Middle, each cooked for thirty-five to forty people.

The people had no kitchens in their homes and were totally dependent on the communal kitchens for their food. In the late 1800s everyone had their meals in the dining room, and as the dining room could not accommodate thirty-five or forty people at one time, they ate in shifts. As time went on, older people and those with small children wanted more privacy. They started coming to the kitchen with baskets similar to picnic baskets, in which they had an assortment of containers which they would fill with food to take home and eat in private.

The building housing the kitchen and dining room was quite large. It was one story with a two-story part attached, which was the residence of the Küchebaas (kitchen boss) and her family.

I had been in the kitchen about three weeks, learning to cook, when the Küchebaas and Marie Schneider, who was teaching me, decided it was time for me to do some cooking by myself, namely breakfast. My alarm went off at 4:30 the next morning, in plenty of time to get dressed and ready to go to the kitchen. I do not remember being afraid of being alone in the dark. I let myself into the kitchen and reached for the matches in the cupboard and lit the three kerosene lamps. Next, I had to make a fire in the long, low brick hearth, the kind used in all the kitchens. I got kindling wood from the warmer, which was a 3-cubic-foot space built into the hearth that we kept full of kindling, because the warmth dried it and it would burn quickly.

I arranged it on the grate, added some coal and kerosene, put a match to it, and my fire was roaring. I filled the container that was used only for water for coffee. I took the lids off the first two holes of the hearth and put the container of water on one hole and the cast iron pot of cold coffee with grounds (left over from the day before) on the other. After the old coffee came to a boil, I added it to the fresh coffee I was making, thereby reducing the amount of boiling water I needed (four gallons) and perhaps making it a little stronger.

Next, I got the two big cast iron frying pans from where they hung on the wall, added lard from the cupboard, took the lids from holes three and four on the hearth and put the pans on to heat. When hot, I added the boiled, cold, sliced potatoes prepared the night before. About half an hour later, they were brown and crispy.

All that was left to do was to heat the two gallons of milk in hot water. That was accomplished by putting each gallon of milk into a larger container of water. I am not sure why they wanted the milk hot; it might have been a custom brought over from Germany. The milk was delivered in the regular milk cans and later transferred to gallon pails which were taken to the basement and put in a trough of cold running water to keep the milk from turning sour. Incidentally, the gallon pails were made by the local tinsmith.

Breakfast being well underway, I went to the dining room, lit the kerosene lamps and checked the tables which had been set for ten to fifteen people by my co-workers the previous evening. Then I sliced bread to be put on the table along with butter.

By that time, people were starting to come in with their baskets to pick up their breakfast, and my co-workers were starting to appear too. I got some fried potatoes, bread, butter, and coffee for my breakfast. Hooray! I had cooked breakfast for approximately forty people on my fourteenth birthday with no mishap!

My co-workers would clear the tables, wash dishes, and so on, while I relaxed at home until 8:00 A.M. when it was time to return to the kitchen and start dinner. Dinner was the main meal of the day. There was always soup, meat, and potatoes, and something to whet the appetite, like pickles, sour beets, or in the summer, lettuce with a sour cream dressing. Dessert days were Tuesdays and Thursdays. Tuesdays, the dessert was of the *Mehlspeise* (flour dish) category, namely fritters, puffs, and puddings. Thursdays, the dessert was in the cake and pie category. Of course, we always had coffee. Supper (the evening meal) was light, usually cold meat, fried potatoes, a salad, and tea.

There were seven people working in each kitchen: three cooks, two people who prepared vegetables, the Küchebaas and her assistant. The three cooks alternated, cooking one week, washing dishes the next, then rinsing dishes, and after that, cooking again. The two people who prepared vegetables also washed the silverware after each meal, wiped the white oilcloth covered tables and kept the dining room clean. The Küchebaas and her assistant kept things running smoothly, baked the coffee cake (after the cook had kneaded the dough the previous evening) and did the cheese making and canning.

Bread, meat, and milk were delivered routinely to each kitchen. Ice was made on the Iowa River and the Lily Pond in the winter, buried in sawdust in the ice house west of town, and delivered to the kitchens in the summer.

The communal way of living ended in 1932. Was I sorry? I don't know.

■ *Marietta Moershel*

Marietta Moershel is a former teacher, the mother of two daughters, and Oma to two grandsons, a granddaughter, and a granddaughter-in-law. She still lives in the Amanas, near Lily Lake in a townhouse in Lakeview Village, a retirement community.

VIGNETTES OF A HIGH AMANA CHILDHOOD

Child psychologists have long recognized the value of growing up in an extended family. I consider myself fortunate in that my child-hood was lived in an extended family, an intimate circle of relatives. But I had another extended "family" that consisted of a whole vil-lage. It is this "bonus" family that I would like to picture.

I was born in 1920 in one of the smallest of the seven Amana villages, High Amana, with a population of about 100. The main occupation in High Amana was farming. The village had a baker, a cobbler, a part-time barber, a carpet weaver, and a blacksmith, who was my grandfather. There were three communal kitchens, a machine shop, a carpenter shop, a post office, and a general store that still exists today. In the early twentieth century, before the com-ing of the rural electric cooperatives to the Middle West, this store sold farm light battery sets all over southeastern Iowa.

My home by the time I was born already had seven inhabitants: my mother and father, my maternal grandparents, and my mother's sister and two brothers. The home was a typical, ten-room Amana frame house with a commodious attic and a full basement. Even now I could draw a quite detailed floor plan of the house and the furnishings in it.

Still, as I write this on a gray, dismal February morning, what I recall best is the gloriously colorful flower garden my grandmother grew. There was a large rectangular flower bed on each side of the front walk. One featured red and the other yellow cannas in a tiered array with fountain grass, spiky red salvia, blue ageratum, dusty miller, and fragrant alyssum. A Seven Sisters rambler rosebush cov-ered a long, wooden fencelike grid and an exotic "cinnamon" vine spun over the lattice work at the sides of the front door canopy. There were peony bushes restrained by wooden peach basket rims and a cluster of moonflowers in a corner. The north *Rabatte* (raised bed) was filled with a yellow speckled, green, hostalike perennial. The *Rabatte* that fronted the trellised grapevines on the other sides of the house was filled with geraniums that had been kept as houseplants during the winter and were now surrounded by mounds of bright annuals. These were mostly petunias, but also coleus, zinnias, cosmos, and marigolds. The German name for marigolds is *Stinkende Hoffart*, which translated literally becomes the wonderfully descriptive "Smelly Arrogance."

One of my chores was to keep the lawn clear of dandelions. Early on it was merely picking the blooms off. When I was a bit older, it was twisting the plant out by the roots with the aid of a kitchen knife. I learned then that a nice garden or lawn doesn't just happen. You have to help it grow. I realize now that my grandmother's flower garden was a brilliantly colored outburst against the somber house furnishings and the dark clothing that was Amana style.

High Amana had nice hills for sledding, and in the winter after school we would all head for the hills, most often to one certain hill called the *Huppel-de-Hupp* (Bumpety-bump). This hill had two sledding runs. One was a smooth, quick glide to the bottom, the other an exhilarating, bumpy, bouncy flight that might jolt you off your sled halfway down. When we went sledding, we learned early that we had to take turns with a ratio of three to one in favor of the older kids. One cold school day with snow on the ground (when I was eight or nine), I decided I would not go home for lunch and instead spend the noon-hour sledding all by myself. I did not share my plan with anyone, not even my best friend. I lingered behind, took my sled and pranced off to the hill. I made several trips down and walked up, but I wouldn't admit to myself that it did not seem half as much fun as I had thought, but I pretended it was and kept riding down and trudging up. Meanwhile my family was out looking for me. The search was short-lived. Brother Puegner reported that he had seen me walking up the street pulling my sled. There was always someone looking out for me.

↬

An Amana child had to learn early to live on a schedule. That meant learning to tell time before you were six years old and ready for first grade. The steeple bell would ring every Sunday morning at precisely eight o'clock so that all could synchronize clocks and watches. There were no acceptable excuses for being late for anything.

High Amana had a unique way of coping with the changes, interruptions, and delays wrought in the work schedules by the temperamental Iowa summer weather during onion, potato, and grain harvests. We had a town trumpeter, Brother John Geiger, who would stand on the front steps of his hilltop house and blow his own original back-to-work bugle call.

↬

I was a darkskinned, brown-eyed child with straight, dark brown hair in a Dutch bob. I needed lily-white skin, sky-blue eyes and long, curly blond tresses to look like the heroines and princesses I read about in fairy tales and story books. How I longed for the coloring they had! I could concede to my hair being straight, but it *had to be blond!* By fourth grade I thought I had conquered this fixation to be transformed into a fair-skinned, fair-haired vision of beauty. Until . . .

Towards spring, after a long and particularly hard winter, Indians would come down the Iowa River in canoes and make their campsite in the river bottom south of town. Then they would come calling at the communal kitchens to trade their woven baskets and beaded bracelets, watch fobs and necklaces for lard, potatoes, onions, and meats. When the word reached school that the Indians were in town, we could hardly wait for dismissal so we could watch the bartering. I liked to hear the mix of German, English, and Indian languages (the latter needed interpretive gestures along with speech). I knew one Indian word. The word was *chicago* and meant "onions."

The Indians' coming was an adventure. The Indian men with their straight, shoulder length black hair and the women with long, heavy single braids down their backs were friendly. The men, most of them, wore ordinary dark work clothes. The women had full skirts with overblouse tops prettied up with an unusual kind of embroidery and beads. As children what puzzled us was that even in cold weather the Indians did not wear overcoats. Both the women and men carried blankets or shawls for warmth. The Indians brought the tang of smoky, green wood campfires and a look at a different life into our sheltered childhoods.

When I was ten years old the Indian visits were spoiled for this darkskinned, brown-eyed child with straight, brown hair. I have never fathomed why an older person said to me that when the Indians saw how dark-skinned I was they would believe I belonged to them and would want to take me away the next time they came. After that the Indian visits became a trauma instead of an adventure. No longer did I race to see them. Now the race was to my bedroom where I stayed with the door locked and bolted until the Indians left town. Many years later when I told this story, someone dear to me said, "Too bad no one thought to tell you there were Indian princesses too."

One of my favorite townspeople was Brother Murbach, the millwright and beekeeper, who, when we met on the street, always had the standard greeting, "How is school going?" Before I could answer, that question would be followed by a not-so-standard, always different, new question. "Do you know the capital of Montana?" or "How many pounds of honey in a ton?" or "Who is the vice-president of the United States?" If I didn't know the answer, and I often didn't, he would say, "Find out and tell me the next time you see me." He was subtly teaching me you can't know everything, but you should know where to find the answer when you need it.

Then there was Great-uncle Emil Schaufuss. He had me constantly perplexed with threats. "If you misbehave, you will have to go to bed barefooted." "If you don't obey, you will get your head set between your ears." It was frustrating since he and I both knew full well that what he threatened as punishment was already the case. I think I was a serious child, and he thought I needed to lighten up. Only with time did I catch the kindly twinkle in his eyes when he made such absurd threats.

One of the intricacies of the German language is the *du-Sie* thing. It is as much a cultural thing as it is a grammatical rule. I didn't know it when I was growing up, but I soon learned it, when I addressed *Schwester* (Sister) Louise Geiger with the familiar *du* instead of the formal *Sie* that should be accorded to your elders outside the immediate family. I always addressed my *Oma* (Grandma) with *du*, and she and Mrs. Geiger were the same age. One day *Oma* sent me to Geiger's kitchen on an errand, and I did a double booboo by saying, "*Schwester Louise, Oma wundert ob du noch das Strickmuster für die längere Handschu'* hast. ("Sister Louise, my grandmother wants to know if you still have the knitting pattern for the longer mittens.") The *Schwester Louise* should have been *Schwester Geiger* and the *du* should have been *Sie*. I got a severe lecture on how to mind my *Sies* and *dus* and became so flustered that I went home without the mitten pattern. That led to another but much milder lecture from *Oma*, and a grammar lesson.

When I was married I moved to Homestead. After some years, when Schwester Geiger was quite old, she also moved to Homestead to be with her daughter and family who lived in a house just across the street form us. I would visit her there, and we would reminisce about High Amana days. On one visit she turned to me and said, "*Du kannst doch du zu mir sage.*" (You can use *du* with me.) It implied no need to be so formal. I never knew whether by then she still remembered the earlier severe grammar and etiquette lesson, but I did.

Sitting here writing in this High Amana building that was the church meeting house when I was a child, I can look out a window and see the back of the house where I lived the first twenty years of my life. What is no longer there but what I can see clearly in my mind's eye is the wooden, four-foot-high platform *Opa* (Grandpa) constructed to carry the post that held a large kerosene lantern. The platform had a five-rung ladder permanently attached. It looked much like a piece of playground equipment we see in schoolyards today. The platform was off limits to everyone except *Opa* who lit the lantern every evening to light the walk to church where the whole village gathered for vesper services.

I loved the singing. The presiding elder would first intone the line of a hymn and the congregation would repeat it. They would sing the entire hymns that way. So even before I could read well I could sing along. I liked the hymn *Nun ruhen alle Wälder* (the English hymn Now Rest Beneath Night's Shadows). What solace for a small child to sing along the words of one of the verses that is a prayer:

> *Breit' aus die* Flügel beide,
> o Jesu, meine Freude!
> und nimm dein Küchlein ein!
> will Satan mich verschlingen,
> so lass die Engel singen:
> dies Kind soll unverletzt sein!
>
> (Lord Jesus, who dost love me
> O spread Thy wings above me,
> And shield me from alarm!
> Though Satan would devour me;
> Let angel guards sing o'er me:
> "This child of God shall meet no harm!")

The platform lantern's glow that lit the way to church serves as the symbol for the gleam provided by our church's teachings, which illuminated the way for my mind and heart. A whole network of cement sidewalks lead the way to the centrally located church building. A whole collection of lessons lead the way to the spiritual core of the church that served as a tether for my childhood. It is this core of Amana Church doctrines that is the cord that binds my life together.

~

All through the years I have sensed the help and support that High Amana offered during my childhood, and feel surrounded by the love and comfortable security that my "bonus" extended family gave and still provides today.

■ *Barbara Hoehnle*

Barbara Hoehnle has been a resident of Homestead (one of the seven Amana villages) most of her life. In the early 1970s she was a librarian and taught in the Davenport, Iowa school system. She is married to Charles Hoehnle and is currently librarian and program coordinator for the Amana Heritage Society.

EASTER

Easter comes on us without warning. Ash Wednesday and Lent are recognized, but not celebrated here. Holy Week, the week before Easter, is a whole separate story. Beginning with Palm Sunday, an air of anxiety and anticipation pervades our lives as we look forward to the week's special activities.

Years ago a trip would be made to the local dyer for dye and to the furniture shop for glue, or in German, *Leim.* Then eggs were collected and a mixture of dye and glue was stirred up and allowed to gel. Small containers had been saved for this process and were used year after year. Often these containers were coffee cups whose handles had broken off.

One day was set aside to "dye." In Homestead a group of women would get together and form an assembly line. One woman would place the eggs into a large soup kettle which had a towel at the bottom to prevent breakage. The eggs were brought to a boil and, while still hot, were taken by other women (each one seemed to be assigned a special egg color). The eggs were tossed, giving a marbled effect to their shells. Then they were laid on greased tins and allowed to dry.

During Holy Week one was always going to evening prayer services. The services began at seven o'clock, but for some reason everyone began coming earlier and earlier, forcing the church elder to begin the service a little sooner each succeeding day since the entire congregation was assembled and ready.

It was the Wednesday night service which seemed the most special, the one in which the favorite *"Weinstock Leid"* ("grapevine song") is sung in which faith is compared to grape wine.

Thursday was the day to bake rabbit cookies. Legend goes that the Amana tinsmith's son wanted a special cookie cutter so he drew a picture of what he wanted. His father, the tinsmith, made the cookie cutter of a running rabbit a foot long. Soon, more children wanted a cookie cutter just like it.

Mothers baked batches of sugar cookies in the shapes of rabbits, chickens, crosses, wherever the imagination would lead. Rabbits and chickens got frosted and were given chocolate chip or raisin eyes.

On Thursday one was to eat an apple to assure good health. Then came Good Friday! One was to fast from sunrise to sunset. Suddenly, any water or piece of candy looked good. Around 2:00 P.M. one would invariably get a headache and wonder why *anybody* would call this day good.

Years ago church was held both in the morning and afternoon. Somehow when the elder got to the place where Christ said, "It is finished!" one wanted to breathe a sigh of relief. The suffering and death seemed so real. For many Amana people, supper came a little earlier on Good Friday.

Easter Sunday would dawn with all the children parading out towards Sunday School in new Easter outfits. It didn't matter if the new outfits were a new pair of dress pants, a dress, shoes, or even a handkerchief, just as long as it was new and special to welcome what was considered the beginning of spring.

One Easter Sunday the children came to Sunday School to find a "gift" which took one's breath away. One of the tenants who lived in the church apartments had planted crocus bulbs all over the front lawn of the church and had not told anyone about her deed. On that day of days there were dozens of crocuses emerging from the green grass like little Easter eggs.

After Sunday School and Sunday dinner were over, everyone waited for three o'clock to arrive and the annual Homestead Welfare Club Easter Egg Hunt. All those women who had colored the eggs a few nights before now put the eggs into hamburger cartons stuffed with green Easter grass, marshmallow rabbits, and perhaps a cookie or two and hid them.

The best place for these hunts was the local doctor's lawn. Dozens of children would happily walk through flower beds never seeming to notice that a tulip that was just appearing out of the soil might be trampled. The doctor's wife, *Tante Doktor Heinche* (Aunt "Doctor" Henrietta) would laugh and lead a child toward a hidden nest, and then it was over.

A new spring had begun and God was in His heaven and all was right with the world.

■ *Lawrence Rettig*

A former university professor of German and Linguistics, Lawrence Rettig is currently Special Assistant to the Vice President for Research at the University of Iowa. He lives in South Amana with his wife, Wilma. Dr. Rettig is the author of numerous journal articles and a book, Amana Today.

STARDOM FOR OMA

In her later years, my *Oma* (grandma) Susanna Rettig, was a tour guide at the Communal Kitchen Museum, across the street from my parental home in Middle Amana. Much to her surprise and subsequent delight, a tourist on one of her tours one day identified himself as a representative of Betty Crocker Enterprises. He said he had enjoyed her tour very much and was particularly interested in the potato ricer she had demonstrated earlier. Would she mind, he continued, if he asked her to demonstrate it again?

After reprising her earlier performance, she wanted to know

what was up. Would she consider traveling to Los Angles to make a commercial for Betty Crocker Potato Buds, came the reply.

Oma accepted eagerly because the trip represented an opportunity to visit her twin sister, who lived in the Los Angeles area. She made it quite clear, however, that she would not set foot in an airplane.

Arrangements were soon made for the long train trip west. Oma carried with her the ricer she was to demonstrate in the Betty Crocker commercial. Regular phone reports would reach us from Los Angeles, in which Oma regaled us with accounts of her royal treatment. She'd received an entire new wardrobe and even a new set of false teeth! She explained that her uppers broke before the commercial was complete, so Betty Crocker had a special new set made for her.

In the commercial itself, Oma showed how potatoes were riced in the olden days. Then a very modern-looking lady came on and announced that now one could buy Potato Buds and simply add water to get the same result.

When Oma returned home with a copy of the commercial, everyone was invited to view it at the local high school. And when it appeared on national television, she could hardly contain her pride. The commercial ran on and off for an extended period, earning residuals for Oma every time it was aired. She dutifully put all her earnings in a special account which was tapped only at Christmastime, when she treated her entire extended family to a Christmas feast at a local restaurant.

Oma had to endure some teasing, too. In order to perform in the commercial, she was required to join the Screen Actors Guild. Shortly after her return from Los Angeles, the Guild announced that it was going on strike. We almost had Oma convinced that because of her membership she was obligated to parade up and down on the sidewalk in front of her house with a large sign proclaiming "On Strike" in big, bold letters. She caught on quickly, though, and responded with an indignant "Ihr seid doch alle verrückt!" ("You're crazy, the whole lot of you!")

■ *Lawrence Rettig*

CARRIE'S HAIR

In her youth, my mother-in-law was somewhat of a rebel. Being the child of a church elder, she was expected to be particularly well-behaved and a model for her contemporaries. But Carrie had her own ideas about the world. It was not supposed to be a stuffy place where order reigned supreme, but one where spontaneity, creativity, and just a dash of mischief leavened everyday affairs.

She tells of the time she climbed a cherry tree in the front yard, helped herself to the ripening fruit, and spat the seeds on unsuspecting passersby below. One of her favorite targets was her grandmother.

One time Carrie almost carried things a bit too far. It was in the 1920s, when bobbed hair was all the rage among the "worldly" women who lived beyond Amana's borders. Amana women were forbidden to partake of such sinful practices. But Carrie felt not in the least bit constrained and appeared one day in a fresh, new bob. The whole village was abuzz.

Church elders promptly convened to deal with this horrendous transgression. Their solemn verdict, should she be unwilling to get up in front of the entire congregation and admit her terrible sin, was excommunication. She decided that confession might be the prudent course and on the very next Sunday found herself facing the entire village populace. As the church service began, storm clouds gathered outside. Soon brilliant flashes of lightening sliced the air, followed almost instantaneously by loud claps of thunder, rattling the window panes and unsettling the church goers. Any second thoughts that Carrie still harbored about going through with her confession quickly evaporated. Shaken and trembling, certain that she would be struck dead on the spot, she blurted out her confession.

But the storm passed, and with its passing other young women noted the fact that Carrie had survived her ordeal intact. Perhaps, they reasoned, confession was not too steep a price to pay for a fashionable bob after all. Within the week, every young woman in South Amana sported short hair.

■ Dianne Rathje

Dianne Rathje lives in Amana and is the county recorder for Iowa County.

LINA

Moving to Amana in 1992 was one of the best decisions we've ever made. My husband and I were warned by family and friends that living in Amana might not be a wise choice because we would be considered "outsiders" and not made to feel welcome.

We moved in July and found our new community wonderfully quiet. Before leaving for work each morning I walked the six blocks to the Handimart to buy a newspaper. A feeling of euphoria passed through me as I walked past the stores where tourists came to shop having traveled hundreds, and in some cases, thousands of miles to visit a community considered special and unique for its simpler way of life. I felt happy realizing that I wasn't just a visitor. I was a resident.

Walking along the same route each day I noticed an old brick house that reminded me of our prior home. I wondered who lived there. The lilacs and rose bushes that spilled over the old wooden fence tugged at my sleeve, as if to draw me closer. The grapevines were overgrown and tangled on their trellis. An old bird feeder sat on top of a fencepost with parts of its roof missing, and wooden planter boxes hung beneath the large windows of the house. A three foot wide flower bed ran along two sides of the house. Maybe the person or family who lived there would like some help with the shrubbery and flower beds.

At supper that evening, I mentioned my idea of offering to work in that houseyard. Our son, who was living with us for a few months, said, "Mom, you can't just tell someone you've never met that their yard needs some attention!" Perhaps he was right. I certainly didn't want to hurt anyone's feelings. But, on the other hand, maybe someone really could use my help!

By October I had met very few Amana residents. Having no children in school, working out of town, and attending a church located elsewhere afforded me limited opportunities to get acquainted. My husband met people through his work and soon became a member of an historic preservation committee. I decided to host a Tupperware party and invited women who lived within a two block area. They all came to my house, and I enjoyed visiting with them. A few weeks later I was invited to one of their homes for a basket party. During the evening I shared my curiosity with one of the ladies about who lived in the brick house near the museum. My new friend, Barbara, said an elderly woman named Lina lived there and that she always enjoyed having people stop in to chat.

A couple of weeks later I hurried home from work, changed into jeans and sweatshirt and, with gloves and pruning shears in hand, I walked to the brick house. The front yard was guarded by the old wooden fence, but I found a gate, walked down the sidewalk and approached the front door. I placed my gloves and shears in the grass and timidly went up the steps to ring the doorbell. I wondered if it worked. The heavy wooden door was closed, and I couldn't hear any sound. I pressed the button again. After several very long minutes, the door opened. An elderly woman was leaning on her walker. She was dressed in a black skirt and blouse with a shawl around her shoulders and a cap over her hair. I stammered through my introduction, one I'd rehearsed several times, telling her my name, that I recently moved into Amana and lived near the water tower. I had come to ask if she might like some help with her yard work.

Tears trickled down her cheeks, and my heart lurched. I had hurt her feelings. But then she smiled and said, "I'm attending a prayer service tonight to pray for someone to come and help me with my yard." I said, "Well, I think I've been sent." It was a very special moment for both of us, and I remember putting my arms around her and giving her a hug, as if to seal our new partnership.

A few days later on the weekend I worked for several hours piling the branches and twigs in a huge stack near the driveway and feeling sorry for the person who would have the chore of piling it in a pickup to haul away. Lina invited me in for coffee and asked me to sign her guest book. She showed me pictures of her yard when she had been able to care for it herself. One of them showed Lina standing on the front sidewalk between two rows of bright red flowers that grew nearly to her shoulders. The entire setting truly was a showcase, and tourists stopped frequently to take pictures of the beautiful flowers that she so carefully tended.

Working in that yard and becoming better acquainted with Lina was such a special time. Our friendship opened a new circle of friends. I have received so much more from her than I have been able to give. She shares wonderful memories from her childhood. One of my favorites is the story of how, during a blizzard, her family mixed eggs, milk, sugar and vanilla in a small bucket, tying the lid on tightly with a rope and hanging it on the wash line to let the wind stir it into a delicious ice cream dessert.

Memories of working as a young woman in the Amana kitchens where cabbages were piled in walls three feet tall around her and her co-workers, who were shredding it for batches of sauerkraut.

Memories of being married to a colony dentist and how poor they were. His education had been paid for by the Amana Society, and the debt had to be repaid by working for a pittance, all the while trying to support his family.

Memories of the birth of a son and two daughters. After cancer took the life of her forty-eight-year-old daughter, I saw the pain she felt and the faith that sustained her.

Memories of working at the Ox Yoke restaurant for thirty years as hostess and serving as a colony tour guide.

Memories of loving to sing and telling me that now her voice is "not so hot."

Memories of flying to Colorado at the age of eighty-nine, alone, for her granddaughter's wedding and of being the special Oma (grandma) to all family and friends.

My memory of returning home from work one day and finding

her sweet voice singing happy birthday to me on my answering machine.

Lina worries when she corresponds with friends that with her poor eyesight she's not crossed her t's and dotted her i's. I am the happy recipient of numerous thank you notes in my mail over the past several years and have saved every one as a treasure from Lina.

She laughs about her "marbles remembering" when I quiz her about a special phone number she wants to remember. At the age of ninety, Lina's "marbles" remember just fine. I told her she doesn't have marbles up there, just jewels. She laughed. Lina has a wonderful sense of humor, and during my frequent visits I never find her cranky, despite the discomforts of old age.

Lina enjoys the comforts of living in her own home, where she attended school as a child. She has many special caregivers who make this possible: helpers who help locate special glasses and equipment so she can read for a few minutes at a time and watch her favorite travel show on TV; helpers who clean her house, pay her bills, bring her groceries from a carefully prepared list, take her to the beauty shop for her weekly "do;" helpers who bring her garden produce, soups, and baked goods. Lina herself is still a very good cook and asks her helpers to rewrite her favorite recipes in large print so she can read them during preparation.

The telephone is also a good friend of Lina's, and she has network of people who talk with her daily.

Lina wonders why she is still here, with her crippling arthritis and failing eyesight. I tell her I believe it's because she is so very much needed to do what she does best, and that is to share, share her memories with younger generations so they know what life was like in the Colonies "way back when." And to make people feel so welcome in a new community. *Ich liebe dich, Lina.* (I love you, Lina.)

■ *Mary Ann Fels*

Mary Ann Fels was born in Amana in 1929 and has lived there all her life. She married George Fels in 1948; they raised two daughters and a son, and have four grandchildren. Her husband died in 1984.

MY WEDDING: OCTOBER 23, 1948

Amana weddings in the early days were very simple and drab with many rules and regulations. In early times in the Colonies, marriage wasn't considered the ideal, it was thought of as worldly. The spiritual leaders would have preferred people to be celibate. Marriage was regarded as a spiritual fall. By the time my parents were married in 1926, the attitude toward marriage had been modified. My mother's wedding dress was black but a shinier, finer material than other Sunday dresses, and the shawl and apron matched. I think maybe the buttons were more ornate. Of course, she made it herself. In those days when a couple decided they wanted to get married, they had to ask the Great Council for sanction, and a marriage date was set for one year hence.

Weddings were usually set on Thursdays. On that day friends and relatives came to church. It was just a regular service, everyone in their regular church clothes. The ladies in their shawls, aprons, and caps sat on one side and the men in business suits on the other. After a song, prayer, and scripture reading, the young couple stood in front of the presiding elder, who preached a long, serious sermon on the duties of husband and wife and on their duties and obligations to the community. They were then considered married. No vows were said. The Elder then gave a blessing and benediction, followed by a celebration in one of the community kitchen houses and later at the home of either the bride or groom.

By the 1940s fewer Amana young people were getting married in the Amana Church. In order to have a more beautiful wedding they would rent a church in Cedar Rapids, or go to the Little Brown Church in Nashua, Iowa, or have the service in their homes. They would then have their receptions in Amana.

It didn't seem quite right to me that my husband and I had attended the Amana Church all our lives and couldn't get married here unless we wore black. I wanted a long white dress, a veil, flowers, bridesmaids, and candles but wanted to get married in our church. This was a giant step, but friends and relatives encouraged us. So we decided to talk to Dr. Henry Moershel, who was president of the church society at that time and a dear, kind man. We made an appointment to see him and were really scared, but decided it was worth the effort as there were really only two answers, yes or no. We told him why we were there, and he was not in the least bit shocked or angry and even thought it was a good idea, but he would have to bring it up in a meeting of the Board of Trustees. The answer was yes. The only admonition was not to do anything too wild.

Now the panic really set in. What had we done and how would we accomplish all this? We decided to have a small wedding and so chose one of the small outer rooms of the church. The Amana Church has a large center room (*Saal*) where all Sunday services were held when everyone attended. The smaller ante-rooms on either side were used for evening services and smaller gatherings. We decided to use one of those. We asked Dr. Moershel to preside. After that we had no guidelines.

So now decisions had to be made. How many bridesmaids and who to ask? Would we have ushers in that small church? Would the men sit on one side and women on the other? We had many friends who were not church members. Wasn't it customary for the groom's relatives to sit on one side and the bride's on the other? It was also a dilemma for guests. Up to now everybody had worn the familiar black, but this was different. Should they wear fancy hats as was the custom of the day in outside churches, or our black caps? Most of the ladies did not wear the black, and it was never really questioned after that. There have been many weddings since that time, and you are free to wear whatever style is current.

Since we have no altar in the church, we had to consider where the elder would stand. Heretofore the elder had sat at a large table covered with a green tablecloth at the front of the church. That would not do. With the florists we decided on candelabra and tall baskets of flowers which made a nice place for the elder to stand. We walked up to him on a white carpet. This was also a suggestion of the florist. Considering the trails we were blazing, I think we did quite well.

Another thing we wanted was organ music and a soloist, something that had not been done before. Where would we get an organ? We moved one from the Sunday School. It was one that had to be pedaled or pumped. Luckily we had a cousin's wife who could play the organ and a dear friend who sang. But what songs would we use? What kind would be allowed? Two of my favorites of the day were "Because" and "I Love You Truly." Not really church songs, and definitely not Amana Church songs, but they are what we used, along with "The Lord's Prayer."

It was truly a beautiful wedding on a perfect fall day. I wore my long, white dress. It was heavy satin with little satin covered buttons down my back and long, pointed sleeves with more buttons and a train. The neckline was trimmed in lace. I can still feel the elegance of that gown. I carried a large bouquet of white roses with an orchid in the center. My sister, who was my maid of honor, wore heavy, blue satin; my bridesmaids were in gold. They carried bouquets of mums. I also had a flower girl, my cousin who was sick the night before and looked a little pale in white but did fine. She too had a part in Amana church history. The men in the wedding party wore business suits. The ties and boutonnieres matched the bridesmaids' dresses.

In those days photographs were not allowed in churches so you had an appointment in a studio in Cedar Rapids for your wedding portrait that was taken after the ceremony but before the reception. All the members of the wedding party plus the wedding cake went. Then we still had a wedding dinner before the wedding reception and dance in the evening. What a day that was, and I was only nineteen years old! The only reason we were able to do all this was because we came from a good community, a good church, and had good relatives and friends who made it all possible.

Our wedding reception was held at the Amana Welfare Association Clubhouse, which was the community building at that time. Most receptions were held there. You invited everybody and everybody came. It was the social center of the community at that time. Everyone had a good time, including the children. You could eat and drink all night long and weren't watched as closely as usual. You could make new friends, run around and slide on the dance floor, and stay up late. We thought we had it all, and I think we did. I remember going home with my future husband on our first date at a wedding three years earlier.

For our wedding we hired a six piece band from a nearby town: Leonard Reyman's Rythmairs. After almost fifty years the band is still playing in the area. I think he charged us $45 for playing till midnight. I wonder how much they would cost now?

The food at the reception was simple but tasty. We made sandwiches out of ground ham or chicken or pork mixed with pickle relish and mayonnaise. There was also a very special cheese spread. These were made in assembly line fashion at the Amana Meat Market by the friends and relatives of the bride and groom. In the evening these same people served in the kitchen. With this we also served pickles (homemade, of course), pretzels, crackers, beer and wine, coffee and delicious cakes, again made by relatives and friends. The cakes were wonderful, all different kinds: white, gold, chocolate, nut, poppy seed, marble, bundt, angel food, and all beautifully decorated. It was an awesome sight to behold. Every lady had her specialty, and you almost knew what to expect from each one. My mother's specialty was angel food cake and at that time it was still made from scratch with twelve egg whites. The only trouble was she always used the twelve yolks to make a sponge cake for us, which was not as good, and we always felt cheated.

The wedding wine was the responsibility of the bride's father, and so you had to make your plans fairly early so the wine had time to age. Most men made wine every year in those days, but wine making was not as much of a science as it is now, and some years it was better than others. If you had a daughter of marriageable age, some of the really good wine was saved in hopes that she would find someone to marry her.

As the evening wore on people began feeling quite happy, and then they began harmonizing in song. They sang many of the old German songs that we all grew up with, as well as the popular songs of the day. It wasn't always great singing, but everybody had a good time. It would be fun to go back to one of the earlier weddings.

■ *Gaycia Neubauer*

Gaycia Neubauer lives in Amana with her husband, Allyn. Her son, Brent and his wife, Ann, live in Homestead. Her daughter, Heather and her husband Mark, also live in Amana.

JUST PLAIN GOODNESS

My family members were always good caters. They were not picky. I especially liked the true Colony food which originated in the communal kitchens. Because we were all good eaters, it stands to reason that all the women in the family must have been good cooks. Some of the dishes prepared by Mom, Aunt Helen, Aunt Marie, and a few other ladies, stand out in my memory.

Mom stuck to the plainer, easier-to-prepare food, tasty, none the less. Nothing was more plain than *Rahmsuppe* (cream soup). The buttered bread in the cream was what nourished us when we were sick. That's the only thing Dad could eat when he was in the hospital once when he was very ill. My Aunt Lu said that when she was a cook in school and Mr. Selzer, the superintendent, wasn't feeling well, the head cook, Marie, would ask, "Should I fix you some graveyard stew?" Because if you felt like you were on your last legs, this soup could sustain you.

Part of my husband's favorite meal at the folks' was *Karbonade* (breaded and baked pork chops) and *angemachter Salaat* (lettuce salad with sour cream and onion dressing). I looked forward to Mom's *Katerbohnen* (yellow dill beans) and yellow bean salad with eggs and sour cream dressing, after the bean harvest in the summer.

Two kinds of *Küchelchen* (fritters) sweetened my youth, Mom's golden fried apple fritters and Lizzie's fritters at Zuber's Dugout Restaurant. In my teens I worked as a waitress at Zuber's, where Lizzie, a sweet older lady, made the fritters only on request and invariably had to make them on the busiest Saturday night. Like magic, the deep-fried airy rounds would appear, enough for the help too.

Some special pudding dishes were *Windbeutel* (cream puffs) and cocoa *Stärkpudding* (corn starch pudding). Cream puffs could only be made on dry, non-humid days, or the crisp hollow outer puffs would get soggy. Mom made both vanilla and chocolate filling for them. *Stärkpudding* was one of my favorite desserts. I made this once for my family. They looked at the gray-brown mass in the bowl, jiggling in the lighter gray sauce, and refused to try it. I had my fill for a week and never made it again.

Another popular dish, which did not appeal to my family, was fried *Speck* (fat). The sliced pork fat, which was breaded and fried, was not their "cup of tea." This generation is picky.

Mom and her friend, Marie Selzer, exchanged birthday cakes. Mom made the most scrumptious upside down cake, and Marie made a marble bundt cake that my brother and I thought was out of this world, and one year it truly was. Mom's birthday was approaching and the heavenly cake had not yet arrived. That night at supper, my brother blurted out, "Let us pray for Marie's marble cake! It turned out that Marie had had surgery, but thanks to my brother's and the Lord's intervention, she felt well enough to produce the cake on Mom's birthday.

The staple food of Colony people was *geröste Kartoffel* (fried potatoes). I liked them best for Sunday lunch, accompanying eggs and bratwurst. My eighty-seven-year-old father-in-law still needs his fried potatoes every night for supper. After years of hearing, "They're not as good as grandma's," from my son, I've finally gotten them close to resembling her brown crisp slices. My son, who is now married, has made them for us for brunch. But I must say, "They're not as good as Grandma's."

Aunt Helen was a tall stocky woman and goodness just radiated from her and projected itself into her cooking. She lived in South Amana and when my family lived there at *Oma's* (grandma's) house, she sometimes came and helped prepare meals. I only remember helping Aunt Helen once, and that was to make *Ziggoriesalaat* (dandelion salad). Before her arrival, *Oma* and I went out early that fresh spring morning. We walked to the farmyard behind our house, while the dew was still on the dandelion leaves. She admonished me to dig only the smaller, pink-tinged, young and tender dandelion greens, since the larger, dark green ones would already be tough and bitter. We carefully avoided the pungent cow pies, which had nourished our fresh pickings. Guess whose job it was to wash the greens, four times at least, which was a necessity, considering where they came from?! The bacon-and-egg-laced creamy salad was such a treat, and a harbinger of spring, along with the robins and crocuses. My present family would not think of eating a salad made from weeds, which were gathered in the farmyard. It must be nine years since an older family friend gave me some. My taste buds remembered the savory salad, and my mind sped back to that sweet spring day with Aunt Helen at Oma's house.

A favorite meal Aunt Helen made was *gekochtes Rindfleisch* (boiling beef), *Spinat* (Spinach), and *gekochter Meerrettich* (cooked horseradish). The beef was really a cheap cut, but boiled tender it was as good as the best steak. Colony spinach was cooked and creamed with the beef broth and browned bread crumbs. It looked very unappetizing, like a fresh cowpie in the spring. That never bothered me, spinach being one of my favorite prepared vegetables, and my husband even learned to like it. I served this at a recent family holiday gathering because I knew my brother liked it. Everyone was good enough to try it, but very few ate it with gusto. The hot creamed horseradish's sharp flavor complemented the blander beef and spinach. Fresh horseradish, whether sniffed or eaten, is also a great decongestant for clogged sinuses. A local restaurant features this wonderful meal about every other Wednesday in the winter. It is advertised in the *Bulletin*, our local paper, and the dining room is full of virtually all Amana people.

A tasty soup prepared by Aunt Helen was *Spätzle*, or dumpling soup. We also ate the *Spätzle* separate with browned bread crumbs. A hearty variation using the dumplings is pot pie, where the *Spätzle* are cooked in a broth with pork chops, bratwurst, and potatoes. These dumplings have become one of my daughter's culinary specialties, and she often fixes them for all of us. My family used to call *Spätzle* "Spatze," which is the German word for sparrows. This confused me, even though I knew I was eating dumplings and not birds.

Aunt Helen's *Kartoffelklösse* (potato dumplings) made from riced, cooked potatoes were exceptional. Riced potatoes were made with a metal utensil called a potato ricer. You put the boiled, peeled potatoes in the cup part of the ricer and bring the upper handle down, squeezing the potatoes through the small holes in the cup, and they come out resembling grains of rice.

Obstkuchen (fruit pie) for dessert, from Aunt Helen's kitchen, completed a delightful Colony meal. Cherries or peaches, nestled in that rich, cream-filled crust, just makes my mouth water thinking of it.

Holidays brought delightful Colony cuisine. For New Year's, Aunt Marie's pretzel was the very best. The sweet dough (the same as she used for her *Wecke*) was shaped into a large pretzel and covered with a white fluffy frosting. Eating pretzel in the new year was sure to bring you good luck.

Easter brought *Bockwurst* and *Hasenkecks* (bunny cookies). Bockwurst was a special fresh pork sausage made by the meat market. It was like bratwurst, except milk, eggs, and chives were added. We always ate it boiled, and it was and still is only available at Eastertime. A typical holy week meal in our family now is *bockwurst*, *Spätzle*, and cottage cheese with fresh chives.

Making bunny cookies was a big deal. It took Aunt Helen's strong arms to stir the large mound of rich brown dough in the enormous dish pan. Batch after batch of bunny cookies, with raisin eyes, slid in and out of the oven. They were topped with Mom's rich creamy frosting. These cookies were made before Good Friday. A sweet baked bunny was the first thing I ate after fasting from morning till late afternoon on Good Friday. Our church still follows this custom of fasting to remind one of Jesus' suffering on the cross. This was really tough when we were younger, but the thought of those bunny cookies at the end of the ordeal pulled us through.

Mom and Aunt Marie prepared the meals at Thanksgiving and Christmas. Mom's dressing for the Thanksgiving turkey was a meal in itself. It's savory aroma of bacon, onions, and apples stirs my senses even now.

Christmas dinner at Aunt Marie's meant *Lappebohnen* (dried, creamed green beans) to go with the roasted pork loin. I was envious of her table setting. Not only did we eat in a dining room (we had to eat in the kitchen at home), but they would make neat little favors for everyone at the table. Since Uncle Dan was a carpenter, these were often made out of wood. I still have a dear, little red sleigh he made that I put out every Christmas. One Thanksgiving I spent all afternoon creating construction paper turkeys for the place settings at our house. They were appreciated, but I bet no one kept one of those turkeys to use as a Thanksgiving decoration.

These family cooking and eating sessions from my past were not only necessary to nourish the body, but also the soul. As a little girl, I felt so safe in the cocoons of Mom's and Oma's kitchens when my aunts would come and converse with them about local and family news, laugh about comical events they had shared in the past, and even sing, harmonizing to old favorite songs and then laugh again, when they ended up way off key, all the while preparing and cooking a meal.

Now when my family comes and we're working together in the kitchen preparing a meal, we are continuing the legacy of those earlier cooks from my childhood that not only filled my stomach with good food, but also penetrated my heart and memory with their warmth and love.

■ Roy Moser

Ray Moser was a farm manager at the Amana Colonies for many years.

FIELDS AND BUILDINGS

Prior to the late 1960s, there was not a big problem of field identification on the Amana farms. At that time there were seven different farms with their own field names and/or numbers. Any new farm worker had to learn the field locations, along with the names of all the buildings for that certain village. After the farm consolidation started (and it took over eight years to complete), the workers were being sent to different villages and had to learn more field and building names. There was, of course, the inevitable duplication. Every village had a mix of horse, cow, dry, sheep, steer, hog, heifer, first, last, sow, bull, straw, hotel, ox, salt or loading chute barn, along with the threshing machine shed, the sawmill, seed houses, lumber sheds, fire shed, wagon shop, ice houses and whatnot. Prior to 1932 and shortly thereafter, there were even more, such as the harness shop, cooper shop, tailor shop, and a host of others that were not around in the sixties anymore.

It was always fun to send a new worker to the heifer barn where the steers were, or to the red shed that had been painted grey for fifteen years, or to the manhole on the south side of where the granary had been. Never having seen the granary or knowing even where it had been was frustrating to that new person.

Working with the government program produced more names and numbers. One such name was the "Ever-Normal Granary." If you expected a building, you would be looking forever. This is a field so named by a former farm manager because it seemed the oats were in the field so long that they seemed to be stored there. The government has its own terminology for grain storage.

Today, with all the farms consolidated under one management, there are approximately 300 field names and/or numbers. To confuse it even more, the names are used for general descriptions, but there are official numbers used for government or record keeping purposes. For instance, a field simply known as number one (there are two of them) has a different official number for the computer. There are a number of fields with the name "100 acre field," ranging from 83 to 117 actual acres, but these fields were named long ago, when precise measurement was neither a priority nor a necessity.

More than one town had a "millfield," "hog lot," "lake piece" or "brickyard," all of which were plausible and understandable names. Others, such as "Johnson," "Pleasant Valley," "Ruddicks," and "Whiting" are linked to the time they were purchased and possibly from whom. Some were appropriately named because of their shape: the "Pie Piece," "Triangle," "Half-moon," "Seven Hills to Hell," "Goat Mountain," "Swamphole;" or named for their early use such as "Celery Garden," "Orchard Field," or "Sheep Hills."

With the advent of larger farm machinery came the combining of two or more fields into one. A few fields retained both names such as "Cherry Tree-Maas's." "Samson's" was incorporated into "Sow Bush." The "60" was swallowed up by "#1." One lake piece disappeared and became part of a village. "Noah's Ark" is not a boat or a building. It is a terraced hill, jutting to the edge of the road, so named by the farm manager because it supposedly resembled the bow of Noah's Ark. One field name I won't mention describes a person's anatomy, so named by a disgruntled worker thirty-some years ago because of the difficulty of farming among the undulating, terraced dips and turns of the hilly makeup of the field. This field, by the way, is bordered on one side by the "Rubber Road."

Field names have changed over the generations. Some of the older workers remember "Laracheks," "Olsons," "Renner Farm," and "Baughs," all of which depict the same area, now called "Cuddles." Most of the "Pine Grove" fields are still around, but the "Doctors" fields have been lost. A few names like "New Umbruch," "Lebencutts," and "Esbenlaub" are still viable, but not used much. "Foxes" was a field name shared by both Amana and Middle. When the dividing fence was taken out, and the field thus enlarged, it didn't cause any problems with name association.

The employees became accustomed to my abbreviation of certain fields: NML for "No-Man's-Land," TCA for "Tin-Can-Alley," MLF for "Middle Line Field," or PP for "Pie Piece." A field at the West Amana curve got its name of "Robber's Cove" because robbers supposedly hid in the brush alongside that stretch of road.

The forests or timbers also have their various names, and to me still sound better in German, such as Inschebush (Indian Woods), Dammbush (Dam Woods), Mühlbush (Mill Woods), or Schulwald (School Forest).

■ *Emilie Hoppe*

Emilie Hoppe, her husband, Bob, and their triplets, age nine, live in

West Amana. Emilie publishes Wilkommen, *a tourist information guide for the Amana Colonies.*

THE PRAIRIE SKIFF

My *Opa* (grandpa) once told me of a boat that was built to sail the floodwaters of the Iowa River. The river is wide and whenever it flooded commerce stopped between the villages of West and South Amana, so a boat was built complete with tall mast and sail. What must it have looked like, this prairie skiff slipping atop the grassy meadows swept by the wind? Could you really sail it from one end of Amana to the other? And when the river fell, did they set her in the mainstream and take her down river? Where did she go, the prairie skiff, whatever became of her?

If I could climb aboard such a boat and sail across the meadow, I would land at the point just below High Amana where the Mill Race levee bridge is located. The levee here is a full eight feet above the prairie and from on top you have a wonderful view of the river bottom to the south and the village of High Amana to the north. In the bottom is the forest of softwood trees and marshy bogland through which the Iowa River flows. Every spring the river floods and muddy water fills the low-lying meadows and fields. The Amana farmers who have the responsibility of caring for the cattle in the low meadows understand the river's habit of flooding and herd the cattle upland when the snow begins to melt and the rain to fall. The cattle are kept in stockyards at the edge of High Amana and all 100 village inhabitants fall asleep each night and wake each morning to the sound of their lowing.

With the flood came the waterfowl, and when I was a girl, thousands and thousands of ducks and geese seemed to drop out of the sky. I have never since seen so many flocks as were visible from my High Amana home on almost any spring day during my childhood.

After school I would shove a candy bar in my jacket pocket and ride my blue Schwinn bike through town to the barnyard. From the barnyard there was a narrow, dirt farm road that led to the Mill Race levee and the old canal bridge. Once on the bridge, I would park my bike and climb up on the topmost bridge railing. Below, the dirty canal water swirled, carrying twigs, leaves, and pearl-like drops of foam. If you watched the water long enough, you became so dizzy the world itself began to whirl, and you felt as if you were about to be sucked beneath the wooden bridge planks never to be seen again.

Overhead the sight was equally dizzying as hundreds, even thousands, of birds swirled and glided, landing gracefully upon the shiny silver surface of the flooded fields all around me. Birds in the air, upon the water, landing and taking off in perfect synchronization, a ballet for my benefit, I thought.

In all the hours I spent watching the birds upon the flood plain, I never once wished for an Audubon bird book. It made no difference to me that the beautiful, green-headed speedsters were teal and the squat, dirt-colored ducks were mud hens. The snow geese and Canadians were easy to spot, of course, and I who had grown up in a household of hunters knew a mallard when I saw one, but beyond that my knowledge of waterfowl never expanded. For me it was enough that they were there; species and subfamily were unimportant.

I especially loved the geese. Their trumpeting call was the anthem of my childhood. Spring and autumn evenings when my friends and I were outside playing basketball or football, we would see them as they flew over our village, their magical song carried by the wind. If they were low enough, we could actually hear their silver wings beat the air.

When I grew up I married and moved just a mile down the highway to West Amana. My husband and I built our house facing the river bottom and spend hours watching the coyotes trail across the meadows and the deer feeding in the fields. I watch for the ducks and the geese, but few come. The waterfowl population has decreased enormously these past twenty-five years and their flight paths have, by necessity, moved west where they can feed and nest in undrained marshland protected by federal law. I suppose if my boat could carry me far enough west to the wide, flat wetlands of the Nebraska rivers, I would sail there to see the geese and to hear them call.

⌐

For several years my husband and I tried to conceive a child, but could not. I visited doctors and spent long, dreary hours in waiting rooms where truly I waited and waited. Finally, after years of trying, I became pregnant. We were overjoyed. Nothing dimmed the happiness or sense of wonderful promise, not even the news that I was carrying not one child, but three: triplets. Listening to the admonitions of the doctors who told us that chances of carrying triplets safely to term were slim, I was oddly unafraid. I, who worried about everything, was not the least bit worried about the prospect of carrying, delivering, and caring for three infants. I knew that this might be our only chance, and I wasn't going to rob myself of one moment's happiness by worrying. I felt it would be okay and by sheer force of will I tried to make it so.

In the twenty-third week of the pregnancy, I went into labor. I was at home and had been working all afternoon on the bookkeeping for my small business. At first the labor could hardly be called such, for all I felt was a general sense of unease and fleeting, almost imperceptible, nervy sensations along my back and legs. When my husband Bob came home from work, we went for a short walk and I felt better. Then we went out for a pizza before settling in at home to watch an Alfred Hitchcock movie, *Rear Window*. Although I was sure it was only indigestion or the effects of the movie, I began to feel uncomfortable, and fearful. To allay my concern I phoned the OB office and talked to the doctor on-call, trying to describe my feelings. He very kindly and patiently listened as I explained that I wasn't in any pain, nor did I feel crampy or display any of the usual symptoms of labor; I simply felt very ill at ease. He said that it was probably nothing, but since I was carrying triplets I ought to be cautious and so we should come to the hospital, St. Luke's in Cedar Rapids.

I gave Bob the news. He was worried, but not overly so, and told me as much. I remember switching off the TV and wondering if I could continue watching the movie in the ER waiting room. We decided not to phone my parents or his. "Why worry anyone? This is no big deal," we told one another.

We took nothing with us beyond Bob's billfold and my purse. We left the house unlocked. We thought we would be back in a couple hours. As it was, Bob didn't return that night, and I didn't come home again for nearly eight weeks.

At the hospital the ER nurse told me that Dr. Wessel, the OB on-call, was waiting for me on sixth floor in the OB wing. The examination would take place there and while they put me in a wheelchair and wheeled me into the elevator, the first contraction hit. I was in labor. Dr. Wessel simply confirmed it and announced that not only was I in labor, I had already dilated some three centimeters.

Bob and I and our family-to-be were in serious trouble and we knew it. Three tiny babies born at twenty-three weeks, some seventeen weeks early, had little chance of survival.

All that night we tried to stop the labor. Medicines were administered to slow or hopefully stop the contractions, my hospital bed was tipped head down so that gravity could do its thing, and everyone, even the pleasant cleaning lady who came in to clean up after I vomited on the fetal heart monitor, told me to relax. Relax.

I was sick, tired and very, very frightened. Sometime after midnight I asked the two nurses who sat beside my bed to turn the lights off in the room. Dr. Wessel and the resident on staff had been coming and going all evening. They were so plainly worried that all their professional demeanor could not conceal it. Bob was there, too, holding my hand, trying to make me feel as if the world wasn't really coming to an end, spinning down, painfully grinding to a halt right then and there.

One of my nurses, a sweet, dark-haired young woman, tried to comfort me as best she could, and I found that listening to her voice, a lilting half-southern voice (for she was a transplanted Louisiana girl) was a kind of relief. She kept me from focusing upon the labor contractions and anticipating them. She told me of her home and her nurse's training, and while I remember that I asked questions and listened as if God himself was speaking, I cannot recall one thing she told me. All her words are lost in the foggy despair of that long night.

After 2 A.M., one of the nurses finally convinced Bob he ought to rest for awhile and took him to an empty room where he could stretch out for an hour. The labor contractions had slowed somewhat, but had not stopped. The drug they administered by IV, Yutopar, was working, but if the contractions did not stop soon, birth would be inevitable. It was very quiet in the hospital. Though I could not hear them, I knew that in other rooms up and down the hall other women were laboring like me, but unlike me they were laboring to give birth. I, however, was laboring to stop.

The nurses urged me to try and doze between contractions, or at least close my eyes and rest, but I was too scared to try.

So I prayed. I have never in my life prayed so fiercely as I prayed that night. With every heartbeat, every vibration of my soul, I prayed that God save my children and me. I prayed for their lives and for mine. And in my imagination I saw myself literally giving my fear, pain and grief to God, saying, "Here, take this, I can't bear it."

In my prayers I saw myself lying still upon the bed, all the anxiety and pain gone. "After all," I told myself, "you gave it away, it's not yours to do any more."

"Think about something calming. Get away from here," I told myself. So I thought about home and about watching the deer shadow the forest's edge walking meekly out to feed in the cornfields and how they step into the shallow water of the grass sloughs to drink.

From out of the tall, green slough grass comes the skiff, lightly loaded and sail aloft. It comes toward you and bumps gently against the sandy shore just where you stand.

"Come along, climb aboard!" he calls and so you do, stepping into the small boat and settling upon the seat.

"We'll just go down river a while. We'll let the current take us," he says. So you do and you feel the boat moving bouyant upon the water, slipping through the plume grass and cattails toward the main channel where the boat will turn and drift away downstream.

I don't remember when the contractions stopped, but they did, and afterward I fell asleep and slept I don't know how long. Sometime after dawn I woke up. Bob and my mom were sitting there, and I asked Mom to open the curtains on the window. She drew the drape, and from my bed I could just see the storage bins of the Quaker Oats plant which stands beside the Cedar River. In the sky were at least 150 wild geese, circling above the river, wings silver like those of angels.

Postscript: Seven weeks after the night of the prairie skiff dream, my children were born, two girls and a boy. Healthy and happy, today they love nothing better than to watch the eagles and cranes that live along the Iowa River.

Commentary: The Amanas

Today the Amanas are a major tourist destination for many thousands of people, most of whom are probably less acquainted with the history of the colonies than they are with its food. On almost any summer day or evening the many Amana restaurants are packed with people eating what are known as "family style" meals, entrees that come with large bowls of corn, cottage cheese, sauerkraut, and bread, with as many refills as you can eat.

The town known as Main Amana receives most of the business, for it has most of the stores. The other villages are primarily collections of houses, some of which are built of large blocks of dark sandstone, set on well-trimmed lawns with vegetable and flower gardens cut in neat rectangles and set beside small outbuildings. The Amana writing workshop was held in a stone building with a plain interior which once housed an Inspirationist church. My wife and I stayed in another portion of the church, and in the morning when we first looked out we saw a scene—lawns and potting sheds, clothesline posts and wire, gardens and homes—that made us think of *Spring in Town*, one of Grant Wood's last paintings. We knew that Wood had been a frequent visitor to the Amanas; one of his friends and pupils, Carl Flick, was an Amana resident. We had been told by several other Amana people that in the days when he was short of money, Wood would visit the colonies where he liked to paint and knew he would always be well fed.

It is easy to understand Wood's attraction to the Amanas: at those times when cars and tourists are not jamming the streets and sidewalks, each of the villages seems the image of the idyllic rural town. While most Midwest towns are bleak affairs, the downtowns especially (mostly two blocks long with no side streets for business, and no public places besides the sidewalks for socializing), the Amanas bespeak prosperity, permanence, and beauty. The residents have prospered in this age, not just by catering to tourists and by their proximity to Cedar Rapids and Iowa City, but by the various businesses which they have established over the years (some before the Great Change), including a microbrewery, six or seven wineries, a woolen mill, three furniture shops, and Amana Appliances. Iowa's oldest professional theater, the Old Creamery Theatre, recently moved from Garrison, Iowa to Main Amana. Amana tourism no doubt owes much to the absence of fast food restaurants and other chains which would destroy the towns' architectural integrity. The extremely active heritage society is now seeking to restore some of the original landscaping in the towns, another sign that the Amanas retain close ties to their past.

THE RIVER
AND DELTA

Introduction

Once Free River press assembled a series of books on the Midwest, I decided to create other regional series. With Murray Hudson's *Dirt & Duty*, the press had a book on one portion of the Mississippi Delta, and since I had a familiarity and a fascination with several of the region's cultures, I decided that the Delta would be the next focus for the press.

But just what area the Delta does encompass is a matter of opinion. Some speak of it as extending from Cairo, Illinois (where the Ohio River joins the Mississippi) down to the Gulf of Mexico. But most often when people speak of the Delta they mean the alluvial lands running from about sixty miles north of Memphis to the Gulf, a region encompassing the western portions of Tennessee and Mississippi, and the eastern portions of Missouri, Arkansas, and Louisiana.

Murray Hudson lives in the northern section of the Delta, in west Tennessee. I met him in Nashville in the early 1990s when the press was focusing exclusively on works by the homeless. The press had received a grant from the Tennessee Arts Council to conduct three workshops across the state to develop these works, and Murray agreed to run the one in Memphis. Later, when I began the farm writing workshop, I asked Murray to create stories about his farming days which I could use as examples for the Iowa farmers. That is how Dirt & Duty began.

The events described in Dirt & Duty occur in Dyer County, Tennessee, across the river and an hour north of Helena and West Helena, Arkansas, a major performance area for the great blues musicians of the 1930s and 1940s. These adjacent towns had numerous night clubs and juke joints—small shacks where people gather to drink and listen to music—that probably were as important for the blues as "the Stroll" on Chicago's South Side was to black jazz musicians of the early twenties. Juke joints remain a cultural institution among Delta blacks. Contributor Chris Crawford's semi-autobiographical story, "Lucky Lacey," which deals with the goings-on in a West Helena, Arkansas juke joint, was written in the MATTHEW 25 workshop.

Midge White's letters from rural Mississippi and Louisiana from the early 1940s to her northern family offer a glimpse into rural Delta life and the timber industry, which was then a major component of the Delta's economy.

About the time I decided to develop a series on the Delta I decided to develop one on the Mississippi River too. The two subjects overlap, since the lower Mississippi is central to the story of the Delta. The first river story that emerged was Robert Teff's piece, "Commercial Fishing," written in a Lansing, Iowa workshop. Later I met Jack Libby, a former Mississippi River towboat captain, at a public talk he gave on the subject of river, and asked if he would write a contribution for the present book. The upshot was not only "The Midnight Watch Change," but other stories for a book in progress.

Shortly after I spoke with Jack, I asked former Iowan Lyle Ernst to write a story on river towns. As far back as 1996 Lyle had told me that he wanted to learn to write, and kept asking when I was going to run another local workshop. When I finally organized one for The Northeast Iowa Book, Lyle joined, researched whatever needed researching, and wrote and rewrote until he had crafted some good pieces. Since late 1997 he has been a regular contract freelancer with the *Cedar Rapids Gazette*.

Ken Jones, who wrote "My Mississippi Mistress," attended a workshop in Dyersburg, Tennessee, though when I met him I had no idea that he had any connection to the river. I met Mary Kathleen Julian at a 1998 dairy conference in Madison, Wisconsin and approached her about writing on farm issues. During our conversation she made it known that she had spent all of her vacations for the past twenty-eight years on towboats. Her husband, James Julian, was for many years a Mississippi river pilot but now farms in Wisconsin. As I discovered later, the Julians are good friends of Jack Libby.

The greatest enjoyment I have had working on this section has come from meeting the writers, each of whom has a very distinct personality. (Although James Julian did not write for this section, his stories of the Delta and the river, told in his slow Mississippi drawl, have deepened my understanding of both.) Northerners and Southerners, landsmen and river folk, this small group has strengthened my determination for further exploration of both the region and the river.

THE RIVER

■ *Captain Jack Libbey*

Jack Libbey has worked on the Mississippi River as a pilot and tow-boat captain for twenty-five years. In 1997 he was part of the Smithsonian's celebration of Iowa's sesquicentennial in Washington, D.C. Jack is currently writing a book for Free River Press.

THE MIDNIGHT WATCH CHANGE

"Cap'n Jack! Rise and shine, it's towboatin time! Midnight!"

What a nightmare, I thought. Hadn't I just lain down? "Already?" I slowly replied, realizing that my night's sleep had only been two hours long.

"I reckon," drawled Bright Eyes. "We're comin down on lock twelve. Cap'n George got on in Dubuque. Cap'n Mike missed his flight to Cape Giradeau. He'll rent a car and drive to St. Louis. Regular suitcase parade."

My mind slowly tried to analyze what had happened during my six hours off watch as Bright Eyes rattled on.

"We finally got them other three loaded barges we picked up wired in. Couldn't get them squared up too good, though. Hope you don't care. Took far ever. I'll try to get it out down to the lock."

"Okay," I muttered. He better get them square, I thought, otherwise the boat will sit cockeyed and act as a two hundred foot long rudder, constantly steering us the wrong direction all the way down the river.

The short, stocky Kentuckian had just been promoted to watchman and was obviously taking his new responsibilities seriously. His new found duties included overseeing the barges and boat and deck crew on the forward watch, between 6:00 to 12:00 A.M. and P.M., opposite my watch.

"Want me to bring ya a cup of coffee? Memphis Mike just made some in the pilot house," Bright Eyes asked.

"No, that's okay. I'll get a cup upstairs." I yawned. My eyes were slowly adjusting to the bright light as I surveyed the Holiday Inn style pilot stateroom, the same domicile that I had inhabited every other month for the last fourteen years, my home away from home. Ever since the day this towboat slid off the shipyard ways, brand spanking new, in Jeffersonville, Indiana, I had been her pilot/captain.

My ambitions of becoming a Mississippi riverboat pilot had been reached over twenty years ago. My first trip on a tug was as a deckhand. I wanted to explore the possibilities of becoming a pilot. If it turned out to be a dead end trail, I would attend medical school and become a dermatologist. Now I was hooked on towboating for life, transporting Midwestern grain in barges the entire navigable length of the Mississippi River between St. Paul and New Orleans.

Our route follows the migratory pattern of water fowl that transit the river's flyway each spring and fall. The only difference is that we average one round trip per month. Constantly underway, we stop only to pick up or drop off barges that are dispatched by the company's Chicago office. Reprovisioning of groceries, supplies, fuel, and water are taken mid-stream via tug and barge while underway. Stopping for these items would be costly.

In New Orleans, the loaded grain barges are dropped into a fleet where they are dispatched to grain elevators and loaded onto ships for export destined throughout the world. Unfortunately, with one-hour turn arounds, the opportunity to visit the sights and venues of the Crescent City are nil. We rapidly face up to our new northbound tow and get underway with empty barges and loads of fertilizer, salt, and other bulk commodities bound for the Midwest.

"You awake?" inquired Bright Eyes.

"Yeah, yeah, I am," I replied. My room and bed came alive with vibration. It became difficult for my still unadjusted eyes to stay in tune with my body. Overhead, in the pilot house, Captain George had ordered the engines into reverse and was backing full astern to slow our descent down river and begin his flank, a tactful maneuver used to counteract the river's swift current above the locks and dams.

"Sheeit!" Bright Eyes blurted, "I better get out there to the head of the tow before Captain George kills me!" His thoughts were confirmed by the shrill whistle reverberating through the inside of the vessel. Captain George had pushed the deckhand call button, calling the crew in preparation for the approaching lock.

"Yeah, I better get ready too. I'm sure he's tired."

As Bright Eyes closed the door it began rattling like a machine gun. My makeshift muffler—a folded paper towel damper—had come loose when Bright Eyes opened the door. I dressed rapidly and washed my face.

I opened the door to my room as it let off another round of gunfire. The overbearing rumble of the engines provided a constant reminder of the immense power that would soon be at my fingertips when I assumed my watch in the pilot house. The smell of coffee, a placid aroma, permeated the boat as I meandered the short distance down the hallway past the guest room. Mesmerized, I began my ascent up the darkened stairway. A warm, snug feeling of belonging emerged as I reached the top of the pilot house stairs.

"Man, am I glad to see you. I'm tired!" George called out as I opened the door and entered the pitch black pilot house.

"I hear you. Welcome back. Have a good time at home?" I asked, fumbling in the darkness, trying to locate my personalized coffee cup. Towboats run on coffee and diesel fuel. "Did he make Brim or Folgers?"

"I had him make Folgers. Figured you wouldn't mind. Besides, I needed the caffeine. Didn't think I'd survive till you got up here!"

"I need some tonight too. Stayed up too late watching a movie," I confessed.

My eyes swept the pilot house as they began to adjust to the darkness. George's upper torso was silhouetted by the faint yellow sweep on the radar screen; his face was barely recognizable in the glow of the swing meter. He flipped on the search light, directing the beam toward the head of the tow. He had not lost his touch. As always, his flank was perfect. We were sitting crossways in the river. The current was beginning to push the head of our 1,200-foot tow toward the lock wall faster than our stern, as it should be. If all his timing, skill, and luck worked simultaneously, the lockmen would be able to throw a small, handy line to our deck crew earnestly awaiting on the starboard head of the tow. In response, the crew would attach and return a 600-foot lock line, three inches in diameter. With the lock 110 feet wide and our beam 105 feet, there is little margin for error. Lock line is used to keep the tow flat against the lock's guide wall during an approach.

A total of twenty-seven government locks and dams must be transited during our voyage down river. Each are strategically placed along the river's course, creating a stair case system to allow for the changes in elevation above sea level and maintain a controlling navigation depth of nine feet.

To raise or lower the vessels from one river level to the next requires a process that normally takes between one and two hours to complete. Only a few of the newer lock chambers are 1,200 feet long. The older locks are only 600 feet long and require the towboat crews and assisting lockmen to break the 1,200 foot tow into two sections. Winches and cables along with the towboat are used to move the separate sections in and out of the lock chamber.

Lockmen not only assist the crew in locking the vessel from one river level to another, but also provide invaluable services. Deckhands and lockmen trade everything from the river's latest rumors and jokes to dogs, fresh fruits, vegetables, books, and wild turkey calls. The only form of currency normally exchanged during these barter sessions is a can or sometimes a case of Folgers coffee, taken from our large stockpile in the galley pantry.

My eyes had slowly adjusted to the darkness of the pilot house. I watched carefully as the xeon search light beam swung slowly toward the upper guide wall of lock number twelve, silhouetted by the lights of downtown Bellevue, Iowa.

Ironically, George and I share many of the same piloting techniques. We always feel comfortable relieving each other's watch. Unfortunately, this is not always the case. I have worked with other pilots who were not as skilled as George and would cause me grief at watch change.

Uttering the traditional towboat change of command, I voiced with certainty, "I gotcha." Everything looked perfect so far.

"I'm ready for bed. You can have it!" George said wearily. I moved in, taking the controls, as he backed away from the regal wheel house chair.

Here I was again, overlooking fifteen barges, three wide by five long (105 feet by 1,000 feet), containing a total of 24,000 tons of grain. Including the towboat, the entire tow reached out to a total length of 1,200 feet. Laced together with turnbuckle ratchets, chain links, and steel cables called wires, they floated harmoniously as one sturdy unit. No ship on the earth was longer. We were the length of four football fields, three hundred feet longer than the Exxon Valdez, and yes, even longer than an aircraft carrier.

A bright full moon slid out from behind the clouds, casting the towboat's shadows onto the Mississippi River's surface, forty-five feet beneath my feet. This rumbling titanic vessel supports a self-reliant crew of twelve. Like the early lumber camps, towboats have always provided plentiful amounts of food and comfortable living conditions for the crew, helping to ease the minds of crew members while away from home. We live on board for a month at a time, in an environment much like that of home, but with the internal complexity of the space shuttle, including electrical generators, twin 4,800 horse power diesel engines, comfortable sleeping quarters, lounges with TVs and VCRs, a library, and galley.

The galley's cook, Marie, from Mississippi or Miss'ippi as she always corrects me, provides smorgasbord style breakfasts, lunches, and dinners, not to mention unlimited snacks and anti-acid tablets.

"We got any Rolaids on here?" George asked in agony. "I had some of Marie's famous breaded pork chops tonight. I missed them when I was home, but I'm not so sure now." He fumbled, searching through the top wheel house desk drawer with a flashlight.

"Nope," I replied. "Ordered some in St. Paul and Winona when we got groceries. Both places said that new goofy kid working in the St. Louis office told them we didn't need em, and that he wasn't going to pay for them!"

"What the—! First the shrimp, now the Rolaids? Ever since that damn grain embargo! Those new office idiots don't know which way the river flows," steamed George.

"Want to hear another one?" I blurted. "With the river coming up over a foot a day, Mike and I told them we only needed twelve barges this trip to be safe. How many do you see? They said, 'Take em!' "

Recovering slowly, the river industry is still feeling the effects of the Russian grain embargo instituted during Jimmy Carter's administration. With reduced exports, many tugboat companies realized that they had over-built their fleets. With less cargo to be moved and an abundance of barges and towboats, not to mention crew members, times became tough. Merger mania, layoffs, and all the other complications of modern day business struck the river industry head on. To cut costs, many companies eliminated the once revered port captains, replacing them with lesser paid bean counters who have no practical boat knowledge. These port captains—highly skilled senior captains—held positions in the office acting as liaisons between company officials and the vessels, oftentimes saving the towboat companies large amounts of money by making efficient decisions in boat dispatches, equipment purchases, and crew hiring.

I had been monitoring the plodding cluster of deckhands' miner style head lamps as the crew meandered from the towboat, towards the head of the darkened tow. Watching the crew prepare to secure the tow to the lock wall, I thought of accidents caused by the cheap line that all the boats had been sent. It wasn't the normal poly dee fiber, which starts at three inches in diameter and should be able to get down to the size of a silver dollar under a good strain and not break.

One locking maneuver I'd heard of came to mind. The current was running fast toward the dam, not making it easy to steer the tow into the lock. One of the men had wrapped the line around the deck fitting in a figure-eight style, tethering the tow to the lock wall. He began to check it. The captain was doing all he could to keep the boat in place. The boat was tucked into the bank, keeping most of the current cut off. It should have been an easy check.

But the line was no good. One deckhand was leaning back, holding the line when it melted on the fitting. The strain was too much. The line broke, snapping him like a whip, knocking him out of his boots and life jacket into the river. That was the last was seen of him.

The relief crew reached the head of the tow.

"I gotcha Bright Eyes," Tommy said. "How come yawl don't have us through the lock yet?"

"We figured you guys didn't have anything else to do for the next two hours," Bright Eyes chided back.

"You're abreast the wall. Thirty-five feet wide and coming in," mate Tommy yelled into the tow speaker. The confident Arkansan had just relieved Bright Eyes.

"How are you tonight, Tommy?" I asked, mostly to acknowledge the fact that I could hear him on the speaker in the pilot house.

"Great. Ten wide coming in. Except for those pork chops."

"You too?" I inquired.

On the speaker I heard the familiar "thunk" produced by the lockman's handy line landing on the barge's steel deck. The crew hastily returned our lock line to the lockmen on the wall.

"How are you fellows tonight? They been keepin you busy?" the lockman asked.

"Finer then frog fuzz, Mr. Lockman, cept . . . You got any Rolaids?" Tommy belched. "Five wide comin in. Two hundred to the bull nose and you will be in the lock."

The tow was still sliding perfectly toward the lock. "We won't need to catch a line, Tommy. She's going our way," I added.

"I'll trade ya a box of Rolaids for a case of coffee," answered the lockman.

"Tommy is a genius!" George added with a sigh of relief as he slammed the desk drawer shut. "We're one up on the office kid now!"

As I steered the tow flat onto the guide wall and entered the lock chamber, Tommy called out, "All clear the bull nose. Inside the chamber. All's well here."

Yes, it is, I thought, and I wouldn't trade it for the world.

■ *Mary Kathleen Julian*

Mary Kathleen Julian is a Catholic school principal and the wife of

James Julian, a former Mississippi River pilot, and now a farmer in south-west Wisconsin. They have one daughter and two sons.

MISSISSIPPI TOWBOAT RIDES

Raised in LaCrescent, Minnesota as a daughter of a lifetime railroad man, it was a shock to the family when I started dating and later married a towboat pilot. For four years during high school and in the summers while at college, I worked at an answering service in La Crosse, Wisconsin. We placed ship-to-shore calls for the captains of the towboats. The summer of 1969 I talked on the radio with James Julian of Tennessee. We met that summer and married in the summer of 1970.

Afterwards, I started going on the towboats as a guest. I often got on the boats at Lock #7 by LaCrescent and rode to the Twin Cities and back out. This was a vacation for me to sit back and relax, visit, sleep, eat, and read. During the school year I was and am a teacher.

One time I got on the boat at Lock #7 and the cook had to get off because of a death in her family. The relief cook was being flown into the Twin Cities in a day or so. James volunteered me to cook that trip so I was given a quick tour of the galley while the boat was locking up stream and before the cook got off. She had pork chops out for supper—among other items.

I was raised in a family of seven kids, so the kitchen held no fear for me. My surprise was the sheer volume of food the men consumed. They would walk into the galley and take six pork chops, mountains of potatoes, vegies, rolls or biscuits, salads. I thought we at home knew how to eat, but we were pure amateurs. For breakfast the menu was biscuits and gravy, pounds of bacon, sausage, grits, eggs, and pancakes. The men going off the midnight-to-six watch would come in and order six to twelve eggs over easy. James had to keep reminding me just to serve the food. The grocery bill wasn't my concern.

The crew works six hours on, six hours off, for at least thirty days straight. Meals on the boat are 5:30–6:30 A.M., 11:30–12:30

P.M. and 5:30–6:30 P.M. This, of course, takes care of the two crews—the ones going on watch and the ones coming off. The kids and I would raid the galley at 11:00 P.M. and make pizzas for the men at midnight. The crew always seemed delighted to have a midnight pizza party. Another delightful surprise on the boat was shrimp. Not the amount we got at home or a restaurant, but large mixing bowls full of boiled shrimp. The first time I experienced shrimp at this volume I had diarrhea for a day or two.

Over the twenty-five years I visited the boat the men were great to visit with. I could relax and enjoy the fabulous scenery of the bluffs from LaCrescent to the Cities. The boat travels slowly up river so you truly can sit and enjoy watching the river and land. The most beautiful part of the river is from Dubuque, Iowa to the Twin Cities. Below Dubuque to St. Louis there are no bluffs, and the going is not as interesting.

From the time our three children started to walk until about age four I did not take them on towboat trips because of the potential dangers involved. This is a work boat, not the Delta Queen. Because of this there are cables, retches, and numerous other pieces of equipment around.

From about four years old on I took them on trips with us. This would not have been possible if they didn't obey us all the time. The first time I took my four-year-old daughter we got on at Lock #7 at LaCrescent, Minnesota and rode to the Cities. I was sure that by Winona, Minnesota (thirty miles north) she would be bored silly. Boy, was I wrong. She was so busy in the galley "helping" the cook. All the men would play and visit with her and the boys. The boys spent a lot of time in the engine room helping the chief engineer.

Janet would get up at 4:15 to help make biscuits. Then after breakfast she would stay in the galley to make pies for lunch and supper.

On another trip the children roamed the boat. One of the deck hands taught Janet how to make bumpers (braided rope dropped over the side of the boat) and she spent hours making miniature bumpers, playing games, visiting, and hosing down the hot decks. When it was time to blow the horn Dad would lift her up to pull the cord. The kids waved at all motor boats and towboats and at all the visitors on each of the lock walls. By the time we got back home they still wouldn't be ready to go off.

Sometimes as I relaxed and watched the men work I would get a case of guilt. I figured I should do something useful. So one trip I washed and scrubbed the smoke stacks and decks, and painted the steps. We all remember from our childhood how jobs were more fun at someone else's house. Well, it was the same way on the boat.

Having been raised on the Chicago-Milwaukee Railroad I love the motion of the train as it moved down the tracks. The sound and shaking would put me asleep in a very short time. Well, the river boat also has its sounds and motions. After a little bit of time this too would relax me and make me sleepy.

One time I caught the boat in Memphis, Tennessee and rode it a little above St. Louis. I got on the boat just a day or two after school let out for the summer. I got on with seven books to read. I believe I slept that entire trip and did little else. But while I was waiting in Memphis at the fueling spot the Delta Queen was there being cleaned and restocked for another trip. The captain allowed me to visit the boat and look around. Being I'll never be able to afford a trip on the Delta Queen this was truly a pleasure. The carpets, china, and furniture made me feel like I'd stepped into the past. Pure heaven.

When you run the river in speed boats you get no feeling of the river or its history, but when you're on a slow towboat you surely can relate to all the stories Samuel Clemens wrote of Tom Sawyer and Huck Finn. The Upper Mississippi is all that real writers have said and more.

■ Robert Teff

Robert Teff lives in Lansing, Iowa and is employed at the Interstate Power plant. He married into one of the commercial fishing families that once formed an important part of Lansing's economy. Robert wrote this story for a Lansing writing workshop.

COMMERCIAL FISHING

I'm glad it's Friday and the end of the week. What a drudge. But tomorrow will be different. Tomorrow will be a working holiday because I will be on the river all day with one of the commercial fishing crews. My father-in-law is a commercial fisherman and his brother-in-law is his partner. I go along as often as I can as the river is like a magnet.

Early next morning it's down to the shanty before five and load the boat. We'll need extra tarred nets, for changing, anchor stakes, knitting needles with twine for patching holes, and ice for the fish bin. Also coats, boots, lunch buckets, thermoses, gloves, aprons, and you name it.

It's time to get out on the drink. We climb into the boat, untie and push off into the channel to buck the current with ripples lapping at our sides, the fog and the chilly, damp morning air. The old man huddles at the engine and reaches for his coffee. His partner stands in the bow facing into the wind, as burnt, dark, silent, and rigid as a cigar store Indian. They both have burnt, leathery, and wrinkled skin from their eyes down, as hats protect the top half of their faces. The sun, mirrored off the water, sears everything else in sight. All river men look like this.

The statuesque figure in the bow of the boat only moves his head side to side to catch a shadow on an island, a coon on the beach, a fish jumping. The red hot ember of his cigarette glows at the end of his nose and the hint of tobacco tickles my nose, almost lost in the fog, as I huddle in the bottom of the boat. He moves with every ripple, every movement of the boat as if he is a part of it. It is dark and eerie and we are wrapped in fog as we slip under the bridge and round the corner to come face to face with a ghostly downstream towboat. We deftly veer aside and dodge the monster and steal by as unnoticed to the towboat as a flea on a dog's back. The drone of the engine follows us, never seeming to catch up.

Daybreak explodes on us out of the dark and the fog, and brings us out of our dreams as we slide past the town of De Soto, which is also nearing life. The old man never seems to shut up and no one seems to listen. The words he throws hits the statue, his partner, in the back of the head at the same time that the wind hits his face. They seems to balance him. "No rain today." "Sun will be hot." "Let's get the lower rip rap first." "River's up." "Nets will be full of leaves."

Does anyone hear him besides me? Is he thinking out loud? We're six or seven miles upriver now, and we must be getting close as the statue comes alive and sheds his coat, finds his gloves and apron. The engine slows, and we ease toward the bank: the statue picks up the rope and the grabhook. The old man hollers, "Grab out from the little willow, it's a four gang," meaning there are four nets hooked together in a string. Sure enough, the hook flies and makes a "ker-plunk" as it breaks water. The rope dances in the statue's hands. I prepare to grab whatever comes up first. We grab the lead line ahead of the front net, which makes it easier to land them.

We will have to hand-over-hand our way back to the last net and the anchor rocks. The string of nets sing and vibrate in our hands because of the current and the fish jumping in them. The string of nets with their lines and the rocks tied on behind will stretch out one hundred fifty to two hundred feet. The nets jerk and snap in our hands as the current flows through them and the fish go wild in them.

We get the anchor rocks into the boat, and as the nets break water they shimmer and spray everything in reach. We bring each net into the boat one at a time and fold them flat, pull out the funnel and pour the fish into the bottom of the boat, throwing the net back on the fish bin and bringing in the next one. When all are emptied, we angle the boat at a right angle and back out, beating the nets with a stick and splashing them in the river to clean them as best we can. As the last net goes into the water, we toss in the anchor rocks with a "ker-plunk" and a splash. The rocks insure that the nets will stand up and stay stretched out.

The nets that we are raising today are fyke nets, better known as buffalo nets. The fish have to swim upstream against the current to enter these nets, and once through the funnels they can't get out again. We will raise between ninety and one hundred of these nets today, which are sometimes baited with cheese or soy bean cakes, but we will not be baiting today.

Having dropped the anchor rocks, we run upstream several hundred yards and grab again. As the nets come aboard the old man hollers, "Change the first net, it needs tarring. The third one has a hole in it." So we empty the nets and tie the lead line to the bow of the boat and untie the first net and replace it with a fresh tarred one, roll the pile over and find the one with the hole.

With a couple quick cuts with his knife, the statue has the hole ready for patching, and with flying hands and knitting needle the hole disappears like magic. I have a little trouble doing my job sorting fish, as his movements are almost hypnotic. In sorting fish the little ones and the gamers go overboard and the keepers go into the bin. Grabbing them without getting horned as they flop around splashing slime in your face takes a little practice and patience.

Untying the rope, cleaning the nets, and backing out to lay the nets we hear, "Were the hoops round? Were the funnels straight? Was the license tag still on?" And you guessed it, no response. I learnt a long time ago, when I thought no one heard, not to stick my nose in. Well believe me, they are communicating.

The next gang is trouble. A towboat has nosed into the bank to ride out the fog overnight. Two nets are flattened and the last net, along with the anchor rocks, are gone. They could be out in the middle of the channel or still stuck under the towboat up river somewhere. We ease into the rip rap and find a couple of new rocks, back out, replace the damaged and missing nets, tie on the new rocks, and lay them back out. We make several grabs around to see if we can get lucky and find the missing net, but no luck. Other grabs will be made other days if time allows, and so go the profits.

The old man must have lost his concentration as he has to refer to his trusty book to figure out where the next gang is and how many nets are in it. His book is filled with a series of numbers and symbols that even his partner can't understand. Number of nets, which banks they are located on, and what the marks are. Marks can be trees, rock piles, broken branches, and even spray paint on limbs and leaves. The mark is always at the lead stake and any changes are updated in the book.

All of a sudden he hollers, "Get this 'bleeping' hook all the way across the 'bleeping' river." Silently we nose toward the bank, the hook flies and with a "ker-plunk" and a splash we swing around at the end of the taut rope.

When we finish this net we will have a half to three quarters' mile ride upriver, as this next strip of rip rap belongs to the Gibbs brothers, cousins of the old man. All the established crews have their own territories and spots to fish and everyone respects them, and they guard and care for their spots. It is an unwritten law among them.

So we carefully wash our hands in the river and then wipe them on our slimy clothes. As we run upstream the dinner buckets and thermoses come out for a well deserved snack.

On approaching the next bank I am bored with sorting fish, so I take the grab hook out of the statue's hand. He doesn't seem to resist, but a smile crawls through the wrinkles and across the leathery mask. This goes on till noon and we ease in beside a dead fall, under some branches and lay out our picnic with radio music and weather and all. Weather being the bible of river men on open water.

I not only stay in the middle of the boat, but I am the center of conversation, fielding fish stories, weather, and politics from the old man, and mostly baseball from the statue. But this talk is quite superficial, as we had a hard time concentrating on the subjects with the nature around us. Quack! quack! quack! Some mallards in a pot hole back in the woods are braying at each other like a couple of jack-asses. Then the soft cackle of their feeding call. A phantom goose hooks its way past the tree tops. Then some chattering and scratching on a tree, then silence, only to have that shattered with some barking up that same tree. The squirrel seems to be laughing at us, saying, "Ha! Ha! You didn't get me!" We look around a little and sure enough there he is, peeking through a crotch of the tree at us.

The solitude is usually overwhelming, and then these sounds come at you almost like blaring trumpets. We reluctantly get up to leave when we hear the snort and the crashing of brush. I don't know who is more startled, us or the deer, as all we see is their white flags disappearing through the brush and trees. All this is punctuated by my thermos clattering into the bottom of the boat. Good thing it is a stainless steel one. This causes us to pause an extra moment before we get back to reality and the rest of the day and the job.

The first gang of the afternoon is not only a short gang of two, but also more trouble. An "alien," a "foreigner," a "bleep" has decided to try and take over the spot and has driven his tail stake right down through the lead net. Not only is the air blue, but this guy didn't even have a license tag on the net. And like the tow boat situation earlier, this guy isn't going to find his net either. After repairing the damage and resetting the nets we proceed on. This will not be the last time you are going to hear about that situation either, for that story will be repeated, added to, subtracted form, multiplied and divided over time.

By the middle of the afternoon we sink our last gang, cover the bin, scrub out the boat, rinse it, and bale it out. It is time to relax and enjoy the ride home. The old man listens to the radio and talks to the wind and the statue, and I stretch out on the bow and talk baseball, sports in general, and about the up and coming Fish Days.

It's so peaceful on the river, the engine drones and drowns out a lot of the small sounds like a fish jumping, ducks splashing in the water, a crane flopping overhead, searching for its next meal. There goes a train a mile away along the hill, roaring down the track. Laying lazily on the bow we know the bridge is coming up as we hear cars and trucks whining across the grated floor. Then the busy sounds of town reach us as we run by Main Street, nearing our destination.

After this pleasant ride we ease in alongside the dock at the fish market, which comes alive with activity. We unload our bin into boxes waiting on the dock, sorting the fish for size and kind. The market employees carry the boxes into the market to be weighed. Of course, the b.s. flies, along with all the local gossip. It's a fun time that punctuates the day. We scrub out the fish bin, get a cold drink of water, snitch a sample of the smoked carp, and then slide up the bank to the home port and empty the boat.

This is it for me. I can go home to the wife and kids with a good feeling inside. But for them it's several hours more work getting ready for tomorrow when they will raise wing nets. That will be a bigger job than today's.

I go up the bank on the old wooden stairs and pause at the car to take one last look at the river. Us river rats, born with our feet in the water like the roots of a tree, have it in our veins. I drive on home and kiss the wife and tease the kids and think how much fun it would be to go again tomorrow, but I can't abandon my family again on my only other day off this weekend.

Is the river a magnet? Does it pull and drag at your very heart and soul? I rest my case.

■ Lyle Ernst

For many years Lyle Ernst was a traveling salesman covering Iowa, Wisconsin, and Illinois. He is now a contract freelance feature writer for the Cedar Rapids Gazette *and manager of the Best Western motel in Prairie du Chien, Wisconsin.*

RIVER TOWNS

Before trains and other means of land transportation, rivers were used to transport people and goods. Thus, towns and cities sprang up all along the Mississippi and other rivers. These towns were much tougher than towns further inland. In the early 1800s raft boats were regularly engaged in towing logs down the Mississippi. The raftsmen who steered these boats were tough and hard. They were feared by the local citizens, and most were of the opinion that "a raftsman would just as soon stab you as look at you." The riverfront dives in these towns were basically brothels, containing thieves, bullies, and crooked gamblers.

My home town, Bellevue, Iowa, population 2,000, is a good example. In the late 1800s the owner of the local hotel was involved in all types of illegal activities, including cattle rustling. He and his gang pretty much ran the town as he saw fit. The county sheriff was having a problem getting the "goods" on this "upstanding" citizen.

Finally, things got to the point where the sheriff deputized a couple dozen men and informed the gang that they would have to leave town or be arrested. The gang holed up in their leader's hotel and a shootout began. When it was over a couple of the bad guys were dead and the remainder were tied to a raft and sent down river with instructions never to come back.

As a youngster I remember Bellevue being a rough and tumble town. Saturday was the day most people came to town to socialize, which for the men usually meant spending the day and night at one of the local taverns. My father enjoyed this type of socializing, so my mother and I would attend the Saturday night feature at the local movie theater. One night I was witness to an incident involving my uncle, who was the Bellevue chief of police. There was a man named Buck who was big and mean and lived by himself somewhere in the hills. Once a month he would come to town to raise Cain. He would always get into fights and beat people up. Sometimes he would be arrested and other times not. I don't know what started the ruckus, but I remember he and my uncle fighting in the middle of main street. Uncle Elmer was a little man, about five foot six inches tall. The part I remember is Uncle Elmer hitting Buck with his billy club, causing the big man to fall to his knees. Buck would get up and pound on Uncle Elmer with his fists. Then Uncle Elmer would rap Buck again with his billy club, and Buck would sink to his knees, then get up again and pound on Uncle Elmer some more. This went on for quite some time, with both men becoming quite bloody. The best I can remember is that Buck went to jail and my uncle went to the hospital.

I also remember three tough and hard rivermen who were brothers. They would be around town for awhile and then would disappear, only to reappear a year or two later. I recall people saying that they had served time in prison for burning down someone's house, after beating them up.

The oldest and biggest of the three was named Bill. He was also the only one who was cordial. He was much more easy going that the others, but at the same time had enormous strength. They hung out in bars most of the time, and Bill's favorite thing was to bet someone a beer that he could bend a bar stool with his hands. He always won the bet. I saw him do it once and was truly amazed at his strength. He also could pick up the rear end of a car.

The middle brother, named Ray, had a very surly attitude and was not friendly to anyone. I was scared of him as were many other people in town. If my memory serves me correctly, years later I heard that he had murdered someone and was given a life sentence in prison.

The youngest brother, Joey, was a little guy with an attitude problem. He was a loudmouth who often caused fights. He always wore a belt with a big metal buckle on the front of it. When a fight got going he would wrap the belt around his fist with the buckle protruding from it. A punch from him could do a tremendous amount of damage to a man's face.

One Saturday afternoon I was having a Coke and visiting with Bill when Joey started yelling and cursing at someone at the other end of the bar. The atmosphere became more and more tense. After a few more exchanges Joey whipped off his belt and began to wrap it around his fist. Without saying a word, Bill took one step, picked Joey up and threw him all the way across the room, slamming him against the wall. Joey got up very slowly and quietly put his belt back on.

In the 1920s and 1930s bootlegging was common in all the river towns. My father would relate stories of being recruited to "run" moonshine at the tender age of thirteen. He was young and adventurous and especially enjoyed driving the moonshiners' brand new Dodge automobile.

In the twenties and thirties hunters and fishermen built cabins on the many islands that dotted the Mississippi across from Lansing, Iowa, located in the extreme northeastern part of the state. Some of these cabins were used as permanent residences, and many of the people living in them built stills for making moonshine. The stills were not a big secret to anyone, including law enforcement officials, who did nothing about them. They knew that people needed to make a living. Something the law enforcement people may not have known is that much of the illegal booze was sold to the infamous

Chicago gangster, Al Capone. There would be a phone call to someone in Lansing and later that night, long after midnight, a boat loaded with metal containers of booze would make its way to the Wisconsin side of the river where it would be picked up by Capone's men for delivery to Chicago.

Lansing also had another connection with Chicago. One of the local doctors patched up gangsters wounded in gun battles in the city.

River towns were known for fighting and Lansing was no exception. There were fights every Saturday night in one or more of the bars. Some fought just for the sake of fighting, but mostly it was to settle an argument. Many times, after the fight was over, the participants would have a drink together.

There were also loosely organized boxing and wrestling matches, with each town having its own champion. Fighters would come from other towns to take on the local champ. One of Lansing's town champions was also a policeman.

Some of the bars in river towns are still rough and tough places to go. There is one in particular in Lansing that has had its share of fights. One Saturday night last summer the place was buzzing with activity. There were many patrons from out of town and as the night wore on, things became tense. Joe and Bill were shooting pool when one of the guys from another town said to Joe, "You look familiar. I think I remember you from last year. You made some nasty remarks about my girlfriend." He then punched Joe in the face. Shortly, there were three and four guys pounding on Joe, so Bill joined the fracas. Sherry, Bill's girlfriend, got up on a table and jumped on the back of one of the guys, beating him on the head. Sherry is no bigger than a peanut, but she held her own. Someone yelled, "The cops are coming!" Sherry, Bill, and Joe ran out the door and drove away before the cops got there.

Another time, in the same tavern, a woman was sitting at the bar drinking while reading a book about vampires. Suddenly she clamped her teeth onto the arm of a woman seated next to her. The woman she bit was screaming, but to no avail. The "vampire woman" would not let loose of her arm. The police were called, and after some difficulty, managed to get the situation under control, and take the "vampire woman" into custody.

Fifteen miles south of Lansing lies Harper's Ferry, also a tough little river town. About a dozen years ago, the body of a man was found inside his boat, which was drifting aimlessly in the backwaters of the Mississippi. There were two bullet holes in his back. The county held an inquest at which it was determined that the man died from an act of foul play. Many citizens of the area claimed to know who the murderer was, but no arrest was ever made. Some of the townsfolk were of the opinion that "things" happen when someone steals fish from another man's net.

The biggest drawback to living in Lansing and the other little river towns is the lack of decent paying jobs. This area is near the bottom for per capita earnings in the state of Iowa, while being rated one of the highest for alcohol abuse in the entire United States. Low income and alcohol consumption always seem to go together. Many of the high school graduates, either because of a lack of ambition and/or money, settle for low-paying jobs and entertain themselves by drinking alcoholic beverages, mainly beer. They begin drinking beer at the ages of thirteen and fourteen.

On Friday night Main Street, Lansing is parked full of pickup trucks and four-wheel drive vehicles, most of whose owners are in the bars spending their hard-earned money. These are some of the same people who come into the convenience store (where I work) on the following Thursday and make their purchases with quarters and dimes while anxiously awaiting payday.

There is a tremendous amount of money spent on lottery tickets in this little town. Too many residents think this will be their escape. One woman, who drives a rusty, beat up car, buys lottery tickets on a daily basis, sometimes spending as much as twenty dollars. In addition, she buys cigarettes. One day her little boy was with her and said, "Mom, can I have a treat?" She answered, "No, shut up and go to the car." She then proceeded to buy more lottery tickets.

Social workers and counselors are kept busy in this area of the country. There are many low income people with drinking and drug problems along with the unemployed. According to these professionals, there are an inordinate number of persons with mental problems.

It appears to me that most of these people are merely existing, instead of living. Apparently, they have given up hope of a better life. It makes me sad.

■ *Ken Jones*

Ken Jones teaches biology at Dyersburg State College in Dyersburg, Tennessee and spends his summers on the Mississippi River. He is also a freelance journalist.

MY MISSISSIPPI MISTRESS

I have had a love affair with the Mississippi River for most of my life. It really started as a sort of puppy love when as a member of a Boy Scout troop I first camped along her banks. Later, as an adolescent, I duck hunted in her backwaters, fished in her oxbow lakes, and camped on her sandbars. As an adult I tried to leave her. I went west for graduate studies in wildlife biology and had a brief love affair with the gorgeous canyon lands, mountains, and deserts of the American Southwest. Of course, I eventually returned to my roots, and my river, the mighty Mississippi.

My hometown, Dyersburg, Tennessee, is not exactly a river town, since it is not located directly on the river's bank. But it is within about fifteen miles as the crow flies on the nearest high ground. This high ground is actually wind blown dust and silt (called "loess" by geologists) that accumulated over the last hundred thousand or so years. Left over by receding glaciers of the Pleistocene, this silt was blown eastward to form massive dune fields all along the river's eastern bank from Illinois to the state of Mississippi. It's on these islands of loess that most towns of any significance are located because all the flat and low ground is in the floor plain, the Delta.

This rich, alluvial soil makes great farmland but poor town sites because of the occasional high water that inundates it seasonally. Even with all our levees, dams, and other floor control structures, mostly built in the last fifty years following the big flood of 1927, the mighty Mississippi still gets rowdy! The recent flood of 1993 proved that no river can ever be completely controlled, as the folks along the upper river can surely testify.

We call this flat land, from Cairo, Illinois south to the gulf, the Delta. This is really a misnomer. It's really the floodplain, as a delta is really defined as the fan shaped deposition formed at a river's mouth, in this case, just south of New Orleans, Louisiana. But because this floodplain is so fertile and productive an agricultural resource, it continues to demand our attention as we attempt to control one of the world's great drainage systems, the Mississippi Valley.

I fell in love with this region, and more precisely the river herself, because she was then and still is a wild and untamable mistress. In times of low water she provides more wilderness area along her course than all the rest of the parks and preserves designated as such in the entire eastern United States. Huge sand and gravel bars, islands forested in bottomland hardwoods, sloughs and inlets, old oxbow lakes, all combine to form an immense region of unique riparian habitats. And it changes constantly.

A favorite summer swimming and fishing hole may be completely destroyed in one flood, and another one created a few miles downstream. On the outside bends where the river cuts and erodes, her currents will consume whole forests, fields, and—sometimes—communities, while just a mile or so away on the opposite bank, new land will accumulate, forming a point bar, soon followed with the vegetation of natural succession. This meandering is characteristic of all old flood plain rivers.

Along with her meanderings, come her changes of mood. At low water she's seductive, a kind and loving stream, free of the debris and silt that normally muddy her waters. At high water she is treacherous with currents in excess of ten knots, with whirlpools and suckholes capable of sinking small boats, with floating logs and newly uprooted trees, with hidden rock dikes, pilings, sunken barges and other hidden hazards to navigation. A river in flood, large or small, is nothing to trifle with. Only with due respect and thorough knowledge of her ways should any pilot ply her waters.

I have spent close to twenty years cruising her length from St. Louis south to the Gulf. I have yet to get intimate with the upper river, because above St. Louis the river ceases to exist. It has been tamed, it has been destroyed. It is no longer a river. Locks and dams hold her back to form twenty-seven lakes upstream that make commercial tow navigation possible. When you dam a river she loses her sex appeal. No longer a moving, constantly changing force of nature, a damned river is a river no more. Lakes are okay, but they attract marinas, shoreline development, home sites, jet skis, bass boats and all the other common trappings of civilization. Who wants to share their mistress with the rest of humanity? I am a selfish lover, but that is why the lower river won my heart. It is one of the most hidden, overlooked, natural resources in our country, partly because it is feared and misunderstood, but mainly because it is simply inaccessible.

THE DELTA

■ *Marjorie White*

Midge White lives with her husband, Zeb, in Hammond, Louisiana. She is an accomplished artist with many drawings of the Delta done during the early forties to accompany these letters.

CARTHAGE, BOOMTOWN

Carthage, Miss.
September 12, 1940
Dearest Mom and Dad:

At long last we are in Carthage, the place at the end of our journey that we have been looking forward to and dreading for a week or more. It seems that every small town that we have come through in Mississippi has looked worse than the last, with ugly unpainted houses and stores hugging the gravel roads. It is hot, the roads are dusty and bumpy, and we are tired out from the three-day trip in our little Ford. "Well," we thought in some relief as we scanned the little white one-storied houses, the new courthouse, and the new imposing post office, "at least this town has some pretty houses and a bit of prosperity. We should be able to find a decent place to stay." There was the square with the courthouse in the center with an array of stores on all sides and a new Coca-Cola bottling plant on one corner. We would explore the town later, but the first thing we had to do was to drive back out to the edge of town to the logging camp where the office was located.

So in the heat of the afternoon, with all our boxes, bundles, and luggage still jouncing about in the back, we started back the way we had come to see what we should do next. A logging camp was an entirely new experience for me, and I was much excited to see the logging trucks piled high with immense logs, bigger than any I had ever seen, tearing down the road, followed by billowing clouds of dust. The camp was huddled in among incredibly tall pines. Little board shacks clustered around the large, rambling commissary. The sawmill was in back, out of our immediate sight, but I could hear the whine of the saws, the humming and the buzzing of the machinery and the grinding of the trucks as they brought in new loads of logs to feed the saws.

I waited in the shade of the commissary porch while Zeb went into the office to check in and ask what we should do next. At long last one of the timber cruisers came out with Zeb to ride into town with us and show us where to go. We passed the little new house that he and his wife were staying in, then he pointed out to us an ugly sagging and unpainted structure set ghoulishly behind two waving trees and rank, weedy grass trying to grow alongside the wooden steps.

"There's your room on the second floor corner," he said, and my heart did a double flip into the pit of my stomach. There was nothing to do but try to be stoical about it since this was it—the end of our journey. Out came a colored man to carry in piece by piece our various goods and chattels. We were led into the barnlike interior with plank walls and up a flight of stairs patched with pieces of old linoleum and smelling of kerosene to a bare upper hall and into our immense corner room. There were three huge windows with dirty shades, walls with stained and peeling wallpaper, and a board floor. There were three large double beds, all of different sizes, with lumpy covers, a boarded-up fireplace, and a light bulb hanging from the ceiling by a piece of wire. In one corner were a few cigarette stubs and an empty Coca-Cola bottle left by the former occupant.

To say I was horrified would be to underestimate the shock. As our paraphernalia was brought up the stairs, all I could think of was to escape from there. Not till a while later did I realize that this was the only hotel in town, and that we were in the annex. As for a bath, there was one down at the end of the hall to be shared with everyone else on the floor. Each had to wait his turn at the end of a long, hot day.

Meals were eaten in the main part of the hotel next door: a building older but no better than the annex. In the dining room there was one large table with all manner of dishes: fried chicken, tomatoes, stew, rice, cold biscuits, vegetables, canned fruit, corn bread, iced tea, milk, all presided over by a funny, little old woman with white hair and big horn-rimmed spectacles, who ran about passing out the food. Everyone sat down together, roadworkers and timber cruisers, girls and women and children, and doctors and merchants eating practically in silence. The thing to do was to eat as quickly as possible and then get out to the porch, there to watch the life of the town, people going by the filling station across the street or in and out of the pool hall on the corner.

The next morning I started out to try to find us a place to live for the few weeks we will be in Carthage. To my dismay the oil people and the road workers had come before and all the boarding houses and the like were full. At last, on the third day of hunting, we found satisfactory room and board with the Baptist preacher, Brother Bragg, and his family. We lost no time moving in that very night.

I'll tell you more later. Hugs, Midge

Carthage, Miss.
September 14, 1940
Dearest Mom and Pop:

You will die to hear that we are residing in the home of a Baptist preacher and his wife. She is quite young with two small children—a boy and a girl—and calls her husband Brother Bragg in the good old Baptist way. We stayed in that hotel for two nights and believe me that was two nights too many for me. This was the only decent spot I could find for us, and it's pretty good. Surrounded by their families, pastors seem to be no different than any other of the citizenry. In fact, Brother Bragg is quite a good egg, we find. It was difficult at first to understand his southern language, but I am gradually getting the hang of it. On Sunday we had to go to both Sunday school and church, and that Sunday school was the biggest farce I ever attended. The church is tiny, not even as big as the chapel at Eastern Point and is practically in the back yard.

Brother Bragg has a herd of eight goats that nibble in the space between the church and house and what he does with the goat's milk is more than I have figured out. Anyhow, it is pretty chummy: us and the Baptists and the goats all together in one big, happy family.

We went over to Canton the other evening with a couple of the boys who are working with Zeb. Canton is the town where we will stay in a week or two, and we are looking forward to the move because Canton looks like a bigger and better town. Carthage is very small: a boom town with a logging mill and sawmill, road builders, oil crews, Indians, and black folks all over the place. I have been out on several roads—they are all gravel or dirt—to sketch the scenes. The houses are a revelation to me, nothing but shacks and logs cabins with mud chimneys and an occasional weather-beaten bungalow. In the doorway of one of the cabins that I saw yesterday there were no less than five kids, with two more in the yard. There doesn't seem to be much difference in the living conditions between white and colored in the country, and such poor land. It's disheartening to see the aridity and erosion after the prosperity of the Ohio farms. Here each homesite has only one patch of cotton and one of dry looking corn.

On Sunday afternoon one of the boys who works for the company and his wife took us out to see some truly virgin timber. Never have I seen such huge pines as towered above us for at least a hundred feet and more. There were acres and miles of it. The timber is gorgeous. We have seen some cypress trees but no Spanish moss yet. The rivers are muddy and winding with pure white sand banks at each bend. The sloughs have cypress knees sticking up out of the brown water.

Well, Zeb is due to come in from the day's timber cruising pretty soon and roar into the bathtub leaving behind wet boots, frayed hat, pants full of red clay, and a shirt the worse for grime and briar holes. The guys sure do cover some rough territory in a day. Initiation into Mississippi timber cruising is making him wade through the Pearl River bottoms in water up to his waist in some places. We will have to have typhoid shots this week although the water here is pure and very good, but we may run into some bad water out in the hinterland somewhere, no telling. Well, it's time to quit and send our love. Write to us at Box 421, Carthage, Miss.

Hugs to you,
Midge.

Zeb adds his to the above letter:

Midge has expressed my sentiments exactly. She has written a swell letter. We were certainly relieved to get out of our hotel room and are enjoying it very much here with Brother Bragg, et al.

Pomeroy, one of the bosses, was here to see us this evening and admired Midge's art work very much. She has done some wonderful pencil sketches this past week, mostly old country cabins and landscapes. Pomeroy will be here for a couple of days, and we should have some enlightening conversations. My stay here in Mississippi is indefinite, meaning a month or perhaps three, I don't know, but it won't do us any harm to get an insight into the living habits of the people in this section, which seems to be one of the poorest we have seen. As Midge says, it is a intensely interesting to say the least.

I need art supplies to keep Midge busy at her observations, since she isn't able to get them here. Could you please send us a dozen or so sheets of tinted paper, some pastel paper, and watercolor paper, lithograph crayon, etc.? I will send a money order for it in the mail. Much thanks.

Love, Zeb

Carthage, Miss.
September 18, 1940
Dearest Mom and Dad:

Our landlady, Mrs. Bragg, has introduced me to a man named Lundy. He is a timeless old Negro with a battered hat and patched-up blue denim clothes. Some say his father and mother had been slaves before the war, but no one knows how old Lundy is. He mows lawns and tends yards for some of the more charitable people of Carthage. He carries an old burlap bag bulging with unseen booty wherever he goes. Anything that might in any way be used for his house—some outcast, rusty, or wornout object—goes into Lundy's sack. The little children believe that Lundy carries bad little boys and girls in the sack, and they look at him with fearful eyes.

One afternoon Mrs. Bragg and Miss Maggie Lee took me out in the country to see his house. I was all for doing a sketch of him, but when they suggested it, he refused with vehemence to let anyone draw his picture.

"No, suh! What anyone want with mah picha? Ah don want none of it!"

So when we again drove out the dusty road to his house, I smuggled in a sketch pad and some pencils.

Up on a high bank squatting in the shade of a tall pine forest, and hidden from the road, was Lundy's fortress. Lundy himself was laboriously sawing wood by the edge of the pines. He looked up impassively at us. "Yassuh, you can go in ef y'want to." He wasn't going to talk much to white folks. A rusty corrugated iron stockade with a gate, complete with someone's discarded lock, was the welcoming note. After entrance to the first areaway was granted there was another gate through a fence of closely bound saplings. This second gate was made of odds and ends of boards crudely nailed together and secured from marauders by a long wire wrapped around some nails.

Inside this gate was a corrugated tin lean-to with a few broken-down chairs and odd pieces of lumber under its roof. The whole thing sat upon a bit of bare, hard clay. This was sort of a summer house, but we weren't sure what it's purpose is. This space is enclosed with various kinds of fence strung together.

Yet another gateway with a different and more ingenious lock (held in place by wire and a rusty chain) led at last into Lundy's garden and house. Such an intricate maze! Lundy seems to be taking no chances with any thieves that might be lurking on that lonely road. I was startled and inclined to laughter to see his humble little abode. Made entirely of bits of cast off lumber and sheets of tin pieced together in a haphazard manner, it stood on a patch of dry clay soil surrounded by his flower garden. In spite of the weird building materials, the lines of his simple shack has some picturesque charm. A wide window set in mud and stone took up one side. Another was taken up by a low doorway and windows with tiny panes. Next to the door, secured by a long piece of chain nailed to the wall, was a chair that might once have been fastened to the floor of a school-house. In the garden grew a bit of crepe myrtle, a few rose bushes, some vines, and a few native flowers.

Of course we had to sneak in and see the inside. It was dark as pitch, with no windows except in the little entryway, but gradually I began to see the fireplace and the mantel which must have been salvaged from a derelict home in the nearby countryside. There was an iron bed in the middle of the room festooned with garments hanging from the ceiling on hangers. Women's dresses and Sunday-go-to-meeting suits, trousers, and some odd britches. In the back was a wee room, sort of a porch or kitchen, though all of the cook-ing was evidently done over the open fireplace.

Miss Maggie Lee went out to keep Lundy busy in conversation while I quickly began to scribble in the outlines of the house and jot down all I possibly could on paper while the time went by and they began to signal frantically for me to come out or surely Lundy would think something was queer. Then, while they talked to him, I man-aged to hide my pad behind a convenient fence and sketch him as he sat with his back turned, smoking his pipe in the late sun.

"I didn't know you had a woman, Lundy. I thought you didn't like women," said Mrs. Bragg.

"Sho, I laks women as well as the next one. Always did lak a woman," he returned.

But we couldn't get much out of him. He was too distant, so long as there were strangers present, and I was a strange white woman. Now I have the little drawings to remind me in years to come of the day when we had a peek into the life of that colorful old Negro man on a hot and sunny afternoon in September in Mississippi.

Hugs to you, Midge

Carthage, Miss.
September 21, 1940
Dear Mom and Dad:

Mrs. Bragg has taken me to lots of the doings hereabout to give me a slant on their way of life. I have attended her Culture Club and some Baptist get-togethers. One of the Baptist things was held at a country church some miles south of Carthage. We traveled there with some friends of hers who gave me a few scary moments as we nearly side-swiped a large logging truck as we careened over a narrow wooden bridge on one of the gravel roads. They said, "Not to worry, we are all good Baptist ladies." I think it was the Mission Society with lunch served in the pews—many talks by various ones— me doing a chalk drawing—prayers by the dames and money-wringing by a shoutingly eloquent woman executive. I really got quite an education into country churching that day.

We have been fishing for white perch in the Pearl River. Zeb came in early the other afternoon so we decided to go exploring. We took some of the boys in the crew down south of town to dangle out minnows in the Mississippi mud. We latched onto a little narrow boat that was there on the bank. There were five of us trying to balance ourselves in it as we paddled against the current with a sawed-off barrel stave. Zeb caught one, we caught none. Very peaceful, however, and beautiful to drift around between the gleaming white sandbars and the cypress knees snagging our hooks on invisible flotsam and jetsam every now and then.

The other night we did a fun thing. We were invited to go dancing out in the boonies on a bridge that went nowhere. So off we went on a brand new blacktop road till we came to a long cement bridge over a creek. Out we piled in the moonlight and pranced around in the middle of the wide new highway to tunes from a portable phonograph. An amazingly slight amount of traffic passed, and we had a lovely time out in the wide open spaces under the tall pines and the full moon.

Keep well. Love, Midge

Carthage, Miss.
Sept. 24, 1940
Dearest Mom and Pop:

The paper, pads, and all other supplies arrived yesterday. A million thanks for going to all the trouble of getting and sending them for me. I am most grateful.

This is the first rainy day since we arrived here in Carthage, and how we do welcome it! The dust from all the roads has been like a heavy fog every time a jalopy goes by. We went over to Canton last Monday to apartment search because we will be moving there soon. The Denkmann Lumber Company, for which Pomeroy and McGowin are now cruising thousands of acres of timber, has its main office and mill in Canton and owns land for miles around between here and there and on both sides of the Pearl River. Canton is, at the moment, the new boom town, with people flocking there to discover oil. They have a number of new oil wells, and now they claim the boom is on the wane. So it was frustrating to try to find a decent apartment there. After looking over many pretty hopeless, even smelly or musty places about in the same category as the awful Carthage hotel, we finally took one in a fairly new duplex with a young landlady about our age. That should be good, and will be only for a few months, anyway.

We'll let you know what happens. Love, Midge

Carthage, Miss.
October 9, 1940
Dearest Mom and Pop:

Mrs. Bragg wouldn't allow me to leave Carthage without doing a large Santa Claus for her roof at Christmas time. So, in the middle of September the citizens of Carthage were surprised out of their boots to see a huge Santa and reindeer emerging from a cardboard mattress carton on the front porch of Brother Bragg's residence. Mrs. Bragg called in all her neighbors, who make up nearly the whole population of the town, to show them what was to be her prize-winning surprise in December. Honestly, that woman is a human riot and Brother Bragg leads her a close second. They have invited us back for Thanksgiving dinner with a wild turkey, if the preacher manages to bag one on one of his wild game forays. It seems to me that the guy does nothing all day but fish or hunt. What a life! He claims to be a vegetarian but isn't above eating bear meat, as he has told us all about going hunting for bear in the surrounding wild land.

One time he told us about driving with his young daughter on a gravel road near Walnut Hill and was stuck behind a logging truck spewing out clouds of red dust. The men riding in the truck bed behind the cab were getting a big laugh at his discomfort until he reached into his glove compartment for his big .45 pistol and pointed it at them from his side window. The riders got the message to their driver in a big hurry and Brother Bragg wheeled on by.

It has been perfect weather, and since we have been in Mississippi it has rained only two days. So I have been going out into the highways and byways quite often with brush and pencil. I'm becoming used to the sight of cotton everywhere, as I did the corn in Ohio. I should send you a picture of cotton wagons going to the cotton gin across the street. There seems to be one every few minutes lumbering along, drawn by two mules and usually driven by a sleepy black man sitting on the white fluff piled up over the tops of the wagons.

The black folks take along a few straight-back chairs from their cabins and travel to town on Sattidy evenings sitting in the back of their buckboards. There they hitch up their mules on the square where all the action takes place. One in particular caught my fancy, and I have been working on it because it had the whole family sitting in the wagon and made a typical scene of life in the town that I would like to remember.

I will write from Canton. Love, Midge

■ *Christopher Crawford*

Chris Crawford hailed from West Helena, Arkansas, where this story takes place. I have little doubt that it is based on a man whom Chris knew from time spent at a juke joint similar, if not identical, to Hot's. Chris wrote the first part of this story at MATTHEW 25.

LUCKY LACEY

Lacey, for the benefit of those who don't know him, was the town drunk. But Lacey was not your average wino. No, Lacey had been blessed with the gift of song and dance. I don't know where he was from, but it must have been a swinging place, because Lacey was a cat, a cool jerk so to speak.

Hot was an old guy who owned a juke joint that most of us used to hang out in. Old Man Hot would put a quarter in the juke box and play some of those down home blues that Lacey loved so well. In fact, Lacey's favorite part of Hot's was the juke box. That's where he lived from sun up to sun down.

Slime was a friend of mine who loved to imitate Michael Jackson. He was crazy. And Christopher was the one guy Lacey would talk to sober or drunk. For some reason Lacey trusted him. So the music started, and away Lacey would go, spinning, turning, and twisting. Now the only thing that was different about this wino is that he could do all this with a fifth of redeye, and not spill a drop.

It goes without saying that to Christopher and Slime this was totally amazing. So amazing that Slime started imitating Lacey. (See, I told you he was crazy!) Old Man Hot found it unbearable to see a sixty-five-year-old drunk acting this way. But as I said in the beginning, Lacey was far from the denture-grip, rubbing-alcohol, and rocking chair kind. No indeed, Lacey was a rocker without the chair. As a matter of fact, there might have been a few moves Michael Jackson might have stolen from him.

"Set yo old drunk butt down sumwhere, Lacey!" Old Man Hot shouted. "Hell! You want to dance sumwhere, go on Soul Train and get the hell outta here!"

"I's dances wheres I's pleases!" Lacey roared back. "Besides, it's my money you're spanning in that old raggedy juke box anyhow's!" He was still holding that fifth of redeye in his hand, as if it were the

"S" on Superman's chest. Boy, what a fifth of redeye will do to some people!

You see, Hot's Cafe meant a lot to the people of West Helena, Arkansas, a small town right across the bridge from the Mississippi state line. Hot's was a place where the blue collar worker making $3.35 an hour could go to unwind and forget about the bills he or she wasn't making enough money to pay. Hot's didn't have a liquor license, so most people would go across the street to Alp's Liquor Store and buy it, then come back to Hot's and drink it.

Now Hot's was your classic juke joint. The ceiling hung low, there were two little gas heaters that kept you warm in the winter, one big five-foot fan that kept you cool in the summer, and two pool tables that worked when they felt like it. The floor was solid unfinished concrete and cracked in some places. The seats were plywood benches. If you weren't careful, you could almost bet that your old lady would get a splinter in her fanny before the night was over.

The average wino you picture in your mind is smelly and dirty, with raggedy clothes and shoes holier than a Reverend Ike sermon. But that was not the case with Lucky Lacey. Lacey smelled, but like Wild Irish Rose (old redeye wine). He wore sweetwater pants with pleats and brogan shoes, spit shined. A sort of George Michael Beard with his hat turned either sideways or backwards. Christopher and Slime used to run straight from school to Hot's to hear the juke box blast and to see Lacey, the Fred Astaire of winos, dance.

Now you can take this rumor with a grain of salt; I mean it's up to you. But it was said that the first paycheck on the one job Lacey ever had, was consumed by a case of redeye. The rest was spent on Hot's juke box. Now Lacey was a brick mason and averaged anywhere from ten to twelve dollars an hour, so he wasn't playing with chump change. That day he must have danced twenty-four hours non-stop. I know if I'd spent that much money I'd still be dancing today.

"Oooowww! Sang that song, baby!" he'd scream at the top of his voice.

"Now that's some sanging you's young jittybugs don'ts knows nothing about," Lacey said as he turned up his third fifth of redeye.

"Why hell, when I use to sing with B. B. King, Bobby Blue Bland, Little Milton and Z. Z. Hill, man, I use to pull all kind of women!" The lies would ooze out of Lacey's lips.

We didn't mind listening to his pipe dreams: it kept him young and us out of mischief. "Back in fifty-seven and forty-seven . . . . Hell, but y'all don't remember them daze. Hell, you wasn't even bone then," Lacey continued. "Man, times was so hard then that if we'd a had food stamps we'd a ate them too! I used to drive a Rolly Royce with two t.v.'s inside the glove box, a.m. & f.m. radio, cassette player with t.v. dinner, four speakers in the dash, four under the hood, five in the backseat, and a pool table in the trunk."

Now I don't know about you, but even though I may not have been born back then in fifty-seven and forty-seven I do know that they didn't even make remote control cars with all that in them.

"Lacey, you ain't got long to live telling all them damn lies to them kids!" Old Man Hot rudely interrupted.

"Hot, if I was twenty years younger I swear I'd get up from here and . . . and . . . and . . . "

"And you'd what?" Old Man Hot shouted.

"Hell if I know, Hot. You just gonna have to wait till I'm twenty years younger and finds out," Lacey chuckled.

Yeah, Lacey was a character all right. Maybe that was the reason Christopher and Slime dug him so much, because in his own right Lacey was a rebel. He said what he felt and what was on his mind, to anybody. You know, there's a saying that goes, "If you don't stand for something you'll fall for anything."

Lacey was no newcomer to saying what he felt was right. He'd been through four decades of injustices. He'd been run out of his hometown of Dumas, Arkansas at the age of twelve for spitting on the sidewalk. He'd had the police dogs turned loose on him for failing to give information to the whereabouts of a friend who stole apples out of farmer Jack's orchard. He'd been beaten on his head so many times by a billy club he couldn't wear a hat for years.

He also had the water turned on, and I don't mean because he paid his bill. I mean water hoses. He marched in a couple of Martin Luther King's nonviolent marches. "A pause for the cause," he called them. He was in and out of the county jail so much that the guards and the judge thought of letting him run for captain of police. I mean, what could they lose, right?

But with all that in his favor, Lacey never touched a drop until Amos and Andy were cancelled. But those are the breaks.

∽

It was six a.m., and a hot, very hot morning. Instead of being awakened by alarm clocks, the residents of West Helena were awakened by slapping themselves in the face and everywhere else mosquitos were feasting on their bodies. It was the middle of summer, and the sun wasn't even out yet, but the people knew one thing, that when it did come there would be nowhere to run and nowhere to hide.

A broom swept drearily across the floor of Hot's Cafe to remove all evidence of the good times that were had the night before. Ms. Bea, Old Man Hot's wife, was doing the honors of cleaning the cafe, and as usual was swearing her head off. "I git so damn tired of these lazy, nasty-ass niggers breaking bottles and fighting in here I could shoot every bastard an' his mammy without a second thought," she mumbled to herself. "Hell, I done told Hot a thousand times we ought to close dis damn place and let the bastards drank in the streets and be picked up for public drunk."

Christopher and Slime were neatly tucked away in a corner somewhere laughing their heads off while Ms. Bea continued the x-rated conversation with herself. "But tat's all right. One of these here days they gone wake up and dis place gone be up in goddamn smoke!" she swore.

"Well, as long as you's wake me up 'fore the fire start I's be fine, Bea," Lacey answered back crazily. Almost shocked to death by his voice, Ms. Bea turned and looked and there was Lacey, waking up from a good night's drunk inside the men's toilet. And as stinky and smelly as it was, I guess you'd have to drink a lot of redeye (like three or four gallons) to fall asleep on the floor.

"If you don't git yo' wine drinking ass out of here, I swear fore living God I'm gone kill yo' black ass!" Ms. Bea threatened. And boy, she took that broom and chased him all over the place. And you know, for a seventy-five-year-old woman she wasn't half bad as a sprinter. She chased him out her back door to Alp's front door, and for Lacey the merry-go-round was off and running again.

One night Lacey was standing near his next of kin (the juke box), hollering and screaming with the music as usual, when a weird thing happened. This slow song came on and it just stopped Lacey in his tracks. It was the kind of reaction that you get in the middle of your birthday party when someone tells you your mother just died.

"Goddammit Bea, I thought you took dat damn song off the juke box!" Lacey said with a touch of hatred in his voice.

"You don't pay the damn bills here, wino," Ms. Bea replied. "So sat down and shut up before I cave yo' skull in."

And sit down he did. You see, this certain song, a slow song, told the story of a man who had had it and lost it all—wife, job, car, house, etcetera. Slime and Christopher had never seen him this way before. It was a side of Lacey that no one had ever seen before. The song struck a nerve in Lacey that hurt him more than if Alp's had gone bankrupt. As he sat there lost in himself, his joyful smile turned into a frown, his eyes saddened and tears big enough to choke a horse rolled down his cheeks.

I never found out exactly what meaning the song had for him, and I didn't bother to ask. You see, even misfits like Lacey are entitled to their privacy, don't you think?

After that night no one saw or heard from Lacey for months. Christopher and Slime started worrying about what had happened to the slap-happy wino who made their day—and nights as well. For some reason Hot's just wasn't the same any more. To Christopher and Slime, leaving school and going to Hot's to watch Lacey was like going to Wimbley Stadium to see Michael Jackson perform Billie Jean in the raw. If no other people on Earth took Lacey seriously, these two kids did. Where could he have gone? Did he leave town? Did he go back to jail? Did he get so pissed that he swore to himself never to come back to Hot's again? Or maybe, God forbid, please don't let it be true, loveable Lucky Lacey was dead?

Part II

Somewhere in the chill of a cold and frosty dark night, Christopher and Slime stand face to face between two shotgun shacks. Between them is a half bottle of T-bird wine, which they use as a blanket to shield themselves from Mother Nature's punishment. It is the middle of winter and God bless those without a coat. The boys are in conference with their favorite joy juice, and are already lit up like two Christmas trees. They are almost at at the bottom of the bottle when . . . .

"Damn, Slime! Are you gonna sit there and hatch the bottle and hope it has twins or something?" Chris asks in disgust.

"Yeah, that would be great," says Slime. "Hell, then I wouldn't have to hear dis song and dance you givin' me."

"Well, until you sprout wings and your feet fit a tree limb, let's jus' play football wit it," Chris replies.

"Football?!!" says Slime.

"Yeah. You be the quarterback and I'll be the fullback and you hand off the damn bottle so I can make it touch down the back of my throat," Chris sarcastically replies.

Although this is a very exciting moment in the history of West Helena, Arkansas, let us get back on the beaten path to the highlight of this story. First of all, Lacey is still missing, and those two would-be detectives are, believe it or not, still hot on his trail. (Another prime example of mixing business with pleasure.)

Lacey had been staying at a five-dollar-a-month rooming house and managed to get five hundred dollars behind in back rent. Don't even bother trying to figure this one out, only his local liquor store owner knows for sure. The rooming house was really a flop house for winos with a check coming in every month, and for women who chose to make a living on their backs. It was run by Big Erma, who was Lucky Lacey's ex-wife, which might explain his rent problem.

Big Erma is five feet, nine inches tall, two hundred fifty pounds, and cockeyed, which might explain his drinking problem. But all in all she had a heart as big as a whale. Lacey, as I said before, was a brick mason (one of the best in Phillips County) and in his day had made enough money to own a ranch in Las Vegas. But Lacey showed a weakness every time he passed Alp's Liquor Store. He was once an upright, upstanding citizen before his drop to the skids. Rumor has it that he was even once a town hero, and here's how the rumor got started.

It was a very hot and sticky July summer in West Helena, so hot that if your swimming pool wasn't filled with iced tea (including the ice), you were in trouble. Lacey was laying bricks at a house in the white section of town.

Now I want to stop here for a minute to give you the setting. It was 1965, a time when the nation was facing its most evil enemy, racism. This was when water hoses were being turned on black people and dogs were ripping and tearing into their clothes and even tearing them. It was a time when civil rights were as taboo as incest, and signs were posted that read "WHITES ONLY" and "COLORED ONLY." When a white person said, "Those are colored people," I'd say, "Really? What color are they?" We fought oppression, the Klan, the police, and sometimes even ourselves in those ever-changing times.

So Lacey was sweating like a boar hog trying to finish up a house owned by a man named Buddy Bailey. Buddy Bailey was an old and bitter white man who was confined to a wheelchair because of the war. He didn't mind letting you know, if you were black, where your place in life was. One day the old fuddy duddy was making a mess in the kitchen, trying to cook, and he had one of the eyes of his stove up too high and Lacey happened to notice the flames and smoke coming out of the rear window.

"Help! Help!" Buddy Bailey screamed. "The damn house is on fire! Somebody git in here and save me!"

Hearing this, Lacey ran around to the front door. Now the front door was locked because Mr. Bailey's philosophy was, "Never tempt a colored by leaving a door unlocked or a window open. They're already bound for hell, so don't give 'em no more room to sin!" Lacey had to kick the door in. "Mr. Bailey," he yelled, "You's all right in there?"

"Boy," Buddy Bailey screamed, "what da hell you doin' comin' in my front door like dat? You git yo' black ass outta here and come through dat back door like you supposed ta."

Lacey stood in awe a moment, then ran around to the back door. Seeing it engulfed in flames, he went back to the front door. "Hey, Mr. Bailey!" he said with an evil grin on his face, "Yo' back door is on fire, so's I guess I'm gonna have ta stands here an' watch you's burn up."

"Boy, you cain't jus' stand there and watch a white man burn up!" Bailey said in terror. "Why it's jus' in-human is what it is."

"Well, I guess I'm gone ta have ta, cause you knows us colored folks ain't allowed in y'alls front door," Lacey replied.

"Boy, please come and save me from dis fire and I will give ya all the money ya want!" Bailey pleaded.

So Lacey ran in and got the old coot out to safety. Once outside both of them were gasping for breath.

Buddy Bailey said, "Boy . . . . . I wants ta thank . . . . . ya fer. . . . savin' ma life . . . . . How much money does ya want?"

"Mr. Bailey . . . . . I's . . . . . don't wants . . . . . yo' money . . . . . I jus' wants . . . . . one thang," Lacey said.

"What's dat . . . . . boy?!"

"I's wants ya to stop callin' me . . . . a damn BOY! Okay?"

"Okay . . . . . boy," Bailey said.

Some people never learn. I guess you really can't teach an old dog new tricks.

After this episode got around town, the people (black and white) sort of looked up to Lacey as a hero, which might have led to his downfall, because some people can't deal with overnight stardom. It can help or hurt the individual. In his case it caused more pain than glory, or so it would seem.

Now we return to those misfits, Chris and Slime, who seem to have fallen off cloud nine a little, and are out to find their fellow comrade Lacey.

The night grows colder as the snow falls silently to the ground, and a gentle breeze moves slowly across West Helena's plaza street.

The boys are tired and still a little tipsy from the joy juice they've been drowning themselves in.

"Outta all the damn wine heads in the world, how the hell did I become friends wit dis one?" Chris mumbles. "You think he'd find hisself an alley or ditch to fall in like any other wino."

"Well hell, if he did dat we wouldn't have ta look for him. He'd be laying there stiff as a board in dis kind of weather, fool," Slime replies.

"Ya know, Slime, when I want your opinion I'll give it to you, so shut up!" Chris snaps. "You know, old Two For A Penny was one of Lacey's friends at one time. He might jist know where he is."

"Yeah, man. I think—"

"Slime, if they paid you to think, you could cash yo' checks at a penny arcade," Chris rudely interrupts. "So let me do all de damn thankin', if you don't mind."

You know, these two guys must be some friends to cut each other up like this and still look for someone the town wouldn't spit on if he was on fire. But they say the Lord works in mysterious ways, and I guess these two are as mysterious as one can get.

Now this guy they're going to see—Two For A Penny—was no prize. He got the nickname Two For A Penny years back when candy and cookies were real cheap. As a matter of fact they were exactly two for a penny. He was the kind of bum that all the other wino's feared and he loved it, every moment of it. Why it was even once said that when the police sicked the dogs on him and one bit him, that he bit the dog back and a day later the dog died.

Two For A Penny was an old World War Two vet who had been kicked out dishonorably for pulling a straight razor on the mess ser-gaent for serving him cold corn flakes. In his mind Two For A Penny was still with his troops.

On cold nights such as this he'd stand around a garbage barrel with fire inside it and talk to himself. Nobody else dared to. "A bunch of sissies is wat I got for troops," he is muttering. "The whole damn lot of ya needs to be hung by the balls and then beat wit a two-by-four. I'm goin' in there and git them damn Japs, and when

I comes out the whole bunch of ya better be gone, or I'll give ya wat I'm gonna give them sonsofbitches."

A real nice guy, huh?

"A yo! Two For A Penny! I need to holler at ya, man!" Slime shouts.

"Punk!" Two For A Penny yells back. "My mama was da last somebody ta holler at me, and when she did I slapped her ass down and ya kin gits the same thang she gots if ya wants to!"

"Hey, man, it was jus' a figure of speech, ya know. He didn't mean any thang by it," Chris replies.

"Well Got damn it," Two For A Penny rudely cuts Chris off. "Is dat all he is, missin'? The best thang that coulda happen ta dat maggot is dat ya find him, but when ya do, make sure he's dead. If he ain't, brang him to me and I'll kill the damn fool myself. HA! HA! HA! HA! Now git the hell away from me. Your beginnin' ta stank up my alley."

"Dis alley was stankin when we came in it," Chris snarls, "and it will be stankin when we leave . . . . if you still got yo' funky ass in it!"

"Why you little piece of SHIT! I oughta—"

"Yeah, you oughta take a damn bath and help dis town cut down on da air pollution in dis alley," Slime cuts in.

And with that the two take off, running down the alley, leaving behind footprints in the snow and a human being (if you can call him that) who, when God was giving out hearts, good sense, and compassion for his fellow man, was in line trying to get a drink with the fellows in hell.

As the two run packing the snow to the ground, Chris looks at Slime and (almost out of breath), says, "Ya know, man . . . . . I hope . . . . . when they bury him . . . . . they bury him . . . . . face down . . . . . so he can see . . . . . where he's going."

It's dawn now, and day is about to open its sleepy eyes. For the residents of West Helena, the coming of a new day means starting from scratch, looking forward to a new beginning. Those who are lucky enough to be employed are getting ready to face their nine-to-five jobs. Their coffee and cocoa are brewing to help them get started.

A few of the children are up and thinking of making snowmen. There will be no school for a few days, because the streets are too icy for the school buses.

So there are joyful noises all up and down the block. Storekeepers are shoveling pathways for the few customers who will make their daily runs for supplies. Those who are unemployed try to think of ways to pass the time of day. Some will be out in their yards with their youngsters, helping them make snowmen.

And, of course, there are always the gossips—girdy women— who will fill their front rooms with soap operas in order to have something to talk about when they see their neighbors. It's sort of a customary thing in this little town.

At 7:30 the morning air is filled with the sounds of cars stalled in the snow and of cars that just refuse to start. At 11 a.m. you have to walk lightly and be ready to duck, because a few of the neighborhood pranksters will be hurling snowballs everywhere. Needless to say, these pranksters aren't very popular with the postman.

Christopher has managed somehow to pour himself out of bed with one hell of a hangover. "Ooooohh! God!" he moans as he tries to rise to the occasion. "One of these daze I'm gonna learn to drink something dat don't say 20% alcohol on it." He does everything but crawl down the hall to the bathroom. When he makes it there he takes a look in the mirror, stares at it a while, and goes, "Who the hell are you?" and "How da hell did ya git into my house?"

He turns on the faucet, grabs a handful of cold water, and throws it in his face, hoping for some sort of a miracle. He takes another look and goes, "Damn! I liked you better the other way."

About this time there's knock (actually more like a pounding) on the door. Wham! Wham! Wham! "I'll tell you one thang," he roars, "if this ain't a raid somebody's ass is in trouble!" He opens it and there is Slime.

"Man, have you heard?" Slime says frantically.

"Heard wat, snot face?"

"The police found a body frozen in the snow last night, and they thank it might be Lacey."

"Lord, I hope dis is some kind of bad dream I'm having."

"Well, they got the body down at the hospital morgue. Ya wanta go check it out?"

"You damn right, man. Jus' let me slip on my clothes and we'll move outta here wit da quickness."

So in the blink of an eye the two are at the hospital. They run up to the front desk with fear in their hearts and panic on their faces. Gasping for breath Chris goes, "Ex-x-x-x-cusse m-m-m-mee, m'am. Is there the frozen body of a wino named Lacey here?"

"Well, the policemen brought a body in this morning, but we have no way of knowing who he is, because the man's face was blown off with a shotgun."

Hearing this you couldn't have used a snow plow to shovel the boys' faces off the floor. To them it was like getting the news that you had won a million dollars and then finding out that someone had made a mistake in sending you a check with someone else's name on it. Yes, it looked like the long grueling search was over, but who would have ever thought it would end this way? I mean, the worst the boys looked for was that one day (because of Lacey's careless-ness) some thug would hit him on the head for petty cash and leave him for dead—but that he would be all right later on. Or that he might even drink himself to death. But for someone to brutally mur-der the guy, well, that was totally out of the question.

Lacey had his faults, but not once did he ever do anyone bodily harm. There was a feeling of anger and sorrow in the two boys' hearts and yet there was also a feeling of emptiness. The same empti-ness the world felt when it lost the king of rock and roll, the feeling that someone took away a part of us that we didn't donate to science.

One word keeps digging in the boys' souls . . . . . Why? Although Lacey was no Elvis, to the boys he was something a little more, per-haps to them he was the last of a dying breed of rebels. "I may be down, but I'm not out," he had said on many occasions, and there was one saying that the boys would remember the rest of their lives: "Don't lighten up, tighten up." So with heads hanging down and lumps in their throats, the boys are about to head toward the exit when they hear a woman scream.

"Oh, the nerve of that dirty old man!" a pretty, young nurse shouts as she runs out of a patient's room. "He doesn't need a wheel-chair. What he needs is a good slap in the face, and if I wasn't on duty I swear that's just what he'd get too." She is telling all this to the front desk nurse as she rubs her fanny.

The boys break into uncontrollable laughter.

"Well, I don't see where that was funny at all, young men," the nurse says.

"Excuse us, lady," Chris says with a smirk, "but does this dirty old man have a hole in the top of his gray Afro, bloodshot eyes, and a nose as big as Bozo's?"

"Why, yes! And I believe his name's Lacey Charles. Do you know him?"

"We'd better. He's our Dad."

■ *Murray Hudson*

Murray Hudson farmed for twelve years on the family farm in Dyer County, Tennessee before turning his hobby of map and rare book collecting into a business. His account of his farming experience, Dirt & Duty, *was published in 1995 by Free River Press.*

Selections from DIRT AND DUTY

TREES, LAND AND GENERATIONS

When the Hassels, Turpins, and Weakleys, my maternal forebears, arrived here by horseback in the 1830s, this country was fresh as a bride, little changed in the thousands of years the Native Americans had hunted, fished, and birthed on the mounds and ridges of the Forked Deer River watershed. Oak and poplar thick as hair and tall as towers greeted them. Everywhere around them grew this immense hardwood forest, fine for hunters and trappers, but a tough, long term task for would-be farmers. They chopped and sawed, grubbed rootwads, burned stumps, and gradually cleared enough space to plant corn, peas, pumpkins, potatoes, tobacco. To them the trees were an obstacle. Although trees provided their shelter and fences and firewood, clearing cost them soaking sweat, broken fingers, cracked ribs, hernias, bone-weary nights. The struggle to keep vegetation back in the wilds of west Tennessee wore men and women out. Because trees were everywhere—like the passenger pigeons whose flocks blotted out the sun and whose roosts they blasted—the first couple of generations could not see the trees for the woods.

After the Civil War, when the railroad finally chugged through these bottoms, trees suddenly became a salable commodity for houses in booming Chicago, St. Louis, and Memphis. Most of the hills were cleared by then, except for fencerows and thickets left to shade the cattle, horses, and mules. Yet only the few higher ridges in the lowlands were clearcut. Otherwise my great-grandfather Weakley let hogs run in the bottoms getting fat on acorns and other nuts and wild feed. Game was plentiful in the big woods still.

In fact, my mother's grandfather, George Weakley, bought the big bottom and put together the patchwork of forty acre farms, yeoman farms that had no slaves, into a large tract which his son, my namesake, Murray, added to in the thirties and forties. Fields were small since they were worked by mules and by farmhand families who were paid by hourly wage and lived next to the fields they worked. My father took over our portion of the farm in the early sixties. He was the son of a timber man who had run crews logging the immense bottoms west of Dyersburg. His outlook was closer to that of the original pioneers. He felt that it was a great waste not to exploit all the rich soil in the bottoms where he hunted ducks. During my seven years away in college he cleared three or four hundred acres of ash, oak, and cypress, working as hard as blazes to cut, pile, burn, and pick up the remaining 'chunks' so he could plant soybeans. The land was still subject to occasional overflow, so soybeans enabled him to plant later with less expense and risk than cotton. He opened up some of the best land we farm, but he wanted it all cleared, including all the slough banks and wet woods loaded with cypress.

Mother, my brothers, Jack and Russell, and I balked at losing the last of the bottom woods and waters. I felt that Dad was right about the production potential of most of the remaining woodland, but I also felt that if we could not make a decent living on ninety percent of our land, that sacrificing the last ten percent to the dozer blade would not make the difference.

I can understand both the farmer's tendency to want more land to work, and the conservationist's desire not to clear another acre, but the practical reality is that some land can be cleared without great loss, and some farmland needs to return to forest.

I was not blameless when it came to decisions about changing the land for farming purposes. I saw that one large field could be made out of two or three adjoining smaller ones by getting rid of the fencerows, blading out willows, ditching and diverting water flow, so that we had rows half a mile long rather than a third of that. This meant less turnrows, more acreage in cultivation, less time involved to plant, cultivate, and harvest, and less wear on equipment from the extra turning. In the course of several years I worked this pattern on every field I could, resulting in miles of field edge habitat destroyed, which had harbored lots of rabbit, quail, and beneficial birds and insects.

PLANTING, A SENSE OF PURPOSE

May 10th. We have six weeks to plant twelve hundred acres. Off and on during dry spells in March and April, between equipment repair and servicing, we scratched up the foulness, the early Johnson grass, and smartweeds that we did not disk behind the combines in the fall. Prather ran the field cultivator with its thirty-six small plowpoints behind the 1566, Big Red, our stoutest diesel tractor. He fairly skimmed over the ground, but there was no sense of urgency. Rex sometimes hit the rougher spots with the twenty-one foot disk harrow with its twenty-inch diameter steel disks that sliced the soil, rolled it over, and buried the bean stalks, fledging weeds, and few remaining earthworms.

There's not much chance of a killing frost by mid-May, so we usually crank up to begin socking the seed in the ground between

May 8th and 10th. We have a certain order like an advancing army. Prather leads the charge with Big Red and the field cultivator to root up any escape weeds. I follow him with my 1486, the next largest piece of machinery, pulling a disk harrow mounted with a spray boom, putting down a yellow mist of preplant grass killer, Treflan, from the two hundred gallon tanks mounted either side of the hood. Behind me Rex pulls his beloved "Doall" (Dew-awl) with scratchers followed by rolling blades like the ones that came in old push-mowers, dangling toothed-harrows, and three two-by-twelve-inch boards that smooth the seedbed for the final, all-important planter, which Herman guides with great care and gusto. He's driving the smallest of our field tractors, and needs two one-hundred-fifty-gallon tanks filled with water mounted like saddlebags to hold the front end down with the heavy planter weight on back.

These mornings I have an almost instinctual urge to get to the shop, calibrate my spray rig, and get the whole operation cranked off. On other mornings I stumble out with great reluctance. But during planting a different feeling grips me. I detect it in the men, too, who work as hard all year as I could want, yet now shift into overdrive. There is an unspoken understanding that what we're doing at this moment is what it is all about. We help each other more than usual. We feel united in a larger purpose.

Everything up to this point was a rehearsal, a preparation for this act, and how we handle this stage is crucial to the whole farming operation. If the ground is worked up too wet, balls of clay bake into baseball-sized clods or brickbats, making it hard as hell to cover the seed. If I forget to turn on the spray boom, we'll see a swath of grass in all those rows I forgot. If the seed boy doesn't fill a hopper, or Herman runs out in mid-field, we find a telltale blank space in a week when the plants break ground.

After we finish planting we go our separate ways during the day. I spray the weeds, while the men cultivate the middles two days behind me. That is solitary, concentrated going, and lacks the camaraderie of planting.

JUDGING BY A KNUCKLE

My first crop year back was also our last year for cotton, and we did-
n't even plant it ourselves. Dad hired it done by a neighbor who
planted cotton in the Oil Barn Field flat, not on the usual raised bed.
A frog strangler rain came the day after planting and washed the seed
away. We didn't even replant, and I believe it was the only time we
gave up on a crop. It shocked me that the seed was so vulnerable, and
it taught me to watch seed depth carefully.

Each season when we first started planting, Dad and Herman
always checked seed placement and depth. After Herman traveled
the first twenty feet with his eight row planter, he and Dad would
kneel down on each row. Dad would pull out his trusty Barlow knife
and flick away soil. Meanwhile, Herman would dig with his finger.
When the seed gleamed white and round, they stuck their
forefingers into the hole and used their thumbs as a measure against
the finger. If the soil was dry, they wanted the seed two knuckle-
joints deep to reach for moisture . . . unless they expected rain. In
good moist soil they wanted just one knuckle depth so it would
sprout and break through the crust quickly.

Many's the serious discussion I've seen over a half knuckle difference in setting the planter, because as Dad said, a small miss is
good as a mile.

RAIN: LIFEBLOOD OR FLASH FLOOD

At noon today as I crossed the I.C. tracks at South Fork I saw a dust
devil swirling across a planted field, funneling dry soil and scraps of
seed sacks into the cloudless sky. No rain for two weeks, and none
in sight.

A farmer spends more time than any other human being eyeing
the sky and listening to the weather channel. Last year at this time
we had backwater (the local word for flood) over five hundred acres.
It looked like we'd never stick a seed in the ground, but somehow
we scratched the soggy surface and got in a crop.

When it doesn't rain, folks hereabouts say we haven't been *payin' the preacher.* I haven't heard any term for what causes *frog stranglers,* when a cloud plops five inches on the bare fields in an hour and tons of Memphis silt loam heads toward the Forked Deer, then the Mississippi on the way to build the delta.

Farmers know what to say when a cloudburst ends a drought, or sunshine stabs through weeks of rain clouds, or the small isolated rain saves a far-flung field that's missed out before: "Thank God!"

The major factor that determines the bushels or bales is out of our control. We can't make it rain, and we surely can't cut if off. That's why we are fortunate with the lay of our land. We depend on sky irrigation. Half our ground is on silt loam ridges sloping down into gumbo clay, which holds moisture. In a wet year the high ground produces well and saves us while part of the lowest land drowns out. In droughts, the bottoms with their sub-irrigation from the high water table make up for the BB-sized beans or stunted cotton on the hills. So it averages out. And that I have found is the name of the game.

LAY BY TIME

What a luxury is late August, the lay-by season, when all the plowing, planting, spraying, chopping, cultivating are done. The crop is "laid by" because there's nothing else you can do but watch it grow. The tractors sit quietly under the tin shed, and I sleep late of a morning, with only the sound of birds and insects and the soft chook, chook, chook of the overhead fan. Then comes the occasional thump or bang of a tennis ball sized walnut bruising the soft earth or rattling off the tin roof shed. The first sounds of fall are pretty obvious.

Frogs retire from their chorus by sunup, their places taken by the insistent insects that provide a high, steady background whir that you only realize is there when they stop for a moment. These soft sounds are accompanied by loud solos of larger bugs that rattle the eardrum from one window to the next. Starting with first light (that dim pre-dawn gauze) the crows begin to caw roughly to one another in the distance. ("Get up! Quit your preening and let's eat some corn.") Blue jays squawk from the walnut top and the territo-

rial mocking bird harangues everyone within earshot with his pro-
nouncements. ("This is my place. I claimed it a dozen moons ago,
and I have documents to prove it!")

Time to lie back; bathed in last night's cool dew-soaked breath;
glazed by first light of new day; serenaded by all humming, chirp-
ing, squawking, trilling life as it stretches its wings.

ALF'S STORE

"Where you can hear everything, but ham meat frying!" Herman.

When the tornado roared over Bruceville in 1985 it toppled the
Coca Cola advertising sign: ALF WILLIAMS GROCERY (and Community Center, Tall Tale, Gossip and Medical Advice Station.) There
is a new sign now, but inside things haven't changed much. People's
names are still scribbled all over the unpainted beaverboard ceiling
that a teenager can reach with a pen. The meat display case and cutter, origin of thousands of baloney sandwiches, and the bread and
canned goods aisles are still the same, even a hair net holder from
the forties shaped like a woman's head. Here you know you're down
South with such staples as pork brains and canned gravy. It's one of
the last outposts for RC Cola and Moon Pies.

It wasn't long after the new sign that the TV popped up one day,
intruding into the domino games and hunting tales and crop talks
with "Jeopardy" and "Days of Our Lives." Still, when any four are
gathered together in the store they march out the twenty-eight cer-
emonial black rectangles with the varied spots, and a sacred hush
envelops the figures bent over the raggedy card-table. Most local
players know what numbers are still out halfway through the game.
No money changes hands, just lots of grunts and umms and groans
when BoBill puts down the 'case' five and ties up the game for fifty
points.

The pot-bellied stove warms the backsides and clasped hands of
rabbit hunters in from the chill (some from the front resemble the
stove). It shuffles a lazy plume of split oak smoke out the flue before
sunup in November to late dusk in March. But that smoke can't compare to Big Alf's barbeque grill at full blast nearing the Fourth of July.

The whole neighborhood downwind drools at the husky smells of pork shoulders jazzed with pepper sauce. Alf is famous in these parts for his pulled-meat barbeque, which fanatics fight for at the annual Forked Deer Electric Coop celebration.

The daily crowd at Alf's store gets older all the time, just as the community ages and the young folk mostly go to Dyersburg to work for the rubber plant or off to Memphis to lose themselves in the 7-11s and suburban traffic. Gone are the days when long, lean Willie Lee Stutts in his late sixties broke his fist cold-cocking his son-in-law who had doubted Willie Lee's word. A man's word was his honor in those days (and there wasn't a single lawyer in Bruceville). Now-a-days the conversation consists mostly of high blood pressure, arthritis, who's in what hospital, or who's laid out at the funeral home for visitation.

Most of the cigarettes and chewin' tobacco are sold to the younger folk, as the older ones get doctor's orders to quit or die. It's possible now to see a smoke-free domino game and the strongest stuff going down the gullet is caffeine.

When Alf retires, unless by some miracle someone else decides to keep it open, the hub of the community will go with him. Churches will still provide community on Sundays and Wednesday nights, and at Homecoming revivals and singings in August, but there will be no central place to gather in split oak chairs around a stove and chew the fat. An age will have passed.

Herman summed up the variety of tales served up by Alf and his patrons when he said, "You can hear everything there but ham meat fryin'."

FOLK KNOWLEDGE

My Bruceville neighbors stake out a pretty wide field of basic knowledge. Prather can see a *water dog* (a smudge of rainbow colors) in the nearly clear sky and predict rain in two days, even in a drought. And every cold spell in late spring has a name: *blackberry winter, locust winter, dogwood winter* ...

Because people like Moody Palmer have lived seventy springs in close companionship with the out-of-doors, they felt those chill days when the honey locusts bloomed with dangling white clusters like grapes. It happened again and again, and they named it and remembered.

They are equally acquainted with the earth they walk on, plant in, and will be planted in someday. They prefer rich, deep black "barn yard" dirt for gardens. Slick red clay that holds moisture in a drought but bakes out like a brick bat (and is used for bricks) they plant in okra, or its cousin, cotton. Sticky gray "gumbo" clay in the bottoms (so richly scented it recalls old outhouse diggings), makes great soybeans. They call the white ground on the Pond Creek side of the ridge "buckshot." It is crumbly, poor, and full of hard nodules and barely holds the earth together.

Mizz Bessie Haley knows to plant "taters" and other root vegetables in the dark of the moon. She plants above ground vegetables by the half or full moon. And anything planted on Good Friday thrives.

Folk hereabouts predict severity of coming winter several ways. A cracked persimmon seed has either a "fork" or a "spoon" to show the harshness. Wooly worms or caterpillars with wide stripes augur for a cold winter, and you can tell how deep the snow will be by the lowest wasp nest.

All these sayings come from acute observation of the natural world by people who have had to deal with it day in and day out for generations.

MULE DAYS

When I was first going to the farm with my grandfather World War II was on, and the bulk of the farming was still done with mules. There were twenty-four teams on the Bruceville farm and that many more on the farms Papa rented. The mules were rounded up every morning before daylight at the mule barn, a huge, rambling wooden structure on the edge of a cypress grove. They were mostly big cotton mules used in pairs to pull a single bottom breaker (a large plow). A thin, hoarse-sounding man named Sam trained the mules to *gee* and *haw* with such subtlety that he could stand on his front porch and talk the mules one direction then the other, back up, go forward, halt.

By sunup the train of mules and mule drivers trekked along the gravel road around the Palestine Cemetery and split off at Bruceville Slab to their respective fields leaving a steaming manure trail that a blind man could follow.

Since most of the cotton was grown on hillsides, the mules learned to lean and walk on the upside of the furrows so the plow or disk would keep straight. Inexperienced drivers might whip the mules to get them to stay in the middle of the furrow; after awhile they would realize the mules were smarter than they were, because the rows would wander farther and farther downhill if the team was not allowed to go where they knew best.

A man got to know his team so well that he recognized the personalities, the character traits of each mule. If he didn't, he became a posthole digger or a locust post cutter, which was much harder, hotter work than following a mule.

A DAY IN THE LIFE OF A FARMER

May 8. 5:30 A.M. A swarm of buzzing hornets erupts from my clock radio. I reach to beat down the snooze bar for ten minutes more of shuteye, but I moved it out of armslength the week before to insure that I got out of bed to switch it off. Once up, I twist open the blinds and catch that first light oozing over the back fencerow, spreading our pond with peach light. I leap across the bed to give Bonnie a wake up hug, jump into my jeans and khaki long sleeve shirt, and head for the bathroom humming. I'm not usually this chipper on rising. Today is special. We begin planting soybeans, and I feel a bit of joy rising from gut level up through my torso, which wants to pop out in song. I'm ready to roll.

A light ground fog nestles in the swale of the pasture out the bathroom window. I hear our resident mockingbird already scolding some intruders as I splash cool water on my face. Harry Hardy's rooster next door puts in his two crows worth to start the day, and

Harry's beagles respond with a few yips. (They're just pups, who'll develop deep baying voices by fall.) I pull on my socks and clod-hopper boots as the scent of coffee smacks me across the nose. Bacon joins the aroma trail that lures me into the kitchen where Bonnie rings the iron skillet on the hot eye basting the eggs. Toast smells crisp and brown in the oven. I reach in the fridge for butter, cream, and homemade blackberry jam, vintage last summer.

"You're awfully cheerful this morning, what's up?" Bonnie asks.

"We start planting behind the shop today to get the equipment set and calibrated for the big push. I've got to get down there early, like 6:15, so I can check things over before Rex and Herman and Prather start talking to me all at once."

I fork half an orange-yoked country egg into my mouth, fol-lowed by half a strip of thick-sliced bacon, wash it down with coffee so hot that it catches me by surprise. I slow down stuffing my face; I'm twenty minutes ahead of my usual pace, so I can really enjoy each bite and Bonnie's fit, horsewoman figure beneath the lilac cot-ton robe. Life feels right at this moment. I want to savor every crumb and lift the straw blonde hair off the back of her neck to kiss that long, bread-fresh throat.

We share a kiss, and I'm off to crank the mighty six-cylinder king cab Ford that got stalled trying to pull a trailer out of the seed barn yesterday. It whirs and starts like a charm. "God's in his heaven, and all's right with the world." At least so far this glowing May day. A farmer knows to take the good when it comes because some unpre-dictable mayhem waits him just around the bend in Bruceville Slab.

At 6:15 I'm at the shop. I did not beat the men there. They must camp out on their tractors.

Rex stilts up in his long-legged gait, dipstick in hand. "She's a quart and a half low. I think the oil pan seal's leakin'."

Before I get a word out about his tractor running a quart or more low every morning, up pops Prather with his air filter the size of a wastebasket. "I've bumped it out and blown it out with the air hose, but it still has dirt in it."

"Get another," I start to advise him when Herman pokes his head up from the planter's packing wheels he's been rolling. "There's a bearing down in this one. Can't start til we've got some bearings." I have not had a chance to look at my spray rig and tractor, which take longer to service and calibrate than any other equipment, and which can waste more money than any other if they're not set right. "OK, Rex, I'll look at the seal on the 1206, then I'm going into Halls and get a filter for Prather and bearings for the planter. Is there anything else broken down I need to get parts for?"

Even when I ask that, I know that there will be at least two more trips for parts today. At this point all I want to do is jump in my cab and head for Halls. No, something says in my head, you have to check your tractor first, and the hoses and connection on the tanks and spray rig. I write down "1566 air filter," and "planter packing wheel bearings, get a couple of extra," in my Daytimer notebook. If I don't have my pad, I have to write it on my palm. My mind can only hold so much daily trivia. I've strung out seven years of college, two and a half degrees, and still I can't remember daily chores without writing them down, whereas the men, two of whom can only write their names for checks, can recall when and where and how we planted each field, the weather on that day six months ago, and what they had for dinner this day last year.

I add half a quart of oil, clean my air filter, and ask Rex to fill my tractor with diesel while I'm gone. The hoses all look good, and I can check the fittings better when I have some water in the tanks, so I put that off for an hour. Halls is seven miles away by road, five as the crow flies. And sometimes, when some critical part is needed, I nearly fly to the implement dealers. The hangup is when they don't have the part in stock, and I have to go to Dyersburg or Newbern or Maury City, chasing down a valve the size of my thumb, while the whole shooting match is shut down. Such is life for a farmer. It's never dull when I'm running, because that's just what I do, run. A gopher with wheels. Fortunately my father takes up a lot of the slack by getting stuff when he's not busy. It's always better to take the broken part because it's mighty irritating to go back for the same part again. Wrong size.

When I walk in Halls Implement Company, the usual lineup of half a dozen farmers lean against the parts counter in their khakis or jeans, short sleeves or rolled up long ones, and ball caps of every color scrunched down on their heads. They talk with the two brothers behind the counter.

"Give me two of those O-rings while you're at it, Bob. Might as well have an extra."

"What do you mean you're out of adapters for my 856? You had a slew of them last week."

Those waiting swap breakdown stories, weather reports, and the usually miserable commodity prices. "Ain't no way to make ends meet with beans at $4.90. Hell, it cost me over five bucks a bushel to raise 'em."

"Gonna come a frog strangler before we get done today. Look at them smoky clouds over toward the bluff."

Retired farmers are propped in their accustomed caucus around the coffee maker and the card table with issues of *Soybean Digest*, *Progressive Farmer*, and *Delta Farm Press* strewn around. To the usual machinery, weather, crop price talk they add arthritis, social security (or lack thereof), politics, and who's got what illness in what hospital. Lots of nodding and shaking of white or bald heads. These folks have been through a lifetime of farming. They can complain with the best of 'em, because there's always something going wrong. You don't have to look far for a just cause to moan about. Charlie, one of the biggest farmers in Lauderdale in acres, expertice, and poundage, holds court with political commentary (yellow dog Democrat). His blue heeler dog stands guard in the back of his pickup.

I grab my parts, nod or speak to the various farmers I know, then scoot out the door making a wide swing around the pickup where the blue heeler stands guard. I ask myself if a dog's life is so bad after all.

COTTON CHOPPING

In the straight down sun of midday with plants too small to shade the ground, the soil glares back heat on my dripping face. I tread the middle between two cotton rows, flicking my blade in the left row to get two burs in three leaf stage, then switching the hoe handle to the opposite position and scraping some crow's foot grass beneath the young round-leafed cotton. The straw hat is hot, especially where the band sticks to my forehead, but the alternative is the full blast of late June, thirty-six degree North sun, which nearly blinds me if I take off my prescription sunglasses with thick green-brown lenses that color the cotton camouflage and make the clouds muddy. I kick clods as I walk, look at clouds, count the minutes til we reach row end and cool water.

When the cotton is waist high and deep waxy green, beginning to lap together in the middle, it is "laid by" with one last sweep of the cultivator. If it rains and the ground stays wet for a month during this time, some escape weeds—cocklebur, Johnson grass, and wild cotton—start shooting above the cotton. Then the hoeing crew walks out early mornings to muddy middles and a sea of dew. Halfway down the first row you're soaked to the waist. Khaki shirt and jeans stick like a second skin. Limbs, leaves, pink and white blooms, and small bolls called "squares" bump against your legs every step, creating enough resistance to make it feel like you're wading belly deep in Reelfoot Lake amidst wide flat mats of lily pads and moss green water. And it's nearly as much effort. By noon on the first day, your thighs ache with each step.

My first farmwork as an adult was leading cotton choppers in the summer of 1968. I came with my wife, Bonnie, and our eighteen-month old son, Mac, a cat named Soot, and a horse called Astronaut, to live in my father's "cabin," a twenty-by-thirty foot frame house with red shingle siding.

I had finished my first year in a doctoral program in English literature at Vanderbilt and thought that this would be a pleasant change from the city. A change it was. Instead of getting up for classes at 8:00 A.M., I was in the field chopping weeds at 6:30 A.M. We only hoed weeds out of the sixty or seventy acres of cotton because herbicides were not as effective for cotton as soybeans, and also because that was the way it had always been done.

My chopping crew consisted of three women and their three teenage daughters. The women wore sunbonnets and long sleeve dresses to protect them from the sun. The girls had long-sleeves and jeans and straw hats. I had as much of my skin covered as I could, too, plus a wide-brimmed straw hat. We started at 6:30 because it was much cooler, and we had a lot of ground to cover. Up until mid-morning we would chop for an hour or more at a time before we stopped at the end of the field where the truck stood with the water cooler, and we took a break and drank some cold water. I stayed just ahead of the women, keeping a pace that was just fast enough to give plenty of time to get every stray weed or grass blade.

Ordinarily I heard a constant chatter at my back, like a flock of chickens. I believe they all talked at once, at least some of the time. One July day about noon when the temperature shot above a hundred degrees, we were in the half-mile long rows on the east side of the Oil Barn field and were nearing the end when I sensed something strange, no noise from my choppers. I looked back, and one of the younger girls was flat on the ground. The others were gathered around her fanning and shading her. I asked the mother and another grown woman to take her out to the end, get her a drink of cool water and sit her in the shade. I realized it was too hot to chop at midday, so we cut out the three hottest hours of the day and chopped later in the evening. I had never been around anyone with heat stroke, and I didn't want to start now.

DOWN ON THE FARM

Eleven years into farming the walls closed in on me. Waking was hard, getting up and dressing difficult, going down to the shop every day an absolute millstone around my neck. In fact everything lost its meaning. The thought of mixing chemicals and spending all day spraying them over row after row after monotonous row of soybean plants was as appealing as eating dirt. Even normally pleasurable events such as talking with friends or watching a movie aroused no interest. I was caught in the downhill snowball of depression. I felt down, trapped.

I felt as though I could not leave the work, because it would be like deserting my duty to my family and the land. On the other hand I felt as though I would explode if I listened to one more repetition of some of the farmhand sayings and stories. Not that I did not like the men and respect their experiences they told about, but when you hear the same tale umpteen dozen times, it begins to grate on the ear. Well, nearly everything grated on my mind as well.

I started to feel that there was only one way out—to die! Every day I thought about shooting myself or driving into a bridge abutment at ninety. I put up all my guns, I didn't even carry a shotgun in my pickup for fear I would get the urge to use it in some back field.

One day, as I approached the stop sign at Four Points, a light flashed across my numb mind: "I don't want to kill myself. I don't want to die. I just want out, to change my life." I even thought of ways to fake my death and head to Brazil, but I couldn't do that to my family.

Finally, I went to an Espiscopal priest, who was a trained Jungian counselor. He had me talk about my blackest thoughts, my worst feelings, and my dreams. One night I had a breakthrough dream.

I dreamed I was climbing a stairwell. The walls and steps were all the same rough cypress we had cut in the bottoms, a job that ruined my back in the process. This cypress was so rough it had splinters sticking out. There were no windows. As I trudged up the stairs the passage grew narrower. Up and up I climbed, bearing around to my left until I conked my head. I looked up and the stairwell was slanted, closed at the top with rough cypress. I panicked and awoke.

When I recounted the dream to my counselor he asked, "How did you feel?"

"Trapped," I answered.

"By what?" he asked.

"Farming, for one thing."

"Then you have to tell your father about it."

"But how can I quit farming? My family is counting on me. No one else is there to take over."

"You won't do anyone any good if you get more depressed and kill yourself."

That hit home. I decided to talk to Dad.

FACING MYSELF AND DAD

I drove to the cabin sweating bullets, trying to rehearse what I would say to my father.

When I walked in, he was sitting at the table playing solitaire and looking out at his bird feeders.

"I counted two dozen male cardinals at the feeders this morning."

"Uh-huh. Dad, I need to talk to you about something."

"Go ahead."

It spilled out. "I've been really depressed lately. I don't enjoy farming anymore. Every day I dread going to the shop. I dislike farming so much that I think about killing myself."

Dad looked up at me. I had expected surprise or anger. He replied matter-of-factly, "Then quit farming. It certainly isn't worth ruining your health."

Relief flooded my body. I felt so thankful that I was not accused of failing in my duty as eldest son. Dad was accepting and understanding. It did my heart good, like digging it out of a premature grave.

AFTER THE FALL

Walking down a frozen field road in January, the ground hard, the grass crackling beneath my boots, I surrender to the season. Thin light seeps through a gauze sky. The stark rows of bush-hogged cotton stalks string out over the hill toward the brown treeline across the bottoms.

This field picked two bales an acre, and they harvested every pothole in the bottoms for the first time in years. I should grin with delight. But I did not plant this crop or cultivate it or harvest the fruits. I am just a bystander now. My sweat and energy and thought and blood went into this ground for a dozen crops, and I know this land and love it enough to want to be planted in it myself when I die.

But I have distanced myself from the farming operation, since my choice of successor was rejected and the fencerow of giant oak on my own farm, the Ponder Place, was destroyed while I was traveling. I miss the way the gateway oak framed the far hills, and I regret the feeling that my wish to preserve some of the best of this countryside will not be honored when I turn my back.

WHY WORRY? IT AVERAGES OUT

My grandfather, Murray, who saw over ninety crops come and go, often said that every year he grew cotton there was some time during the crop year when it looked like the cotton would not get planted or would completely fail. Other times promised to produce a bumper crop, but usually the yield was neither pitifully low nor abnormally large, just average, enough to pay the bills and have some left over for the next crop and a decent living.

My father, who sweats the small stuff such as a weed in a twenty acre field or a wrench he can't find, is quite stoic when it comes to the big picture. When back water sloshed out over a third of the beans during the growing season one year, his comment was, "Why worry about something you can't do anything about? We've never missed a crop altogether."

I tended to sweat the everyday pains like flat tires, broken bolts, and escaped weeds as well as the falling bean prices, blown transmissions, or six weeks' drought during growing season. That is one reason I had such a hard time dealing with farming—I took it all to heart, I took it personally, and that is not healthy.

Now that I have stood back from the actual operations I can see that it is crucial in farming—where you have little or no control over so many of the variables like weather, market debacles, equipment failures—to understand that ACCEPTANCE is the key to survival, mentally and emotionally. As long as I make the best effort, mentally and emotionally. As long as I make the best effort, including planning and execution, then I have shown responsibility for everything in my control. Disasters big and small are not my fault, and to agonize over them is futile and self-defeating. That wisdom or common sense would have made farming much more bearable, and I would have slept better in those difficult times when things went haywire. At least knowing the importance of acceptance makes a difference in whatever I do now and how I react, or don't react, to tough situations. I try not to worry needlessly. It is an enormous waste of time and energy. Besides, it all works out in the long run.

EPILOGUE

I still live in the Cypress house the men and I built and my neighbors saved from fiery destruction. It is very quiet now with the boys grown and gone to Arizona and Kentucky.

The land still sustains me. Stray thoughts of past springs cling like the stray tufts of unpicked cotton on the spent stalks. I walk the dogs down the field road remembering the monarchs that danced around me one spring day (like Uncle Remus in Song of the South), the five-leaf clover that caught my eye one June.

The airdales leap into fencerow honeysuckle vines after a rabbit, and I return to the present. I spend much of my time traveling and give the farm very little thought except as a home base to return to when I'm worn out from going and going.

Yet I feel as though there is a magnet in my chest, and this piece of earth is the mother lode that draws me back. Whether the land is bare and the sky stacked with black clouds, or sun lights a fluffy field of cotton and flame-faced sassafras, I always feel realigned when I return to this land, my dust to this dust.

Commentary: Delta History

By the nature of its history, the Delta became a melange of African, Native American, and European cultures and blood lines. New Orleans, with the greatest degree of intermixture, has produced the most explosive and creative culture of the region. When we think of the Delta we think of the blues, New Orleans jazz, Zydeco, Creole and Cajun cooking, the plantation system (slavery, cotton, white aristocracy), docks piled with cotton bales, Mississippi paddle-wheelers, chain gangs, brass bands, juke joints, snake handlers, Evangelical preachers, black gospel choirs, segregation, Civil Rights.

Southern sociologist Howard Odum's work of the 1930s was perhaps the first to draw attention to regional diversity within the South. Of all Southern regions, the Delta, defined geologically by its alluvial lands, is probably the most diverse. Its cultures have been shaped not only by the major racial groups, but by subcultures within them. Thus, for example, musicologists can trace the influences of various African tribes on Delta music. On a more obvious level, differences in cuisine, folk customs, and architecture (or amalgams of influences) can be attributed to the Spanish, French, Scotch-Irish, blacks and others.

Beneath its surface—despite industrialization, national franchises, mass entertainment and communication—the South still differs from other sections and regions of the country. As J. W. Cash pointed out in *The Mind of the South*, there exists a common core of values and attitudes that define this section and differentiate it from others in the country. Southerner and Delta blues historian Fetzer Mills says of the South: "It's definitely a different culture. On the surface there may be an homogenization, strip malls and all that, but deep down it's a very different place." Poet Allen Tate referred to the South as "Uncle Sam's other province."

Perhaps the most obvious element of the Southern character—white and black—is the tendency toward emotional display. The Midwest, settled primarily by northern European races (primarily German and Scandinavian), is restrained by comparison. Religious testimony in a Midwest sermon is a reasoned affair; in the South it is an explosion of the Holy Spirit. Until recent decades, the South had a tradition of political oratory to match its religious raptures. This rhetoric, claimed J. W. Cash, developed during the South's duel for mastery with the North, and "every day became less and less a form of speech and more and more a direct instrument of emotion, like music." It was this "direct instrument of emotion" that was the tool of Southern demagogues, including the Delta's most publicized politician of this century, the Populist Huey Long.

A second prominent characteristic of the Southerner—or rather the white Southern male—is his tendency to violence. This violence arose in the Southern frontier, which also begot Southern individualism. Ironically, the Southerner, while capable of immediate flashes of violence, possesses at times an almost courtly set of manners (which ultimately may have derived from a reading of Sir Walter Scott's novels which are said to have had an enormous influence on Southern plantation culture). Even today Southerners say, "Yes, sir" or "Yes, ma'am" when talking to strangers, a respectful custom unknown to Northerners. The elegance of manners and dignity of elderly blacks has nothing to do with Uncle Tomism but is a fusion of Southern culture with their own nature.

But the politeness among whites is an easily shattered veneer. I saw violence erupt when I was a student at a Tennessee military academy, where boys came from the deep South as well as Tennessee. I saw the pride with which they were imbued, how it could rankle at the slightest perceived threat to their honor. I vividly remember seeing a group of cadets ordering another Yankee boy to remove his pants, then whipping him fiercely with a coat hanger. In echoes of more stereotypical violence, a Southern writer of my acquaintance was severely beaten by three sheriff's deputies in the Delta. "Part of Southern manhood," he said, "is being able to fight, I think. I mean I had to do it when I was a kid. The South is a violent place." In Cash's view the Southern frontier with its rowdyism, fights, brags, and assertive individualism perpetuated not only private violence but the public violence of lynchings and burnings.

The South, and the Delta in particular, has always had large numbers of rural poor, white and black. Even into the twentieth century most of these people had some sort of land from which to scratch out a living. As Midge White wrote: "There doesn't seem to be much difference in the living conditions between white and colored in the country, and such poor land. It's disheartening to see the aridity and erosion after the prosperity of the Ohio farms." Since the 1980s the South's yeomen farmers, who had never fallen to the state of the poor whites, have been finding themselves squeezed out of agriculture. Like their counterparts in the Midwest, they have discovered that increasing mechanization supports fewer and fewer people on the land. Take one example, the Hudson family farm in Dyer County, Tennessee. Up until the first half of this century, their land supported three to four hundred people (twenty-five or twenty-six tenant farm families) but now supports no more than a dozen individuals.

And while the entire South is now industrialized, its factory work is generally poorly paid. Because of this, and because of the mechanization of agriculture, the Delta is said to be the poorest section of the country. According to a 1995 report by the Federal Reserve Bank of St. Louis, the Lower Mississippi Delta Development Act of 1988 "determined that the Lower Mississippi Delta lagged behind the rest of the country in economic growth and prosperity and suffered from a greater amount of measurable poverty and unemployment than any other region of the country."

In response to this poverty, Congress mandated that the National Park Service establish a commission to conduct the Lower Mississippi Delta Region Heritage Study and, according to the commission's first newsletter, "make recommendations on economic needs, problems, and opportunities in the region." The newsletter states: "Despite its rich cultural and natural resources, the delta region is synonymous with hardship and poverty. Housing conditions are seriously substandard; highways, roads, and bridges are in poor condition; and commerce and business opportunities are constrained by limited access to capital and low skill levels among delta workers."

According to Kathleen Julian's husband, Mississippi river pilot James Julian, (who was born and raised in Greenville, Mississippi, a river town): "In 1959 when I quit school, in that part of the country you either had money or you picked cotton or you went to work on a riverboat." He picked cotton as a youngster, from "first grade to about third grade, so I'd get clothes for school."

Beginning in the 1960s, industry began moving steadily from the North to the South. Since at least the 1920s, economists, businessmen, and politicians had been advocating southern industrialization and calling their vision for this section of the country the "New South." The New South is now a reality, but ironically it is experiencing the loss of industry that the Northeast did only decades ago, except that Southern industries are moving their operations to third world nations. Once attractive to industry because of its anti-labor bias and low wages, the Delta is expensive compared to foreign alternatives. Even so, Delta industry is still the largest sector of employment in the region.

For economic as well as social reasons, blacks began moving to northern cities such as Detroit, Gary, and Chicago for factory work around the time of the First World War. Many whites, also trapped in poverty, left too. While no figures are available, some blacks, at least, are returning to retire. On the face of it this seems absurd, inasmuch as when we think of the Delta it is almost inevitable that at some point we think of slavery, lynchings, and Jim Crow. We also think of sheriffs who ran their counties with an iron hand. In his book *The Land Where the Blues Began,* Texan Alan Lomax tells of the harassment he received from sheriffs when he interviewed Delta bluesmen in the early 1940s. This was a South hostile to Yankee outsiders coming to organize labor or to anyone who might fraternize with blacks. In one day Lomax had a hostile encounter with two sheriffs and a meeting with an FBI agent who identified him on sight. The first sheriff knew of every meeting Lomax had had with blacks that day, even of a meeting with a woman on the front porch of her home on a country road, with no other houses or people in sight. The sheriff knew that Lomax had gotten up on the woman's porch, a thing that particularly angered him. ("We don't want to get too intimate with um.") The sheriff pulled Lomax in because " . . . now [that] our country is at war, we've been told to be on the lookout for Jap agents . . . ." Perhaps that fear explains what the FBI agent was doing in Tunica County, Mississippi, absurd as it sounds.

On the surface, relations between blacks and whites today are better than in those days, but beneath the surface there is tension. From antebellum times until the civil rights movement of the 1960s it was common for white and black children to play together. In a forthcoming Free River Press book, Murray Hudson's father, Jack Hudson, describes his childhood adventures with his best friend, who was black. Throughout most of the South such friendships had to end in adolescence; in West Tennessee they did not. From at least the Great Depression until the late 1950s and the incipient civil rights movement, white and black families helped each other out. Jack Hudson said everyone in their community banded together to help one black woman plant and harvest crops.

 ⤳

A great part of the Delta's economy and legend has always centered on the Mississippi River. Etchings from *Harper's* magazine in the late 1800s show Memphis docks lined with huge paddlewheelers, one after another, and the wharfs piled high with bales of cotton. The cotton economy and the paddleboats survived into the 1930s, so that Thomas Hart Benton could still depict black men on cotton-laden wagons headed for docks where roustabouts loaded boats. And Midge White's October 9, 1940 letter from Carthage, Mississippi describes a scene straight out of Benton. "I should send you a picture of cotton wagons going to the cotton gin across the street. There seems to be one every few minutes lumbering along, drawn by two mules and usually driven by a sleepy black man sitting on the white fluff piled up over the tops of wagons."

Towboats, of course, are now the major and most efficient means of transport on the river. One tow with the standard fifteen barges can haul as much as 870 trucks, or two and a half trains with a total of 250 cars. Towboats primarily haul grain, which is grown in the rural hinterlands, stored at farm co-ops in small towns, then transferred to trucks and delivered to the elevators (huge silos) on the Mississippi. From there the grain is loaded onto barges which deliver it to ocean-going ships in the port of New Orleans, which in turn deliver it around the world. Five great multinational grain merchants control most of this system: they buy the grain on contract as well as own the storage and delivery systems—the trucks, barges, elevators, and ocean going vessels. Once the merchants obtained this control, the production and delivery system became rigid and dehumanized. Jack Libby and James Julian both left the river when corporations gave young college graduates who lacked any knowledge of the river responsibility over those who had worked it all their lives—those who knew its markers, currents, and bends. For over two centuries the river was worked by rugged characters: by rough boatmen like Mike Fink, by commercial fishermen, and by hard living, hard working roustabouts. Now these are either gone or, like the fishermen, in short supply. The individual has given way to faceless authority within the corporation.

The river itself is hurting too. Years of chemical runoff from farmlands has poisoned the Mississippi to the extent that people are advised to limit the amount of river fish they eat. Worse, accumulated runoff has created a dead zone within the Gulf of Mexico, severely limiting the fishing catch and driving shrimp farther off shore. In 1997 Vice President Al Gore called for a federally mandated clean water plan. As written, the Environmental Protection Agency's Clean Water Action Plan calls, among other things, for greater regulation of animal manure (a major source of water contamination), the creation of standards for the amounts of nitrogen and phosphorous allowed in bodies of water, and the assessment of chemical pollution on a watershed by basis. Since all watersheds east of the Continental Divide ultimately run into the Mississippi River, control of animal manure and farm chemicals is crucial to the health of the river. As expected, powerful forces, including the American Farm Bureau and lesser entities, including the Iowa Department of Natural Resources, oppose this bill. Money and politics are so deeply intertwined in this issue that the reclamation of the river will entail a prolonged struggle, very likely involving litigation in state courts. Both sides have an economic stake in the matter, but one of them supports a diverse economy—including fishing, farming, and tourism—and a respect for the natural systems the river once supported; the other is narrow and can see nothing beyond the profits of the chemical intensive farming of agribusiness.

Afterword

DEVELOPING REGIONAL RURAL ECONOMIES

The following is a six-part radio commentary on the need for rural Americans to develop self-sufficient regional economies, written for broadcast over KUNI in Cedar Falls, Iowa, a National Public Radio affiliate. The commentary won the Society of Professional Journalist's Sigma Delta Chi Award for best radio editorial of 1994.

When I moved to rural Iowa, almost three years ago, I did not know the troubles it faced. I had heard of rural flight, but as an urban dweller, not facing the daily reality of rural life, I ignored the rural crisis.

I moved here, to northeast Iowa, because I wanted to live in beauty and relative solitude, because I thought it might be possible to have a culturally rich life in rural America. I know now that I was overly optimistic and naive. I had, in fact, very little idea of what it would mean to live on an isolated farm ten miles from either of the nearest towns, trying to earn a living as a writer and publisher.

When I moved here I believed what possibly many others believe: that rural America is a place where people still gather in community, sure in themselves and their friends. I believed the land and water were pure and uncontaminated, even though I had read and heard otherwise. I believed that the best of modern technology had been absorbed, the worst rejected. I believed all these things because I did not live in rural America.

Perhaps I had been affected by the television commercials which try to sell products by identifying them with farms and country towns. I believe that many of us still associate rural America with what is uncontaminated and cleanest in ourselves. It is a myth which helps sustain us. Like the ever-shrinking wilderness, we must have it, at least in our fantasies, a land or town where it is still possible to escape from an ever-more frantic and directionless society.

But that, as I said, turns out to have been extremely optimistic and naive. The fact is that rural America is dying.

There is little energy and self-confidence here. And little work. The farmers are leaving their lands for low-skilled jobs in the cities. What few jobs small towns do offer pay mostly minimum wage. The young people, those who can, leave as soon as the high school diploma is in their hands.

What can we do?

⌒

I live in the Third World, in Iowa, not far from the Mississippi River. Oh yes, Iowa is part of the Third World, and so is most of rural America. If you need convincing, just look at what third world countries do, then look at rural America.

Typically a third world country has natural resources and human labor that it's willing to sell for a pittance, resources and labor that developed countries want, especially at bargain prices.

Does that fit rural America? You bet. Rural America exports its produce and livestock, and in exchange receives a pittance. That is, the family farmer does. The profits from the small farmer's produce, stock, and hard work go to someone else, usually out of state. On the other hand, the corporate farmer makes good money because he's farming in volume. But the corporate farmer, more than likely, does not live in rural America, but in some large metropolitan center like Chicago or Dallas. Thus the profits made from family and corporate farms flow from rural to urban America.

The condition of the third world country worsens as its resources are gobbled up and its workers and farmers become more and more destitute. We see that happening here in Iowa. Corn, Iowa's biggest crop, because it is grown year after year, takes an enormous toll on one of Iowa's greatest natural resources, its soil. But federal subsidies for corn growers encourages this loss. And, of course, Iowa farmers, thanks to the present agricultural system, remain poor and continue leaving the land in a steady stream.

This situation occurs in third world countries when the industry and agricultural methods of developed countries—the colonizers—disrupt the traditional way of life in the colonies. It lures peasants from their land and villages for jobs in factories, mines, and deforestation crews.

Likewise, rural Americans continue to leave the countryside for opportunity elsewhere. Rural America's most valuable export, more important than its grain and livestock, is its high school and college graduates. They can't afford to stay.

The colonizer's economy takes away the native's self-sufficiency in a local economy and replaces it with dependence on the colonizer's economy. Control of their own lives is no longer in the hands of the locals.

That's Iowa's situation, and the situation of every other rural area in this nation, where local and regional economies have been destroyed, first under the development the national economy, later under pressure from an ever-growing international economy.

Meanwhile no one in Washington seems particularly concerned about the state of the third world within its own borders.

⌒

From the urbanite's point of view there probably is no reason to keep rural America alive. Most urbanites don't know where their food comes from, and don't much care. It makes no difference to them whether their food is grown on a family farm or corporate farm. Big or small is irrelevant to the final product, which should be tasty, clean, and brightly colored, if not smartly packaged.

I am afraid that our federal officials and bureaucrats share this sentiment about our food, its source, and the state of rural economies. At least I have not heard of any rural policy positions or programs emanating from the White House or Capitol Hill.

When President Clinton was first elected I did read or hear something about the administration's concern for building a rural development program, and now two years later, this spring, he convened a rural development conference in Iowa. But it was a symbolic gesture, and like much else the president has done, it seemed half-hearted, without passion or commitment.

About a year ago I called Senator Harkin's office, and asked his top aide if he could tell me which think tanks in this country were developing rural policy. He mentioned The Center for Rural Affairs in Walthill, Nebraska, but I knew about that. Nothing else came to his mind. He said he would research it and call me back. That was over a year ago and he has yet to make that phone call.

I now think that Washington's indifference is a blessing. When President Reagan began dismantling federal programs, in the belief that problems were better handled on state and local levels, I was angry. But now I think he was right. National programs cannot be flexible enough to adjust to local conditions. More important, a centrally directed program will not develop what needs to be developed: economic self-sufficiency and local initiative.

No one is going to solve our problems for us. We have only our brains to rely on, and if they are stuffed with inadequate ideas we're going to pay a heavy price. No one from the outside is going to give us a wonderful future. No one from New York or Los Angeles is going to hand us a three billion dollar check.

We create our own future. Either we decide what it is we want, and go after it, or someone else will decide it for us. If we are actively going to create our future, instead of waiting for it passively to happen, we must first decide the kind of future we want. Which means we must work cooperatively. We must think together.

⌐

So long as Iowans and other rural residents believe that they can rebuild their economies and spirits within the existing economic system, their situation will worsen.

When most rural Americans think of improving their local economies, they usually think of either attracting more tourists or of recruiting factories. We have all heard of desperate towns across America giving tax incentives and outright cash to companies that will locate within their borders. And time and again we have heard of these same companies, having gotten a free ride, pulling out for another desperate town or country where costs are even lower. Rural Americans would do better to create their own businesses.

But this will not happen until rural America has banks committed to local development. Perhaps you have that kind of bank in your town, but where I live people complain that the only ones who get loans are those who don't need them.

That sort of conservatism is anathema to healthy commerce. Rural America needs banks like the South Shore Bank of Chicago, which for years has been committed to the economic development of Chicago's black South Shore district. That bank has developed black businesses, and rebuilt South Shore's prosperity. Now it is working for the development of a portion of rural Arkansas.

But some have despaired of the present banking system altogether, including one rural Vermont town that has decided to secede from the U.S. banking system, and has developed its own scrip. Because of disenchantment with so many institutions, I suspect that in years to come we will hear more about the need for rural areas to unhitch themselves from the federal reserve system and build their own banks and issue their own currencies.

What does seem clear is that so long as Iowa and other rural areas remain third world countries, depending on the crumbs from the colonizer's economy for their maintenance, so long as the colonizers run the factories, farms, and banks, so long will rural America be poor.

∽

I began thinking about rural economic development when I first heard Warren Rudman's claim that if the United States does not drastically reduce its national deficit that someday it will become the world's largest banana republic.

Whether or not a deficit would ever trigger collapse, other factors force rural Americans to think about constructing arks, self-sufficient economic and social entities that can survive the hard times that are upon us.

My own town, Lansing, could not possibly be self-sufficient, but what size area could be? For some reason, perhaps because of the shared landscape of hills and winding valleys and their farm economies, I began to think of northeast Iowa, southeast Minnesota, and southwest Wisconsin. I began to wonder whether this area could be self-sufficient.

Someone told me that it has a name, the Driftless Bioregion, so-called because the glaciers did not drift over it. That same person said that northwest Illinois, including Galena, was a part of it.

I learned that people around the country were thinking of bioregions as determinants of future economic and cultural units, not in terms of the nation or of states. The important point when developing an ark is to think in terms of shared values and habits. A bioregion can provide this.

The Driftless Bioregion unifies us by virtue of its topography, which in turn defines agricultural practice. And that practice defines our opportunities and limitations. We are bound together in many ways, some not always obvious.

Most of the counties of this bioregion, for example, are poor, about the poorest in their respective states. And that's because of our topography, which means our farms are not as rich as flatland farms.

But, with the application of imagination and courage, this poor region could be transformed into a land of wealth.

Already imaginative and energetic people from Minneapolis and St. Paul are moving into southeast Minnesota and setting up businesses; people from Madison and Chicago have moved into southwest Wisconsin. Fewer have ventured into northeast Iowa, because of its greater distance from the major cities. But it will happen, I'm sure, it's just a matter of time.

As I've said, a regional economy can provide an ark, a social and economic unit that can enable us to weather these hard times, and those ahead. A self-sufficient regional economy is not a third world economy, nor a region of the colonized.

A regional economy cannot be built directly, but in steps, and indirectly.

In the case of the Driftless Bioregion, encompassing southeast Minnesota, northeast Iowa, southwest Wisconsin, and northwest Illinois, the first intermediate step is to begin envisioning a Regional City for each of these areas.

A Regional City is another name for what has been called the Social City. The Regional City, as it is usually envisioned, is an aggregate of cities, not of towns. The point of the Social or Regional City is to maintain a greenbelt between individual cities to prevent the development of one mass megalopolis.

There are only three cities within the Driftless Bioregion with populations of over 10,000 persons, so the Regional Cities we might build are radically different from what is usually envisioned. But for both kinds, cooperation between towns or cities is imperative to its functioning. If one town or city developed a technical college or a major hospital, others would refrain from duplicating it. The pie, after all, is only so big.

Major economic and cultural domains, such as tourism, industry, and transportation, would be addressed in common planning sessions, to develop overall strategy.

In 1993 Joseph Lambke, studio professor of architecture at the Illinois Institute of Technology, sent a proposal to ten or so small towns of northeast Iowa, stating that for $500 per town the students of his planning class would undertake the task of drawing up a blueprint for transforming northeast Iowa into a Regional City.

The price was modest, and the insight that we might have

gained could have been enormous. But the towns turned down the project.

One of the biggest problems in small towns is their inability to work cooperatively. Towns see each other as rivals, or potential rivals. And to complicate matters, most small towns are divided into factions.

Perhaps the situation will not improve, perhaps it will worsen. But the vision of a bioregional economy connected by Regional Cities remains a possibility, and a vision that is loved, be it good or evil, can be willed, and being willed, can be actualized.

PROVINCIAL HOPE

Regionalism, I think, is an idea we will be encountering with ever greater frequency in coming years. It denotes a specific form of decentralization which is now being generated in reaction to the disintegration fostered by globalization. My first encounter with the word "regionalism" came years ago when I first read *Modern Art*, a book by critic Thomas Craven, in a section devoted to Depression-era painters of the American scene. In it I also first became aware of the work of that great triumvirate of regionalist painters: Grant Wood, Thomas Hart Benton, and John Steuart Curry. At about the same time I learned that numerous writers of that period were also delving into the collective experiences of their locales and regions, including William Faulkner, Oliver LaFarge, Wallace Stegner, and Erskine Caldwell. Regionalism, then, was not a restricted movement, but something shared by writers and painters across the continent. As someone who hoped someday to record the life of the nation, I read and studied them and others of the American Scene avidly throughout my high school years. At that time, however, I associated "regionalism" with nothing more than the depiction of place.

My interest in regionalism was rekindled after moving to Iowa in 1991. I was and am a publisher of folk literature, and before settling here had decided to publish at least one book by Iowa farmers. As I began to learn more about the ongoing farm crisis, I began thinking about economic development and concluded that the survival of rural areas depended on their capacity to generate more of their own products, whatever could be produced and sold. To do this towns had to learn to work cooperatively. Thus I realized that community development must precede economic development, and that the work I was doing—setting up writing workshops for people without literary ambition and publishing their work—was one way not only to foster community but to help develop a regional consciousness. I wanted to promote the development of a body of folk literature that would help unify the experience of the people in my region. They, through their writing, would express their shared experiences past and present, a record of what had been lost through the assaults of modernity, and what had been preserved.

Pondering what shape a rural economy might take necessarily made me an agrarian. My farm neighbors with their simplicity and honesty, their dignity and integrity, contrasted sharply with the involuted psychologies of the urban mentality that I had known on and off for years. I soon came to value farmers as a class more than others, and realized that if civilization needed to start afresh it would do far better with them than with doctors, lawyers, journalists, politicians, corporate executives, and a dozen other classes I could name. This, then, became the basis for my agrarianism, and when I came afterwards to read smatterings of Jefferson, I found confirmation for my thoughts.

Then, about a year into my work with farmers, I read *Grant Wood* by James Dennis. In that book I learned about the Southern Agrarians, poets mostly, who had taught at Vanderbilt University and had decried the machine's intrusion into southern life. These men, including Robert Penn Warren, Donald Davidson, and John Crowe Ransom, wanted the South to turn its back on the North with its mechanization and to preserve its own agrarian roots. In 1930 they published a manifesto, *I'll Take My Stand*. Frank Owsley pretty well summed up the twelve writers' thoughts at the close of his own contribution: "This struggle between an agrarian and an industrial civilization, then, was the irrepressible conflict, the house divided against itself, which must become according to the doctrine of the industrial section all the one or all the other. It was the doctrine of intolerance, crusading, standardizing, alike in industry and in life.

The South had to be crushed out; it was in the way; it impeded the progress of the machine."

Dennis in his book pointed out that Wood and Benton's regionalist theories were stimulated by *I'll Take My Stand*. Aware of the power that art had for the revitalization of American culture, Wood wanted regional art centers established across the country. In her book *Grant Wood: The Regionalist Vision*, Wanda Corn wrote that Wood's regionalism was a reaction to the cultural homogeneity threatening the nation. Wood, then, wanted diversity of folkways preserved, and saw art as a tool for that the preservation. His own Stone City art colony would provide the model for other regional art centers, which would be instruments for cultural preservation.

Before ever learning of Wood's dream of regional art centers I had hoped to develop writing workshops throughout my region, workshops that would remain a vital part of the cultural and civic life of their respective towns. The point I am making here and elsewhere from my own regionalist experiments is that regionalism remains a vital possibility for decentralization, and that local art, literature, and music are the best means available for developing a regional sensibility. As I was later to find out, that was the belief of scores of other regionalists as well.

Within a year of reading various works on Wood I read a biography of cultural critic and generalist Lewis Mumford, whom I had personally known, but hardly as well as I thought. From the biography I found that he, too, had been a regionalist, and that his regionalism had been spurred by the same concern that the Southern Agrarians and Wood had voiced: that the machine was producing a standardized and homogenized culture, and in the process was debasing humanity itself. In his regionalist years Mumford wrote: "At present . . . our metropolitanized populations throughout the world are both witless and wantless: true cannon-fodder, potential serfs for a new totalitarian feudalism . . . "

⌣

In the 1920s Mumford had been part of a group, including Benton Mackaye and Clarence Stein, who formed what they called The

Regional Planning Association of America. Mumford and his colleagues felt that the revitalization of the country depended upon
decentralizing industry and banking, for the webs of the power
complex were and remain centered in urban areas. What Mumford
and his friends envisioned was a limit to the growth of existing cities
by infusing rural towns and areas with industry and the cultural
institutions of the large city. It would mean creating what Mumford
called Regional Cities. Beyond that, Mumford wanted Regional Cities
to aggregate into regions bound together by ties of art and literature, language and folkways. Mumford's biographer, Donald Miller,
says that Mumford believed that these "tied people together more
than social structures or ideology." Indeed, most regionalists, as creative writers and theorists, believed it too. B. A. Botkin, who com-
plied many folk literature anthologies, voiced the general notion
when he wrote that "the motifs, images, symbols, slogans, and
idioms" of regionalism could bring about "regional, class, and other
forms of collective consciousness."

Five years after beginning to theorize about economic and cultural development within my own region, I came upon Robert Dorman's work *Revolt of the Provinces: The Regionalist Movement in America*, 1920-
1945. From Dorman I learned that regionalism embraced far more
writers, artists, and thinkers than I had imagined. Regionalists
included a stellar roll call of twentieth-century writers and thinkers:
Mari Sandoz, Walter Prescott Webb, Bernard DeVoto, John Neihardt,
Oliver LaFarge, Mary Austin, Willa Cather, Van Wyck Brooks, Lewis
Mumford, Robert Penn Warren, Donald Davidson, Howard Odum,
Lynn Riggs, D'Arcy McNickle, B. A. Botkin, John Collier, Constance
Rourke, John Gould Fletcher, Allen Tate, John Crowe Ransom,
Stringfellow Barr, and J. Frank Dobie, among others.

As these writers were clustered about the country, so naturally
the centers of regionalism lay in the outlands themselves, in Taos and
Santa Fe, in Lincoln and Iowa City, in Nashville and Chapel Hill, in
Austin and Missoula. With the exception of Mumford (who lived in
New York City until 1936 when he moved full-time to a rural ham-
let), the spokesmen for regionalism worked outside the centers of
the power complex, the loci of the webs.

What all shared was a desire to bring into existence a quiltwork of cultures spanning the country. Which meant that regionalism was a theory of decentralization rooted in specific locality, and to the earth. But there was not always agreement on how to define a region. Howard Odum and Harry Estelle Moore began their book *American Regionalism* (1938) with perhaps a score of definitions then in use. What bound this mix of regionalists together was the understanding that modern culture—thanks to mass communication, rapid transportation, and assembly line production—was producing a uniformity of experience and thought among Americans. The assembly line offered uniform goods while public relations and advertising created a demand for them. Real needs were often supplanted by artificial needs, which increasingly consumed more of the individual's income. Citizens became consumers. Indeed, mass communications, advertising, and public relations imbued Americans coast to coast with similar if not identical thought and attitudes. Rapid transportation decreased the individual's contact with the land and consequently lessened the importance of his ties to it. Above all, these modern instruments of transportation, production, and communication were producing a new psychology, a new individual: one without rootedness in place, without ties to the land, without community, one who acted from motives of expedience rather than from loyalty and truth. This was Mumford's "cannon-fodder." Thus none of the regionalists wanted a repetition of their own machine-dominated society, but rather a new civilization based upon a renewed humanism, animated by folkways and an art derived from local life. Art for all of them was crucial to the project, a conveyor of meanings.

In retrospect, one of the greatest regionalist achievements in the arts was the creation of the Nebraska state capitol in Lincoln, a monumental work with a soaring central tower that fused the modern with the traditional. Integral to the total conception of the work was a series of bas-reliefs intending, as the architect's collaborator Hartley Alexander wrote, to portray "the history and symbolism of political freedom." Images and symbols of Indian life and thought, along with other motifs, were carved and inscribed on the walls and tower. The meaning of the building, which was meant to be read as a text, began with "the American idea, on the Indian side," as Alexander wrote. The first image (the bison) was intended to convey the autochthonous, or "that which springs from the soil." By his tie to the land which he held sacred, and in other ways, the Indian became a central figure and symbol for many regionalists.

Nebraskan writer John G. Neihardt's book on an Oglala Sioux holy man, *Black Elk Speaks*, was Neihardt's attempt to infuse Native American values into a declining American culture. His venture was repeated by others who valued the Indians' respect for the land, for the cycle of all life, for communal values. Indeed, the problem of reconciling American individualism with the needs of democracy was a regionalist preoccupation. The example of the Native American seemed the most potent to some, including Mary Austin, Neihardt, and archaeologist Edgar L. Hewett. Alexander, who had codesigned the texts for the Nebraska capitol building, told Hewett that Indian values and thought were "ideally gifted for the inauguration of a new humanism."

To others the pioneer and the farmer offered the model folk for the emerging regional civilizations. But to some, the values that motivated the pioneers had led to the modern crisis. Mumford and Van Wyck Brooks interpreted the pioneer experience in this light, and saw the pioneer as a despoiler of land and resources. For Vernon Parrington the farmer had "never been a land loving peasant," but an opportunist who sold land for a profit when he could, and was eventually "transformed into an urbanized factory" worker, "rootless, migratory, drawn to the job as by a magnet." The farmers certainly were not stewards of the land: they had farmed it with such insistency and carelessness that within a hundred years from when the first plow had cut into the prairie, the Midwest had lost most of its topsoil. Who, then, were the model folk? If the regionalists could not agree on who they were, they would at least admit that diverse folkways existed.

The closest that regionalism ever came to becoming reality lay in the Tennessee Valley Authority, a New Deal program run by David Lillienthal, whose book on the TVA, *Democracy on the March*, provided a clear statement of what he thought regionalism was about. "If it is decentralized industry men want," he wrote, " 'family farming,' or pleasant cities not too large, an end to smoke and congestion and filth—there are modern tools which can be turned to just such ends . . . not only for the people but by the people . . . . Democracy can emerge revitalized." Regionalists embraced the TVA, Dorman says, only because regionalism had not been activated on a local level; it had taken the federal government to bring about a regionalist experiment. That experiment, unfortunately, turned out to be more about power plants and controlling flood waters and bringing electricity to rural people than about sustaining a folk culture, including agrarian life and associated arts.

1936 marked the depth of the Depression, and it was a turning point for regionalism. In painting, Wood, Benton, Curry, and their colleagues came under heavy attack from the advocates of abstractionism. While their work was appreciated by the public at large (the common folk of Iowa, for example, loved Wood), they were sneered at and attacked by esthetes and academics. For the theorists of regionalism—the Southern Agrarians, the members of the Regional Planning Association, Howard Odum and B. A. Botkin—1936 was the year in which they realized that they had to enact their ideas or abandon their work.

The crisis of the Depression had created the possibility for reform, but by 1936 the possibility was fading. In that year the Southern Agrarians were breaking up, some having abandoned the cause. Also that year Odum, a professor at the University of North Carolina in Chapel Hill, wrote: "For those who long easily 'to recapture the past' for Jeffersonian agrarianism, it must be pointed out that . . . the task is not so simple in the modern complex America." Sixty percent of the population of his time, Odum said, lived in urban areas, and 76.2 percent earned their livelihood "in manufacturing, mechanical distribution, and social services." The following year Congress killed President Roosevelt's proposal for seven little TVAs. By 1938 B. A. Botkin told Joseph Brandt, another regionalist, "personally, I think the regionalism movement is almost played out."

By 1938 Wood, Curry, and Benton were being excoriated by the press, by gallery dealers and academics. The virulence of the attacks weakened Wood and Curry, both of whom died in the early 1940s. The regionalists, Dorman notes, failed to implement their ideas because they had no method for doing so, and had no feeling for political realities. For most of them, writing was act enough: they were academics and believed that education was sufficient to effect results.

After the 1940s regionalism pretty much died out. A few regionalists continued their work sporadically into the fifties, but no new recruits filled their almost emptied ranks. (Dorman—unconvincingly, I think—places Edward Abbey's books in the regionalist tradition.) Not until the 1980s have writers, spurred by the continued growth of corporations and other collectives, and by the continued spoliation of the land, air, and water, brought back discussion of place, albeit under the mantle of ecology. Ecology is the fundamental force behind bioregionalism, a term coined by California writer and editor Peter Berg. Advocates of bioregionalism rely exclusively on discussion and identification of plant and animal species, geologic formations and other elements of a region's biosystem to convert the population to a new, land-centered culture. Bioregionalism, however, takes no account of how an alternative culture and economy might be produced once the values of the mass of people have been almost magically transformed.

From my experience—rediscovering on my own the concepts and methods of regionalists seventy years before—I am certain that regionalism is the only method by which a group of people can survive the onslaughts of the transnational corporations and the national bureaucracies. Only a region is capable of becoming self-sufficient enough to withstand the onslaughts of globalism. The United States as a whole will not survive, since our national politicians are in the pay of the corporations.

Regional development, however, is more than a matter of pushing matter about; relocating factories or putting land in more hands will in itself solve nothing. For the problem is us—not just with those who despoil the land or create dehumanizing work for others. The root of the current crisis is in our selfishness, which is to say in our distance from our one true Center, and in the thousands of ways we thoughtlessly express our self-absorption. In that lies violence and the root of all that disintegrates society, and in turn causes us to mourn the loss of community. The reconstruction of society must be preceded by the rectification of the individual. After all, corporate greed is simply individual greed writ large. As a farmer friend has said several times: "If you want to know what the problem with the world is, take a good look in the mirror."